BLACK OUT LOUD

BLACK OUT LOUD

The Revolutionary History
of Black Comedy from
Vaudeville to '90s Sitcoms

GEOFF BENNETT

HARPER

An Imprint of HarperCollins*Publishers*

Without limiting the exclusive rights of any author, contributor or the publisher of this publication, any unauthorized use of this publication to train generative artificial intelligence (AI) technologies is expressly prohibited. HarperCollins also exercise their rights under Article 4(3) of the Digital Single Market Directive 2019/790 and expressly reserve this publication from the text and data mining exception.

BLACK OUT LOUD. Copyright © 2026 by Geoff Bennett. All rights reserved. No part of this book may be used or reproduced in any manner whatsoever without written permission except in the case of brief quotations embodied in critical articles and reviews. For information, address HarperCollins Publishers, 195 Broadway, New York, NY 10007. In Europe, HarperCollins Publishers, Macken House, 39/40 Mayor Street Upper, Dublin 1, D01 C9W8, Ireland.

HarperCollins books may be purchased for educational, business, or sales promotional use. For information, please email the Special Markets Department at SPsales@harpercollins.com.

hc.com

FIRST EDITION

Designed by Bonni Leon-Berman

Library of Congress Cataloging-in-Publication Data
Names: Bennett, Geoff (Journalist) author
Title: Black out loud : the revolutionary history of Black comedy from vaudeville to '90s sitcoms / Geoff Bennett.
Description: First Edition. | New York : Harper, 2026. | Includes bibliographical references.
Identifiers: LCCN 2025032097 (print) | LCCN 2025032098 (ebook) | ISBN 9780063418172 hardcover | ISBN 9780063418196 ebook
Subjects: LCSH: African Americans in popular culture | African American wit and humor | African American comedians | African Americans in the performing arts | Comedy—United States | African Americans—Intellectual life
Classification: LCC E185.625 .B46 2026 (print) | LCC E185.625 (ebook)
LC record available at https://lccn.loc.gov/2025032097
LC ebook record available at https://lccn.loc.gov/2025032098

Printed in the United States of America.

26 27 28 29 30 LBC 6 5 4 3 2

For those who laughed
against the odds—and made
that laughter a legacy

CONTENTS

Prologue		1
CHAPTER 1	Billy Kersands and Minstrelsy	7
CHAPTER 2	Bert Williams and George Walker	17
CHAPTER 3	Stepin Fetchit	29
CHAPTER 4	Hattie McDaniel	38
CHAPTER 5	Amos 'n' Andy	55
CHAPTER 6	Pigmeat Markham	71
CHAPTER 7	Moms Mabley	80
CHAPTER 8	Redd Foxx	90
CHAPTER 9	Dick Gregory	119
CHAPTER 10	Flip Wilson	130
CHAPTER 11	Bill Cosby	147
CHAPTER 12	Richard Pryor	185
CHAPTER 13	Eddie Murphy	210
CHAPTER 14	*A Different World*	223
CHAPTER 15	*In Living Color*	232
CHAPTER 16	*Family Matters*	259
CHAPTER 17	*The Fresh Prince of Bel-Air*	265
CHAPTER 18	Martin Lawrence	276
CHAPTER 19	*Living Single*	282
CHAPTER 20	*Chappelle's Show*	291
Conclusion: Punch Lines and Progress		299
Acknowledgments		303
Bibliography		305
Index		309

BLACK OUT LOUD

PROLOGUE

On Sunday, April 15, 1990, after watching the irreverent antics of the Bundy family on *Married . . . with Children*, viewers of the Fox network got their first look at a daring new experiment in television. It was a sketch comedy show created and controlled by Black artists, intended to pose a direct challenge to NBC's long-running *Saturday Night Live*. *In Living Color* was the brainchild of Keenen Ivory Wayans. He was the head writer and star, supported by four of his brothers and the rest of a cast—and dance troupe—made up almost entirely of people of color. Americans had never seen anything like it before. And they loved it.

I sure did.

I was ten years old, sitting wide-eyed and slack-jawed beside my brother in our family's living room. It felt like someone had kicked open the door to a party I hadn't even known I was waiting to be invited to. I'd seen Black faces on TV before, but rarely had I seen so many, all at once, being this funny, this free, this in control. *In Living Color* didn't just make me laugh, it reflected the rhythm of the barbershops, family reunions, and cookouts I knew so well. It was comedy that looked like my world.

That moment wasn't an accident. It was the product of a deliberate strategy set in motion when Barry Diller launched the Fox network in 1986 with a mission to disrupt the television status quo. Back then, the Big Three—ABC, CBS, and NBC—offered a steady stream of safe, interchangeable programming. As the scrappy new contender, Fox had to break the mold. Diller, along with programming chief Garth Ancier, set out to build a network that was alternative by design—unafraid of risk.

The breakthrough, Diller told me, came with a script for a show pointedly titled *Not the Cosbys*—a riff on the wholesome, top-rated sitcom *The Cosby Show*. That script became *Married . . . with Children*, that gleefully subversive sitcom that set the tone for everything that followed. "It was as alternative as you could get in terms of what the American networks were offering to viewers," Diller explained. "Once we knew we were an alternative and that we had to be edgy, it dictated almost every decision we made."

That ethos produced groundbreaking successes—*The Simpsons*, *Cops*, and a slate of shows that challenged everything about what network television could be. But nowhere did it shine brighter than in the emergence of *In Living Color* and, soon after, *Martin*—two shows that would help transform Fox into an unlikely powerhouse of Black cultural creativity. It wasn't a plan; it was a by-product of being open to voices, visions, and brilliance that the legacy networks too often ignored.

"It made Fox the number one network," Diller noted.

What most of America didn't realize at the time was that they were witnessing the dawn of a new era in entertainment, one where Black artists were shaking off cultural constraints and flourishing because of, rather than in spite of, their Blackness. It was a moment that had been a long time coming, carried on the shoulders of giants.

Black comedians had been honing their craft since the days of vaudeville, through the early days of television, and into the transformative decades of the 1960s and '70s, despite segregation and institutional racism. Bert Williams, Jackie "Moms" Mabley, Redd Foxx, Dick Gregory, Bill Cosby, Richard Pryor, Eddie Murphy—these were artists who used humor to subvert the status quo and carve out space where there had previously been none. They weren't just making people laugh; they were building a legacy.

By the 1990s, that legacy had taken root. And as Keenen Ivory Wayans assembled the cast of *In Living Color*, he made intentional choices to elevate talent outside the industry's usual pipelines. "Minority talent is not in the system, and you have to go outside," he told the press at the time. "We went beyond the Comedy Stores and Improvs, which are not showcase places for minorities." He pulled in unknowns and rising stars—his brothers Damon, Shawn, and Marlon, alongside

T'Keyah Crystal Keymáh, Kim Coles, and Tommy Davidson. Jennifer Lopez danced as part of the "Fly Girls," with Rosie Perez as choreographer. There was one white guy: a rubber-faced impressionist from Canada named Jim Carrey.

The show's success kicked off what would become a cultural boom. I didn't have the language then to describe what was happening, but I felt it—this rush of pride, this sense that we were finally being seen not just as characters on a screen, but as full, complex people. The 1990s were the first time I remember being able to flip through TV channels and see Blackness represented in a way that felt real and expansive: from Martin Lawrence's outrageous antics to the aspirational brilliance of *A Different World*, from *Living Single*'s confident cool to *The Fresh Prince of Bel-Air*'s blend of humor and heart. These shows weren't just entertainment—they were reflections of life, mirrors in which my family, my friends, and I could see ourselves.

Of course, tensions simmered behind the scenes. The Wayans family's bold vision for *In Living Color* eventually collided with the instincts of Fox network executives, who increasingly found the show too raw, too provocative—especially in contrast to the pastel wholesomeness of NBC's *The Cosby Show*. But that edge wasn't a bug; it was the feature. The irreverence was the point. It was what made the show matter. And it was what drew comics like Chris Rock and Jamie Foxx into its orbit. Rock famously left—or was pushed out of—*SNL* after growing frustrated with the limited roles he was given. "*SNL* is a pretty white show," he later said. "And *In Living Color* was just hip. The shit was hot."

It *was* hot, because Black creative power was being unleashed at all levels. "I think a lot of Black culture was finding its voice during that time," comedian and producer Larry Wilmore told me. "If you talk about Black shows on television [before that], many of them were created and run by white people." That shift—from being the subject of stories to being the storyteller—is what made the 1990s revolutionary.

I wrote this book because I'm a product of that revolution. I came of age watching Black characters who felt like people I knew, who were messy and hilarious and ambitious and flawed. They shaped how I saw the world and how I saw myself moving through it. I'm a journalist now, but I grew up loving comedy because it was one of the first places I saw truth telling as an art form. Jokes that punched up, that slipped past defenses, that revealed something deeper while still making you laugh.

The boom of Black comedy in the '90s wasn't just about laughter—it was about visibility, agency, and joy. It unfolded against a backdrop of real political change: the end of the Cold War, an economic boom, and shifting demographics that made America more diverse—and more reflective of voices that had long been kept on the margins.

Former president Bill Clinton was famously dubbed "the first Black president" by Toni Morrison in 1998, a nod to his cultural fluency and perceived empathy with Black communities. This was before Obama. Before the world imagined a real Black president. And yet, the cultural groundwork was already being laid—in part by comedians who turned stages, screens, and scripts into battlegrounds for inclusion.

The decade also saw a resurgence of Black political consciousness, inspired by the Civil Rights generation and fueled by modern injustices—from Rodney King to rising incarceration rates. Black TV responded in kind. Shows tackled racism, sexism, colorism, and class. Even sitcoms, cloaked in laugh tracks, were often sly Trojan horses for deeper truths.

The audience was changing too. More Black people were attending college and joining the middle class, which created demand for more nuanced portrayals. Before the '90s, TV ratings for Black and white audiences were nearly identical. But by the decade's end, Black viewers had more options—and made different choices. Shows like *Seinfeld*, while beloved by critics, never broke into the top ten for Black households. Why would it, when *Living Single* felt far more familiar?

This was more than a shift in taste. It was a cultural realignment.

And through it all, the lineage of Black comedy stayed unbroken. Jamie Foxx named himself in tribute to Redd Foxx. Arsenio Hall gave

Chris Rock his big break, which led to *SNL*. Arsenio also mentored Will Smith, paving the way for *The Fresh Prince*, and shared a screen with Eddie Murphy in *Coming to America*. That movie featured John Amos—who'd starred in *Good Times*—and a then-unknown Samuel L. Jackson. Every laugh line, every one-liner, every moment of prime-time brilliance was connected by a thread of legacy.

By 1992, even as the golden age of Black sitcoms was peaking, a struggling playwright in Atlanta named Tyler Perry put on his first play with $12,000 of his life savings. Three decades later, he would be a billionaire, owning the largest Black-owned studio in the country.

Black comedians have had one hell of a century.

This book tells their story. It's an underexplored chapter of American culture, but also a deeply personal one for me. Many of these comics were more than entertainers—they were cultural translators and civil rights figures in their own right. They didn't march on Washington or face down fire hoses, but they climbed onstage night after night, often in rooms where few looked like them, and dared to be brilliant. Every ticket sold by Redd Foxx, every HBO special by Chris Rock, every sketch on *In Living Color*—they weren't just performances. They were progress.

Without them, there would not have been any "golden age" of Black comedy. There might not have even been an opening for a Colin Powell or a Barack Obama. And I don't know that I'd be sitting here, writing this book.

So why this book? It's a question I've been asked often since I began reporting and writing it more than two years ago. I've spent most of my career as a journalist covering national politics. This clearly isn't a book about Trump or Biden or the never-ending churn of political headlines—not because those topics aren't important, but because they already dominate so much of our public consciousness. In a moment when politics can feel both inescapable and exhausting, it's worth remembering that cultural power can be just as essential. And often, more enduring.

And why the focus on TV? While stand-up and film have shaped Black comedy, television is where it reached its widest audience, shifting culture in real time and embedding itself into the fabric of American life. In the '90s, those stories were joyful, pointed, irreverent, beautiful, complicated, and unapologetic.

This is the story of how we got there. The breakthroughs, the battles, and the brilliance that made it all possible.

A language advisory: Comedy thrives on pushing boundaries, playing with language, and sometimes using words that carry weight. This book explores the history of Black comedy with honesty and respect, which means discussing language and including words that are provocative, controversial, or even offensive. Consider this a heads-up: Comedy doesn't always play by the rules, and neither does its history.

CHAPTER 1
BILLY KERSANDS AND MINSTRELSY

To understand how Black comedians came to shape not only television but the broader contours of American culture, we have to start much earlier—long before the breakout sitcoms of the 1990s. The story begins on the dusty stages of vaudeville, where performers like Billy Kersands laid a comedic foundation, joke by joke, amid a nation still reckoning with the scars of slavery and the deep divides of race.

At the height of his fame in the 1870s, Kersands stepped onto a Southern stage and was met with a sight as surprising as it was profound: a mixed-race audience, Black and white patrons seated together. In an era when rigid segregation dictated nearly every aspect of public life, such a scene was virtually unheard of. Black audience members were typically relegated to balconies or back corners. But Kersands was no ordinary performer. His exaggerated comedic antics packed the seats with Black audiences so eager to see him that money-hungry theater owners started bending their own segregation rules.

They let Black patrons take up half the house—balcony, gallery, ground floor, the works. It was America, after all—greed often wrestled bigotry into submission. If there was one thing that could occasionally overpower bigotry, it was the promise of a bigger payday. And when Kersands was in town, the payday was worth the compromise.

"When his name appeared on the billboards, the whole town would get ready for the show, taking on a holiday air," Black comedian Tom Fletcher wrote in *100 Years of the Negro in Show Business*. Fletcher's work as a historian and performer in the late nineteenth century made him an important figure in preserving the legacy of early African-American entertainers.

Kersands was a minstrel performer—which meant, like all minstrels of his time, he performed in blackface. In the years leading up to the Civil War, white performers in blackface dominated the American stage, making minstrelsy the most popular form of entertainment in the young nation, especially among the struggling working class. In its early years, the world of minstrelsy was rigidly segregated; Black performers were barred from sharing the stage with white acts. That barrier eventually began to crack, but only slightly: Black performers were permitted to join the minstrel circuit—but only if they, too, wore blackface. Some accounts from the era even claimed that white audiences couldn't tell the difference between white and Black performers under the burnt cork. That, frankly, strains credulity.

When white audiences packed theaters to see minstrel shows, they believed they were witnessing an authentic portrayal of Black life on Southern plantations—delivered, ironically, through the wildly exaggerated caricatures performed by white men in blackface. These portrayals were anything but real; they were grotesque parodies designed to entertain by dehumanizing. Black theatergoers, for their part, rarely showed interest in watching white men prance around in tattered clothes and burnt cork, recognizing the cruelty and absurdity behind these so-called depictions of Blackness. But Kersands was different.

He was such a gifted dancer that he's credited with originating the Buck and Wing—a high-energy tap style—and pioneering an early version of the soft shoe. But even more than his footwork, what made Billy Kersands a sensation on the minstrel stage was his ability to create wildly popular, if deeply problematic, characters. He often portrayed a slow-witted plantation worker, singing songs drawn from caricatures of Black life in the South. One of his most requested numbers was "Mary's Gone with a Coon," in which an old man laments that his daughter has "run away wid a big Black coon." Despite the offensive content, the song became a hit, emblematic of how minstrel audiences consumed distorted versions of Black identity as entertainment.

Kersands's greatest claim to fame, however, was not his dancing or his characters—it was his mouth. Literally. He built much of his act around his unusually large mouth, famously stuffing it with props like billiard balls. According to lore, he once fit an entire teacup and saucer inside. While touring Europe with a minstrel troupe, Kersands reportedly told Queen Victoria that if his mouth were any bigger, they'd have to move his ears.

The physical comedy helped set him apart from the white performers who dominated minstrelsy. One critic noted that Kersands had "a copiousness of mouth and breadth of tongue that no White man could ever expect to rival" (Toll 1974, 254). It was both a grotesque gimmick and a defining feature of his stage persona.

Kersands and other Black minstrels often relied on the same painful caricatures that had defined white minstrel acts for decades—portrayals of Black people as slow-witted, bumbling, and confused, their blackened faces exaggerated with oversize red lips. These grotesque stereotypes were rooted in the "Sambo" figure, a fixture of minstrelsy since its emergence in the 1830s. The form's founding myth traces back to Thomas "Daddy" Rice, a white performer who popularized the character Jim Crow after writing and performing the song "Jump Jim Crow," which he claimed was inspired by an elderly Black man he had observed in Washington, DC.

Despite this fraught legacy, Kersands became the first Black entertainer in America to achieve national celebrity. While Frederick Douglass rose to prominence by commanding the attention of the educated elite with his fierce intellect and eloquence, Kersands captured the imagination of the masses with his comedic brilliance. Over a career that spanned four decades, he performed for packed houses across the United States and Europe, becoming a global star at a time when Black performers were still fighting for a place on the stage.

At first glance, the journey from Billy Kersands performing in blackface to Dave Chappelle donning whiteface on his self-titled show more than a century later might seem like a vast distance. Yet, there is a direct and traceable lineage connecting these two comic masters. Both rose to become the most celebrated comedians of their eras—artists whose popularity transcended racial boundaries. Kersands, despite relying on many of the same racist caricatures popularized by white minstrels, was deeply adored by Black audiences. Robert Toll, author of *Blacking Up: The Minstrel Show in Nineteenth-Century America*, suggests that most Black viewers at Kersands's shows were less concerned with how white audiences perceived his performances than with the laughter and connection he inspired within their own communities.

"It was the difference between the Black bourgeoisie with their eyes focused on Whites and on middle-class standards and the masses of Black people whose perspectives were essentially confined to their group and to Afro-American culture," Toll writes. "Unlike Whites, they *knew* the diversity of Black people; they knew all Blacks were not like these stage images and that no Blacks were exactly like them. But they also probably knew Black people who shared some of these traits. They laughed at the familiar in exaggerated form. At least in part, theirs was in-group laughter of recognition, even of belonging."

It is a theory that would be familiar to modern observers perplexed by the popularity among Black people of such lowbrow, stereotypical characters as Tyler Perry's Madea. Indeed, the complicated question of who gets to laugh at whom—and why they are laughing—was a big factor in Chappelle's decision to walk away from his immensely popular *Chappelle's Show* after just two seasons.

Kersands's rise coincided with a fervent curiosity among Northern whites in the decade after the Civil War about slavery and the life of the plantation. While Northern whites had been warned of the hordes of newly emancipated people who would invade the North after the war, no such hordes materialized—leaving room for a nostalgic interest among Northern whites in these former slaves. Exploiting this interest, some Black acts billed themselves as "genuine slave bands" or "former slaves" who would perform in plantation clothes and sing slave songs. They would co-opt Black religious music and add "spirituals" to their shows, though often changing the words.

"Reflecting the immediacy of religion in their everyday lives, slaves had used spirituals as work, social, and marching songs as well as for worship in the narrow sense," Toll writes in *Blacking Up*. "In addition to biblical stories, morality, and redemption, they had sung of food, clothing, dancing, and jesting—subjects that Whites, with their more limited concept of religion, felt were irreverent or irreligious. Thus, when Black minstrels included such material in their spirituals, they seemed to be corroborating deeply embedded White minstrel stereotypes of Negroes."

Because of his popularity, Kersands performed with many minstrel troupes during his forty-year career, such as Sam Hague's Georgia Minstrels and Callender's Georgia Minstrels, where he gained notice because of his "gymnastic drumming." Born in Baton Rouge in 1842, Kersands started his career in the early 1860s, as the country was convulsing during the Civil War. By 1882, Kersands reportedly earned $80 a week, which was only slightly less than the featured white minstrels. When he traveled to Europe, his earnings reached as high as $250 a week. In 1885, he started his own troupe, Kersands' Minstrels, whose famous marching band led a Mardi Gras parade in 1886. Kersands reportedly offered $1,000 to any group that could outmarch his band.

Kersands's star shone brightest in the South. In the words of Tom Fletcher, "In the South, a minstrel show without Billy Kersands is like a circus without elephants." When his fellow Black entertainers had moved away from performing in blackface, instead presenting urban shows that had no connection to plantation life, Kersands refused to give it up. Until his last days, well into the twentieth century, Kersands was still taking to the stage with his face covered in burnt cork.

"All of my money came from the people of the South, the White and the colored, while playing down there. Whether they meant it or not, the way I was treated by them, and still am, I feel at home," Fletcher heard Kersands say one night. "I also make a good living with no worries."

He died in 1915 in New Mexico at the age of seventy-two, suffering a heart attack shortly after a performance with his minstrel troupe. Illustrating how far Kersands and blackface had fallen out of favor among Blacks, the last line of his obit in Louisiana's *Donaldsonville Chief* stated, "The prices to see the old-time king of negro minstrels had dropped from two dollars a seat to fifteen cents."

Minstrel shows surged in popularity during the 1840s, fueled by a growing American appetite for entertainment that spoke to the working-class masses. For decades, these audiences had been migrating to cities in search of better opportunities but still yearned for a connection to the rural traditions they left behind. Minstrelsy quickly emerged as the nation's first—and most influential—form of popular culture. Its appeal crossed social and geographic boundaries: Presidents like John Tyler, James Polk, Millard Fillmore, and Franklin Pierce were among its many admirers, and its reach extended far beyond the East Coast. When gold was discovered in California in 1849, minstrel troupes followed, with as many as five companies performing in San Francisco by 1855. These shows thrived along key transportation routes—from the bustling ports and river towns along the Mississippi to the expanding railroad lines of the Northwest and the crowded cities of the Northeast, including New York, Boston, and Philadelphia. In New York, minstrel companies even built dedicated venues, sometimes dubbed "Ethiopian Opera Houses." Once white audiences caught a taste of this new, raucous entertainment, they couldn't get enough.

In trying to explain its appeal, Toll suggests that minstrels "became a major vehicle through which Northern Whites conceptualized and coped with many of their problems." Toll writes:

> Minstrelsy brought the vitality and vigor of the folk into popular culture. Furthermore, minstrelsy was not only responsive to its audiences, it was very much like them. It was immediate, unpretentious, and direct. It had no characterization to develop, no plot to evolve, no musical score, no set speeches, no subsidiary dialogue—indeed no fixed script at all. Each act—song, dance, joke, or skit—was a self-contained performance that strived to be a highlight of the show. This meant that minstrels could adapt to their specific audience while the show was in process.

The minstrel shows used a three-part format that would appear quite strange to the modern eye. In the first part, the performers arranged themselves in a semicircle, with the three leads in the front. The character known as the "interlocutor" sat in the center; he was the straight man, while the comic characters known as "Mr. Tambo" and "Mr. Bones" sat at opposite ends. In the second part, called the "olio," the characters performed song and dance acts. In the finale, they did a rousing walk-around on the stage.

The shows had an additional benefit: They proclaimed to be authentic depictions of Black life, thus satisfying the burgeoning curiosity in the North about Blacks and slavery as it became an explosively controversial subject in the country. Because Northerners had limited direct contact with Black people during slavery—slavery had existed in the North, but in a form radically different than the Southern agrarian model—they tended to believe the exaggerated and often ridiculous versions of Black life portrayed onstage.

Minstrels illustrated the twoness of the Black mindset, performing for Whites while keeping their true thoughts and feelings closely guarded—hidden by a mask of burnt cork. This reflected the double-consciousness of the Black experience in America that emerged during enslavement. W. E. B. Du Bois would write eloquently of this phenomenon in *The Souls of Black Folk*, published in 1903.

"It is a peculiar sensation, this double-consciousness, this sense of always looking at one's self through the eyes of others, of measuring one's soul by the tape of a world that looks on in amused contempt and pity," Du Bois writes. "One ever feels his twoness—an American, a Negro; two souls, two thoughts, two unreconciled strivings; two warring ideals in one dark body, whose dogged strength alone keeps it from being torn asunder."

Enslaved Blacks learned there was a value in entertaining the white masters—but that value came with an incredibly steep cost.

"These behavioral adjustments forced many African-Americans to assume dual social roles: one for a hostile White world, the other the natural demeanor they reserved for interactions among themselves," Mel Watkins writes in *On the Real Side: Laughing, Lying, and Signifying—the Underground Tradition of African-American Humor that Transformed American Culture, from Slavery to Richard Pryor*. "Humor was a crucial factor in dealing with the situation. In interactions with Whites, it eased tensions that might otherwise have exploded into violence. The humor many African-Americans displayed in public, however, often affirmed America's vision of Blacks as naively funny and fundamentally simpleminded. . . . For a vulnerable Black minority, surreptitiousness and trickery were the principal defenses against repression, and humor played a key role in this deviousness. For much of America's past, the two faces of Black humor could not be combined without serious risk."

If they could keep the master laughing—even if it meant playing the ignorant fool—they might avoid the lash. But that "fool" soon hardened into stereotype, becoming the dominant white perception of the enslaved: a bumbling, childlike figure whose supposed lack of intelligence conveniently justified his continued bondage.

The tension between the public humor Black performers used to entertain white audiences and the sharper, more subversive humor shared within Black communities has endured for centuries. It's a dynamic as old as Black performance itself—layered, coded, and often contradictory. Scholars like Mel Watkins trace the roots of Black humor to the rich oral traditions and layered communication styles of West African societies, where enslaved Africans first learned to mask truth with laughter.

For example, the clever wordplay and punning common in Black humor mirror the verbal ingenuity that enslaved people used as a tool for survival and resistance. Practices such as signifying, or "playing the dozens"—a long-standing tradition in Black culture—can be linked to similar verbal contests found in various African tribal groups. In these societies, the griot—the oral historian and storyteller—often combined comedy, trickster-like wit, music, and storytelling to captivate and entertain audiences, blending humor and history in a way that resonates deeply in the African-American comedic tradition.

"The evidence of Africans' traditional high esteem for 'verbal wit' in discourse and their familiarity with the manner and benefits of 'playing the fool' strongly suggest that blacks were not merely imitating Whites or acting in a purely reflective manner to divert White enmity when they struggled to acquire verbal acuity in English or took on the guise of Sambo or the Fool," Watkins writes. "It seems far more likely that they were simply relying on well-established and highly esteemed customs from their own background, both to sustain a connection with their past and to contend with the 'arrogant contempt' they faced as human chattel in the New World."

They found a way to retain respect for themselves at the same time as satisfying their masters.

The slave owners were so clueless about the inner thoughts and feelings of their slaves that in the following exchange between Pompey and his master—taken from Peter Randolph's 1893 slave narrative *From Slave Cabin to Pulpit*—the master doesn't really grasp what the slave is saying about him because he believes the slave is a naïve simpleton.

> "Pompey, how do I look?" the master asked.
> "O, massa, mighty. You looks mighty."
> "What do you mean 'Mighty,' Pompey?"
> "Why, massa, you looks noble."
> "What do you mean by noble?"
> "Why, suh, you looks just like a lion."
> "Why, Pompey, where have you ever seen a lion?"
> "I saw one down in yonder field the other day, massa."
> "Pompey, you foolish fellow, that was a jackass."
> "Was it, massa? Well, suh, you looks just like him."

Clever slaves could use humor to evade punishment, or to barter for some type of favor or reward. In one common tale, after desperately hungry slaves killed the master's hogs for food, they reported to him that the hogs had died from a horrible disease called malitis. What is *malitis*? The "disease" the hogs contracted after being hit between the eyes with a mallet.

"By becoming amusing darkies who entertained the master and their guests, they found themselves a new identity and a way out of the field, assuring themselves better lodging, elevated status, and better and more adequate food," says *The Redd Foxx Encyclopedia of Black Humor*.

With this link between Black people and humor firmly solidified in the white mind, minstrels became a way for the white entertainer to lean on this link as he applied the burnt cork and portrayed stereotypical characters that his white audience fervently embraced and grew to love.

In *Love & Theft*, writer Eric Lott traces the enormous impact of minstrels up into modern America, calling the minstrel show "ubiquitous, cultural common coin."

"It has been so central to the lives of North Americans that we are hardly aware of its extraordinary influence," Lott writes. "Minstrel troupes entertained presidents (including Lincoln), and disdainful high-minded quarterlies and rakish sporting journals alike followed its course. Figures such as Mark Twain, Walt Whitman, and Bayard Taylor were as attracted to blackface performance as Frederick Douglass and Martin Delany were repelled by it. From 'Oh! Susanna' to Elvis Presley, from circus clowns to Saturday morning cartoons, blackface acts and words have figured significantly in the white Imaginary of the United States."

Minstrelsy was so predominant that any Black performer in the late 1800s couldn't avoid it even if they wanted. In the words of the legendary W. C. Handy, who would become known as the father of the blues, "all the best [Negro] talent of that generation came down the drain. The composers, the singers, the musicians, the speakers—the minstrel show got them all."

After minstrels came vaudeville, Broadway, motion pictures, radio, and television—all owing a debt to the blackface entertainers who first pranced across the stage to entertain the American masses in a manner purposely as far from the pretentious European operas and symphonies as they could get. The list of white actors who performed in blackface in the early and mid-twentieth century is long—Shirley Temple, Al Jolson, Bing Crosby, Eddie Cantor, Bob Hope, Fred Astaire, Judy Garland, Mickey Rooney, and even Mickey Mouse all occupy spots on the list.

CHAPTER 2
BERT WILLIAMS AND GEORGE WALKER

In many ways, exploring Black comedy in America is inseparable from exploring American comedy itself. Black comedians have been so fundamental to shaping the nation's sense of humor that their story cannot—and should not—be told in isolation. Few figures embody this truth better than the incomparable Bert Williams.

Williams was the bridge from the racialized posturing of the minstrels of the late 1800s to the bawdy stand-up joke tellers who emerged after the vaudeville era in the mid-twentieth century. Williams donned the burnt cork, but he managed to imbue his blackface characters with a humanity and even dignity that allowed him to be vigorously embraced by Black audiences as well as white. Given the crassness of the racial stereotypes underpinning most minstrel acts, it is remarkable that a Black man could transcend the form to such an extent that he would be applauded by no less than W. E. B. Du Bois and Booker T. Washington—two leaders as preoccupied with Black respectability and representation as any who ever lived. Neither man had any patience for foolishness and buffoonery.

Du Bois noted that after the minstrel was created by whites to mock Blacks, the form was elevated when Black performers like Williams and his longtime partner George Walker were allowed to step into the spotlight.

"Their development of a new light comedy marked an epoch and Bert Williams was at his recent death without doubt the leading comedian on the American stage," Du Bois wrote in *The Gift of Black Folk: The Negroes in the Making of America* in 1924, shortly after Williams's death in 1922.

In 1910, Washington wrote of Williams: "He has done more for our race than I have. He has smiled his way into people's hearts; I have been obliged to fight my way."

Williams's was a career of firsts: the first Black recording artist (with Walker), star of the first Black musical comedy on Broadway (with Walker), the first Black actor to appear in a movie—the 1916 films *A Natural Born Gambler* and *Fish*, both of which Williams wrote, directed, and starred in. When he signed a contract to perform for the famous *Ziegfeld Follies of 1911*, he was the highest-salaried member of the Follies, an otherwise all-white Broadway production, earning $62,400 a year. At the same time as he broke the color line on Broadway, his talent and popularity forced Florenz Ziegfeld Jr. to pay him more than any white performers—a salary equivalent to more than $2 million in today's dollars. That's how good Williams was.

Born in the Bahamas in 1874, Egbert Austin Williams immigrated to the United States with his parents around the age of ten, eventually settling in Riverside, California. From a young age, Bert was captivated by the "medicine shows" that traveled through rural towns—traveling productions featuring pitchmen hawking miracle cures to eager audiences, often the only form of entertainment available in these communities during the 1890s. Drawn to the excitement, he quit school to pursue his dream of becoming an entertainer.

Charismatic and quick-witted, Bert was hired as a barker, whose job was to spin enticing stories about the wonders waiting inside the tent, luring crowds in. These shows combined dancers, singers, and comedians to provide a much-needed escape from the monotony of small-town life. Tall and fair-skinned, Bert often felt out of place among his peers, which sharpened his powers of observation and mimicry—skills that would become the foundation of his unique comedic talent.

"I suppose it was analysis, but in those times, I didn't think anything about it," Williams said of his childhood observations. "If I had, I should probably have accused myself of idle curiosity. But in retrospect, I can go back very, very far in my life and as I live over those old childhood scenes now, I realize that I was storing away little character sketches that were always to serve me. . . . Truly, it seemed that I was and am still, constantly storing away dialects and little bits of mimicry, together with mental pictures."

As a Caribbean immigrant, Williams did not have a natural grasp of Black Southern dialect. In an essay he published in 1918, Williams acknowledged having to navigate the dual pressures of portraying Black life with authenticity while meeting white audiences' expectations that Black characters were supposed to sound ignorant and uneducated. He said it initially "to me was just as much a foreign dialect as that of the Italian."

He met his longtime partner, George Walker, in California. Where Bert was tall, stocky, and fair-skinned, with somewhat of a reserved personality, George was short, dark-skinned, with an ebullient and confident manner. Born in Lawrence, Kansas, in 1873, George—known as "Nash" to his friends—started his performing career working with twelve other young Black boys in a minstrel troupe. He also worked as a barker for medicine shows, like Bert. He said he learned two important lessons in those early years that he wouldn't ever forget: "White people are always interested in what they call 'darky' singing and dancing and . . . I could entertain in that way as no White boy could."

Bert suffered from a debilitating case of stage fright the first time he applied the burnt cork and took the stage in blackface in San Francisco in the early 1890s. "Although the blackface mask hid him, being on the stage exposed him," Camille F. Forbes writes in *Introducing Bert Williams: Burnt Cork, Broadway, and the Story of America's First Black Star*. He began sweating profusely, turning his face into a streaky zebra-like spectacle. When his stage mate threw lines at him, Bert's mind went blank. As seconds passed, the audience thought the painful silence was part of his act. They howled in laughter.

"Even on his worst day," Forbes writes, "Bert had been a hit."

Bert walked away from that experience vowing never to wear blackface again. However, after he began performing with George, his attitude about the burnt cork changed. At a show in Detroit in 1895, Bert decided to wear the blackface again after having gone years without it and was surprised to discover that his feelings about the makeup had changed. He realized that the makeup hid his true self from the audience, serving as a kind of protection, a buffer.

"A black face, run-down shoes and elbow-out make-up give me a place to hide," Williams explained. "The real Bert Williams is crouched deep down inside the coon who sings the songs and tells the stories."

Williams and Walker were quite the performing phenomenon, becoming the most popular Black comedy duo in the country. Audiences clamored for Williams's ragtime hit "Oh! I Don't Know, You're Not So Warm!"—the song he sang on the fateful day when he decided to once again wear blackface. The duo also scored a hit with "The Coon's Trademark," the lyrics of which demonstrated the racially odious parameters in which they were forced to work.

> *As certain and sure as Holy Writ,*
> *And not a coon's exempt from it,*
> *Four things you'll always find together,*
> *Regardless of condition of sun and moon—*
> *A watermelon, a razor, a chicken, and a coon!*

As Forbes points out, the stereotype had now slid from the lazy and unthreatening Southern rube to a violent and dangerous Northern negro with a razor. So-called "coon songs" had exploded in popularity in the 1890s, appealing to the sensibilities of racist whites pushing ugly stereotypes. The phenomenon gained momentum with the popularity of "All Coons Look Alike to Me," a hit song by African-American blackface performer Ernest Hogan. Hogan had reportedly borrowed the melody and reworked the lyrics from an earlier version that used the phrase "all pimps look alike to me," swapping in the word *coons*. He later claimed that he intended the term as a compliment, suggesting that it associated Black people with the cleverness of raccoons. But whatever his intent, the song played a pivotal role in popularizing the slur among white audiences—and cementing the "coon" stereotype in American entertainment.

Williams and Walker made a savvy move when they included pictures of themselves on their sheet music, wearing elegant, tailored suits. In this way, they were announcing to the public that they were distinct from the stereotypical characters they portrayed onstage.

As Williams and Walker scrambled for work opportunities, they were eager to try their hand at a new form of popular entertainment coming out of New York called vaudeville. Developed by Italian immigrant Tony Pastor, vaudeville was his effort to create a variety show that would be acceptable to the middle class, which shunned the loud, uncouth minstrel shows. A necessity to this end was creating a show that would appeal to women, thus giving the show an air of sophistication. Pastor tamped down the drunken merriment at the shows by banning the serving of alcohol.

Vaudeville kept the tradition of showtime segregation alive by requiring that only one Black act be placed on a bill at a time.

"Blacks' participation in this theatrical world was clearly circumscribed and controlled by white performers' mocking characterizations as well as the preference of the white audiences," Forbes writes. "Though black audiences often did attempt to register their dissatisfaction with their treatment in the theater both on and off the stage by boycotting venues, managers were not compelled to accommodate them. They comprised too small a portion of vaudeville's audience to persuade those in power to change their course."

In their vaudeville act, Williams and Walker called themselves "Two Real Coons" to distinguish themselves from the whites prancing on the stage in blackface.

"They attempted to claim the despised term [coon], using it consciously," Forbes writes. "Rather than accept its assumption of inferiority, they took it on so as to assert their 'realness' in contrast to the counterfeit of white blackface performance."

Williams and Walker took a dance they performed, called the cakewalk, and turned it into a national craze. With gliding, dragging, shuffling steps, the dance can be linked to African tribal rituals and was originally performed by slaves mocking the aristocratic ways of their white masters—though whites didn't recognize that was what the dance was doing. When slaves, dressed in their finery, would battle each other for dance supremacy, the mistress of the house might give the winner a cake as a prize—thus the name. Ada Overton, who would eventually marry George and become Aida Overton Walker, was such a skilled practitioner of the dance that she would give lessons to white women of the upper classes.

Aida came to the duo's attention by happenstance. The American Tobacco Company approached them in 1896 and asked them to appear in an advertisement for the company's product, Old Virginia Cheroots. But the company wanted two women to appear with them in the ad. They found a woman in New York named Stella Wiley to appear with them. Wiley brought along her friend Ada Reed Overton. Described as strong, principled, and independent, Ada—she would later change her name to Aida—had had an unpleasant encounter with another troupe, the Black Patti Troubadours, and had decided she wanted no more to do with show business. But Williams and Walker's manager wanted to recreate the foursome that appeared in the tobacco ad, so they asked Ada to join their act. She kept refusing, but eventually Walker persuaded her, with the agreement that she would only perform in New York. They began performing the cakewalk in their act, and Ada—now Aida—became one of the most skilled practitioners of the dance anyone had ever seen. When they took to the road, she was now more than willing to join them.

Williams and Walker were eager to make their mark in an emerging theatrical world that had taken on the all-encompassing name of its hectic hub—Broadway. Their 1903 play *In Dahomey* was the first full-length musical at a Broadway house written by and starring Blacks. The play was an attempt by Williams and Walker to explore African culture and history onstage—though they had to balance that admirable goal with the less admirable necessity of appealing to a white audience at the same time. It was composed and conducted by Will Marion Cook, a graduate of Oberlin College who served as their company's musical director. Cook's father, John Hartwell Cook, had been a member of the first class at Howard University School of

Law and, as one of the first Black lawyers to practice in Washington, became chief clerk of the Freedman's Bureau and eventually dean of Howard's law school.

"They would strive to remain loyal to their Black audience without alienating the white audience, and to entertain their white audience without degrading themselves and their black audience," Forbes writes. "They would create a majestic spectacle that countered the prevailing image of the 'dark continent.' And in the absence of 'Americanized African songs,' to which George had aspired, they would create songs utilizing the African American idiom of ragtime."

In Dahomey had an extremely successful run on Broadway, but the play's popularity outraged many whites, even leading some to gather in angry mobs outside the New York Theater, where it was staged. To appease the whites, the theater owners retained their segregationist practices inside the theater—especially when they witnessed Black crowds decked out in their evening finery flocking to the theater looking for the best seats they could afford.

"Even those who could afford to pay a dollar for such a seat had to accept accommodation in the gallery or forgo the chance to see the company perform," Forbes writes.

This practice moved a *New York Times* writer to declare that the decision was "a triumph in fact for all concerned." They brought *In Dahomey* to London, where they staged a command performance for King Edward VII at Buckingham Palace in 1903—which Bert would later call "the proudest moment of my life." In London, Aida became the master cakewalk instructor once again, teaching British society how to do the dance.

Williams and Walker followed up *In Dahomey* with another Broadway musical, *Abyssinia*, which was even more grand than *In Dahomey*. It also allowed Bert an opportunity to show his range as a serious dramatic actor—something he had been yearning to do. With music written in an operatic style mostly by Will Marion Cook, *Abyssinia* wasn't as warmly received by the white critics, with one questioning why whites would want to see Blacks make a serious musical in the style of whites "when they can have the real thing better done by

White people almost any week in theatrical season." Another critic faulted the play for having "barely a trace of negroism"—which meant the stereotypical characterizations they had grown used to seeing in minstrel shows.

In early 1906, Bert and George returned to the recording studio for what would be George's final session—he never enjoyed making records. During this session, Bert recorded "Nobody," the most popular song of his career. Delivered in a distinctive half-recited, half-sung style that became his signature, the song eventually sold hundreds of thousands of copies. Modern listeners have even likened his approach to the rhythmic spoken-word style used by contemporary rappers. Over the years, "Nobody" was covered by a diverse range of artists, from Nina Simone to Johnny Cash.

In 1908, tragedy struck when George suffered a stroke while performing onstage. It was later revealed that he was battling syphilis, an incurable disease at the time. George died in January 1911 at just thirty-eight years old, leaving Bert devastated. George's wife, Aida, stepped in to perform alongside Bert, but eventually, Bert carried the show solo.

As a solo act, Bert's star continued to rise, but he still faced the relentless sting of racism that shadowed his career. In his memoir, famed vaudeville comic Buster Keaton recounts a story that illustrates the daily challenges Bert endured even as a nationally celebrated performer:

> When Negroes were allowed in white saloons at all they were restricted to the end of the bar farthest from the door. Pop [Keaton's father] ignored this the night he walked into the Adams Hotel bar in Boston, which was conveniently situated, being directly behind Keith's Theatre. Bert Williams, who was again on the bill with us, was standing, as required, far down at the other end.
>
> "Bert," said Pop, "come up here and have a drink with me."
>
> Bert looked nervously from one white face at the bar to another, and replied, "Think I better stay down here, Mr. Joe."

"All right," said Pop, picking up his glass, "then I'll have to come down there to you." (Forbes 2008, 178)

Bert frequented saloons, where he was often welcomed by white patrons, but he was always wary that at any moment his presence could turn into an ugly encounter.

Coming out of vaudeville, Flo Ziegfeld established a variety show featuring comedians and chorus girls and called it *Follies of 1907*, eventually becoming *Ziegfeld Follies*. Ziegfeld was hoping the Follies would be considered closer to legitimate theater than the raucous vaudeville shows; his Follies would become enormously successful. But he would face dissension from his all-white cast when he decided to add Bert Williams to the show. Despite their protests, Ziegfeld considered Bert to be vital to his show and wouldn't budge. But Blacks weren't allowed to buy tickets to the Follies, meaning they couldn't see Bert's triumphant, race-busting performances. Many Blacks called on him to speak up for them, but it wasn't in his nature to protest publicly. He said he joined the Follies cast to break down barriers as a pioneer—even if Blacks couldn't see him.

Bert eventually decided to leave the Follies in 1918 out of frustration that his talents weren't being fully utilized. An article in the *Crisis*, the NAACP magazine founded and edited by W. E. B. Du Bois, reported that Williams walked away "alleging that while his name was carried to help the show, his parts have not been commensurate with his ability or reputation" (Forbes 2008, 329).

After leaving the Follies, Bert recorded numerous songs for Columbia Records, including several "Prohibition songs" bemoaning the disappearance of alcohol and saloons, that were big hits. He also recorded monologues that featured his amusing take on such scenes as a Black preacher speaking to his congregation.

W. C. Fields famously called Bert "the funniest man I ever saw, and the saddest man I ever knew."

When Bert died on March 4, 1922, there was a great deal of sorrow, but also recognition of the magnitude of his career and life. More than 5,000 people crowded into St. Philips Episcopal Church in Harlem to view his body, with thousands more lining the streets outside to be close to him. The Masonic Lodge in Manhattan held a second funeral for Williams at the all-white Grand Lodge, with 2,000 people crowding into the 1,200-seat venue on West Twenty-Third Street. It was the first time in New York State that a white masonic lodge held services for a Black man.

White writers extolled Bert's comic genius and praised his contributions to the Negro race. "Williams put into his quaint songs and humorous sayings the quality and philosophy of the Negro race," wrote the *New York Tribune*. "He did for one side of Negro life and character just what the plantation Negroes did for another. He gave expression to and put into form easily understood and appreciated something of the inner life and peculiar talent of the Negro."

Caribbean writer Eric Walrond, who gained fame during the Harlem Renaissance of the 1920s, wrote a piece after Bert's death that probed the contradicting sides of Bert at war in his soul:

> Although it was his business to make people laugh, there were times when he would go into his shell-like cave of a mind and reflect—and fight it out.
>
> "Is it worth it?" one side of him would ask. "Is it worth it, the applause, the financial rewards, the fame? Is it really worth it—lynching one's soul in blackface twaddle?"
>
> "But it is the only way you can break in," protests the other side of the man. "It is the only way. That is what the white man expects of you—comedy—blackface comedy. In time you know, they'll learn to expect serious things from you. In time." (Forbes 2008, 329)

Over the years, many subsequent generations of African Americans hesitated to fully recognize Bert Williams's genius because his legacy was overshadowed by the blackface he wore—a symbol of unforgivable racism. This painful tension came into sharp focus in 1981, when legendary actor and performer Ben Vereen paid tribute to Williams during Ronald Reagan's inauguration. Vereen first became fascinated by Williams during his Tony Award–winning run as the star of the Broadway play *Pippin* in the early 1970s.

As Vereen explained to me, a man who attended the play gifted him a copy of *Nobody: The Story of Bert Williams* by Ann Charters, published just a year earlier in 1970. Vereen, who knew little about the history of minstrelsy, was captivated by the story of this pioneering artist.

"I started reading it; I couldn't put it down," Vereen recalled. "I had started to think about an act to take out on the road. Something's got to be said about this, I thought to myself. Black artists like me were in the entertainment industry and didn't know anything about our roots in the business."

Vereen developed a one-man show about Williams and took it on tour, recounting Bert's career on Broadway and with the Ziegfeld Follies alongside legends such as Eddie Cantor and W. C. Fields. Vereen recalled the transformative moment in his act:

"I sit down at the table and I slowly become Bert Williams as I put on the black makeup. After I finish, I get up and I sing and dance as Bert. I do the cakewalk that he made famous. Then I sit down at the table again and start wiping off the blackface. It reveals the painful, dehumanizing process he had to go through in order to entertain white folks."

A few years later, Frank Sinatra called Vereen and asked him to perform at Reagan's inauguration. Vereen saw it as a unique opportunity to offer an important lesson in Black history to the new president and his supporters.

"I thought I could smack this cat, this new ultra-conservative president, and show him sectors of our society and history he now had to face," Vereen said with a chuckle.

But Vereen admitted he didn't have enough time to provide the full context for Williams and blackface during the performance. When aired, the segment was severely edited—omitting Vereen's explanation and the crucial moment of wiping off the blackface. Instead, viewers only saw a Black man in blackface dancing and shuffling onstage.

"Oh God," Vereen said when he learned how the act was cut.

The backlash was swift and fierce. Vereen joked that this was the first truly bad cut of the Reagan years. Many Black viewers were outraged; the *Chicago Defender* called him "a disgrace to the race." Even worse, attendance at his one-man show, which had previously been popular, plummeted. When comedian Dick Gregory advised Vereen to apologize, he replied, "Dick, I can't apologize. That's like you asking a Jew to apologize for the Holocaust. I can't do it."

As Vereen's tribute showed, Bert Williams's story is not just about blackface or entertainment—it's about the difficult choices Black artists have long faced to be seen and heard.

CHAPTER 3
STEPIN FETCHIT

They gathered downtown at the Civic Club in lower Manhattan—bright, ambitious, and determined to chart a new course for Black art and identity. Among them were Jean Toomer, Langston Hughes, Countee Cullen, and Alain Locke, all emerging as literary lions poised to reshape American letters. The invitation came from sociologist Charles S. Johnson, the Urban League's national director of research and investigations and editor of its influential magazine, *Opportunity*. That evening in March 1924 would come to be known as the spark that lit the Harlem Renaissance.

On the heels of World War I, this group of thinkers felt that they could use the arts and literature as tools to fight American racism by depicting more complete, more progressive portraits of Black life than the stereotypical Sambos, Mammies, and Uncle Toms.

"While white society had geared itself to resist advances by blacks in employment, voting, housing, and union affiliation, there were fewer obstacles to blacks in publishing and entertainment," Mel Watkins writes in *On the Real Side*.

Locke wrote an influential book entitled *The New Negro* in which he argued that Blacks had moved far beyond Mammy and Sambo as they flocked to the cities of the North and Midwest and became more sophisticated and urbane. However, most of white America had little interest in this emerging artistic movement in Harlem. America was still feasting on the simplistic, offensive characterizations of Black life shown in minstrel joke books and, for the better educated, magazines like *Judge* and *College Humor*.

This is a sample of the fare in *Judge*, in a 1919 column called "Darkeyisms":

> "Seems to me," said Mammy Chloe, "dat sometimes you'd rather sleep than eat."
> "Speck I would," answered Pickaninny Jim. "Cause when I'se asleep I'se liable to dream about fried chicken an' spare ribs an' watermelon—an' I ain't seen no such dinner as dat in a long time."

Or another from *Judge* (1922):

> Doctor (noticing a squalling black child on the floor): Missus Johnson, that baby is spoiled, isn't he?
> Mrs. Johnson: No sah, doctah, all nigger babies smell dat way.

WHILE BLACK WRITERS and artists looked to Harlem as a source of optimism and inspiration, whites saw Harlem and other centers of urban Black life as alluring quarters for their more licentious desires. "They rushed to see and hear African-American musicians, mimicked black dances, and glorified black style while, in private, they retained their disdainful view of Negroes," Watkins writes. "Even as they violently suppressed black efforts to advance in education and employment, and exercise their lawful rights, whites turned to the black community as a model for their rebellion against puritanical rural values."

This was evidenced by their nightly presence in Black population centers such as Chicago's South Side, Watts's Central Avenue in Los Angeles, Beale Street in Memphis, and Harlem.

As the Roaring Twenties roared on, speakeasies and nightclubs popped up across Lenox Avenue and Seventh Avenue in Harlem—many of them owned by mobsters and, despite their location in the heart of Black New York, all of them exclusively reserved for whites, except for the service staff and the performers onstage.

As noted by Watkins, "These clubs generally indulged the white stereotype of blacks as natural primitives."

While the nation continued to search for ways to amuse itself, American popular entertainment was subsumed by two inventions that changed everything: talking films and radio. For Black performers, it was a struggle trying to break into these new spaces. Initially, efforts to put Blacks on-screen were aided by the claims of Black filmmaker and promoter Bill Foster, who said that Black voices were "recorded with better fidelity than white" and were a better fit than whites for sound pictures. That notion circulated throughout the film industry, aided by the discovery that the voices of many of the white silent film stars were too weak for talking pictures. Ironically, Hollywood responded by producing a rash of films featuring whites in blackface—most famously Al Jolson in 1927's *The Jazz Singer*, the film credited with launching the sound era. There were many all-Black musical shorts and feature productions; two of the most noteworthy were the full-length 1929 films *Hallelujah!* and *Hearts in Dixie*. While *Hearts in Dixie* was filled with the typical nonsense such as dancing pickaninnies, the movie did introduce a performer who would become one of the most famous and ultimately controversial Black comedians in the country: Stepin Fetchit.

In his lazy buffoon character, Fetchit would reflect the Black community's long-standing struggle with Black participation in Hollywood and the intoxicating power and destructiveness of Black imagery in film. This struggle really commenced with D. W. Griffith's groundbreaking 1915 *Birth of a Nation*, which mesmerized the country with its glorification of the Ku Klux Klan and devastatingly offensive portrayal of Blacks. So powerful was the film that it led to violence and rioting in dozens of cities across the country, resulting in hundreds of deaths.

Hollywood had no interest in presenting balanced portrayals of Black life. The Black characters that appeared on-screen closely resembled the clownish stereotypes popularized by the minstrels. If they wanted to continue working, Black performers had no choice but to play the role. Their frustration is apparent in a letter Langston Hughes wrote to fellow Harlem Renaissance writer Arna Bontemps, complaining about the seductiveness of Hollywood. Hughes had been asked to write for trite Hollywood productions like Sol Lesser's 1939 film *Way Down South*.

"The bad things I do are the only things that ever make me any money," he writes. "Never take a Hollywood job."

"Hollywood is our *bête noir*," Hughes would later write. "It is America's (and the world's) most popular art. . . . Yet, shamelessly and to all the world since its inception, Hollywood has spread in exaggerated form every ugly and ridiculous stereotype of the deep South's conception of Negro character."

Born Lincoln Theodore Monroe Andrew Perry (his father launched his comic career by naming him after four US presidents) in Key West, Florida, on May 30, 1902, Stepin Fetchit was the nation's first Black movie star. Fetchit perfected the act of the slow-witted, slow-footed, lazy coon so well that his name became synonymous with embarrassing Black stereotypes. He actually dubbed himself "the Laziest Man in the World," bringing to the screen intact the coon caricature he had already honed onstage.

"On stage, he would come shuffling out, scratching his head, looking for all the world as if he were utterly confused and lost," Watkins writes in *On the Real Side*. "Mouth agape, eyes half closed, shoulders slumped, he would embark on his practically incoherent monologue—usually in a whining monotone that had little meaning beyond the visual impression of confusion it conveyed. Then, suddenly, he would begin a controlled dance routine that amazed his audience; as he danced, his facial expressions changed subtly, the half-closed lids lifting, the eyes widening momentarily to reveal the spark of enthusiasm and arrogance that his simpleton mask concealed. Without this contrast, Fetchit frequently moved beyond that thin line that separates the humorous from the pathetic. On the screen, the contrast was often absent."

What distinguished Fetchit from many of his contemporaries was his gift for self-promotion. He encouraged the myth that he couldn't read or write to enhance his coon image—and also cleverly to discourage directors from giving him an actual script, leaving him much more control over what his characters said in the films. He played up his absentmindedness and indolence, dropping items in the gossip columns and newsclips that furthered the image—helped by the publicity machine at Fox Pictures. His slow-footed gait was so indelible that people questioned whether he was even capable of breaking into a run. Commentators noted that shoeshine boys and busboys began to imitate Fetchit's notorious walk in the real-world streets. News reports gleefully described his six houses, his sixteen Chinese servants, his lavish parties, his $2,000 cashmere suits, and his twelve cars—one of which was a champagne-pink Cadillac with his name splashed across the side in neon lights. These antics made him even more famous, though they obviously put a target on his back, as they embarrassed many middle-class Blacks.

By the time the 1950s rolled around, calling a Black person "Stepin Fetchit" was a stinging put-down. But at the height of his influence, Fetchit epitomized the success that was possible if a Black man was willing to demean himself by playing the king of the coons on-screen.

Fetchit made one of his first film appearances in 1927's *In Old Kentucky*, playing a lazy, malingering stable hand. In *On the Real Side*, Watkins recounts a story told by one of Fetchit's relatives—taken from an unpublished manuscript—about how he got his first film role. Fetchit heard the studios were looking for a "colored boy," so he brought his stage act—with comic Ed Lee, he called his act "Step and Fetch It"—directly to the audition.

> He said he just stood there looking like he didn't know
> where he was or why he was there and he was scratching his
> head, which he had shaved clean, and he was just looking
> around like he was lost. I guess he looked so sad and lost and
> everything that he got their attention.
>
> So, one of the directors, he pointed at Step and he said,

"Say, You!" And Step, he looked all around the place acting like he thought they couldn't have been talking to him, but knowing all the time they were, and they called him again. He turned around all slow and wide-eyed and pointed to himself and said, "Is you talkin' to me?" And the dumber he acted, the more they laughed, because nobody had ever seen anybody *that* slow and ignorant. So they told him that he had the part.

Fetchit made his first major screen appearance in the 1929 film *Hearts in Dixie*, the first full-length, all-Black movie produced in Hollywood. Playing alongside Clarence Muse, who portrays a tenant farmer, Fetchit was cast as the clichéd buffoon, lazy and happy-go-lucky. His performance stood out from the hardworking fieldhands around him because of his clever wordplay and his impressive dance moves.

Fetchit benefitted greatly from the period in Hollywood that Donald Bogle called the "Age of the Negro Servant." Bogle links the predominance of servants on-screen in the 1930s to the Great Depression.

"In the movies, as in the streets, it was a time when the only people without job worries were the maids, the butlers, the bootblacks, the bus boys, the elevator men, the cooks, and the custodians," Bogle writes in *Toms, Coons, Mulattoes, Mammies, & Bucks*. "The Black servants of the Hollywood films of the 1930s met the demands of their times. . . . As they delivered their wisecracks or acted the fool, the servants were a marvelous relief from the harsh financial realities of the day. . . . They were always ready to lend a helping hand when times were tough."

Nobody was better positioned to take advantage of this Hollywood obsession with servants than Fetchit, whose characterizations exuded "servant" with every fiber of his being. He was the best known and most successful Black actor working in Hollywood in the early 1930s, appearing in forty-four films between 1927 and 1939. He was the first Black actor to earn a million dollars. Special scenes were often written into movies just for him.

Fetchit's career benefited from his friendship with the humorist and comic actor Will Rogers, who transitioned so successfully from vaudeville to films that he became the highest paid actor in Hollywood. Rogers's homespun wit and political observations were so popular that his weekly syndicated newspaper column reached 40 million readers in 1926. Rogers, who liked to work with his friends, asked Fetchit to costar in four films—two in 1934 (*David Harum* and *Judge Priest*) and two in 1935 (*The County Chairman* and *Steamboat Round the Bend*). But as Rogers's shiftless sidekick, Fetchit was frequently demeaned by Rogers, who would scold him, push him, and even kick him in the behind on-screen.

"It was perfectly acceptable for [Rogers] to talk to Fetchit in much the same manner that one would address a not too bright house pet," one commentator noted of the pair.

As the 1930s progressed, Fetchit's appearances in films like 1934's *Stand Up and Cheer*, with Shirley Temple, became predictable and embarrassing for all who watched. By the late '30s, both movie audiences and studio execs weren't much interested in Fetchit. Black people had grown so disturbed by his characters that they publicly voiced their protests over his work. As a result, his influence inside Fox Studio waned considerably, particularly after Will Rogers died in a plane crash in 1935. Walter White, executive secretary of the NAACP, lobbied the film studios in 1942 to stop portraying Blacks in demeaning, stereotypical roles, specifically citing Fetchit.

Fetchit worked with stars such as Louis Armstrong at the downtown Cotton Club in Manhattan and with Moms Mabley on the Black "Chitlin' Circuit"—though even those jobs dried up eventually. When he made an appearance in 1952's *Bend of the River*, the *New York Times* wrote, "We are sorry to note that Stepin Fetchit is back to play a clownish stereotype."

But Fetchit fought back. Trying to save his career, he attacked civil rights leaders for attacking him. "Me and the civil rights movement don't get along," he said during a radio interview, going on to accuse civil rights leaders of having "un-American interests." Bizarrely, Fetchit reappeared in the mid-1960s as part of Muhammad Ali's entourage. But any chance of a comeback was shut down when CBS broadcast a program in July 1968 as part of its Of Black America series that focused on the harm Fetchit had done to the image of African Americans.

"The tradition of lazy, stupid, crap-shooting, chicken-stealing idiot was popularized by an actor named Lincoln Theodore Monroe Andrew Perry," narrator Bill Cosby intoned, reading a script labeled "Black History—Lost, Stolen or Strayed."

Fetchit filed a lawsuit against CBS three years later, stating that the program "pretended to relieve racial tension through education and understanding by slurring an entire generation of Negro Americans as inept" and seeking $3 million for malice, invasion of privacy, and defamation of character.

"It was Step who elevated the Negro to the dignity of a Hollywood star," he claimed. "I made the Negro a first-class citizen all over the world . . . somebody it was all right to associate with. I opened all the theaters."

His lawsuit didn't go anywhere. After a couple of film appearances in the 1970s, Fetchit suffered a debilitating stroke in 1976; he died in 1985.

In his review of Mel Watkins's 2005 biography *Stepin Fetchit: The Life and Times of Lincoln Perry*, critic Armond White posed provocative questions that still resonate for Black artists today—questions about the boundaries and responsibilities of Black art. The tension between highbrow and lowbrow comedy, and what is deemed acceptable by image-conscious Black middle-class audiences, continues to ignite fierce debate—nearly a century after Stepin Fetchit first appeared on-screen.

"Given the contemporary success of black performers and innumerable hip-hop artists who flirt with shameless, disreputable images, Stepin Fetchit's legacy—from popular figure to pariah—takes on new importance," White wrote. "Should African-American performers be accountable to political correctness? To what degree should they worry that their antics shape the self-image of young African-Americans? Should they follow any standard other than their own conscience? Should they have a conscience?"

Watkins contends that Fetchit's career was a "microcosm" of the Black experience in America during the first half of the twentieth century—giving white people a handy way of delineating the American Dream by offering a group who served as its opposite, thus giving form to the dream. As long as you were doing better than Blacks, the dream remained a possibility for you.

"Without doubt, the image of blacks during this period was distorted and demeaning—in many instances, irredeemably so," he writes. "But subterfuge and playing the fool were indispensable tactics for blacks before the mid-twentieth century. To ignore this point is a questionable attempt to conceal a rich and ingenious part of the African-American heritage."

CHAPTER 4
HATTIE McDANIEL

While Fetchit was establishing himself as one of the most extreme examples of the Hollywood servant, Hattie McDaniel used an entirely different approach to portray the hired help. McDaniel was bossy, sharp-witted, and had no interest in suffering fools. And she was funny. Her magnetic screen presence and acting talents were on full display in her most celebrated work, as the maid overseeing the Tara plantation and the O'Hara family in *Gone with the Wind*.

That role earned her an Academy Award for Best Supporting Actor in 1939; she was the first Black person to win an Oscar. In total, McDaniel played a servant in more than 300 films—though she only got credit for 83. After the Oscar, finding it impossible to break free of the servant role, she became the first Black actor to star in her own radio show, *Beulah*. She subsequently starred in the television version of the show, replacing Ethel Waters and earning $2,000 a week on the popular but controversial show.

Born on June 10, 1893, in Wichita, Kansas, Hattie McDaniel showed her flair for performance at an early age. Hattie was the youngest of twelve children, though only seven survived to adulthood. She was greatly influenced by her older brother Otis, eleven years her senior. Otis—described by Hattie McDaniel biographer Jill Watts as "dashing and debonair"—was viewed as a budding star by the Black community in Denver, where Hattie grew up. Otis worked as a porter at a white barbershop, sweeping the floor and doing various chores, but he had loftier ambitions. He had no interest in being chained to the menial labor that most African Americans accepted as their fate. He saw a path to a show business career in the example set by the comedy troupe Williams and Walker, particularly the work of Bert Williams. The family went to see Williams and Walker in 1897, profoundly affecting both Otis and young Hattie, and also their brother Sam.

When she was six, Hattie declared that she wanted to be an actress. "I always wanted to be before the public," she said, according to the Watts biography. "I'm always acting. I guess it's just the ham in me."

A couple years later, the family was in dire financial straits, so Otis took Hattie to a carnival where he and she might earn some money singing and dancing for the crowd. She earned $5 that week—the equivalent of about $185 today—to contribute to the family coffers. It was an important lesson for her; she could use her many talents to entertain white folks and earn cash.

During her freshman year at East River High School, she won a drama contest, sponsored by the Women's Christian Temperance Union, for her rendition of a touching poem called "Convict Joe" about a man who murdered his wife. She would later tell journalists that it was a pivotal event on her path to show business, though she had been performing for many years at that point. That same year, she and three of her siblings—Otis, Sam, and her sister Etta, who was also a talented performer—appeared with J. M. Johnson's Mighty Minstrels. In 1909 Hattie joined a New York–based minstrel troupe, the Red Devils, when they came through Denver for a few days. She also appeared that year in a play written by her brother Otis, an ambitious spectacle about newly freed slaves called *Champion of the Freedman* that drew a strong crowd.

McDaniel quit high school that year and soon joined a traveling theatrical group started by Otis that consisted of ten members, including Otis's new wife, Sue. After they disbanded the troupe, Otis developed his own act, taking the extremely daring step of performing in whiteface, unheard of for a Black act in 1910. Back in Denver, Hattie won raves for her performance in *The Great $4,000 Electrical Ball*.

"Miss McDaniel is one of Denver's clever little singing comediennes and she brought down the house with applause," crowed a review in *Franklin's Statesman*. Watts pointed out that show business opportunities were rare for Black women in the early 1900s and only one Black woman, Aida Overton Walker, George's wife, had achieved national fame.

"Most African-American women were held to rigid gender conventions, expected to settle down into a traditional marriage with children, and, confronting economic realities and racism, to accept jobs primarily working as servants for white families," Watts writes.

McDaniel was all too aware of this reality, as she was forced to take jobs herself as a domestic. Watts claims that servant jobs weren't that far removed from slavery, as the women, often living in the employer's home, had to be on call twenty-four hours a day, with only Sundays off. After she rose to prominence as Hollywood's most famous servant, McDaniel would emphasize that she considered this "honorable" work—though she added that she never had to work for an entire year as a maid.

In May 1914—three years after Hattie married a gifted piano player named Howard Hickman—she formed her own all-female minstrel troupe with the help of her sister Etta. A crowd of 500 turned out for the first show, which featured a script and two original songs written by McDaniel herself. The troupe was a big hit and continued working in venues throughout Denver's Black community. One of the most noteworthy aspects of the McDaniel Sisters Company, as it was called, was McDaniel's idea to mock the white fixation with the Mammy character. As Donald Bogle notes in *Toms, Coons, Mulattoes, Mammies, & Bucks*, Mammy is very closely related to the comic coons, except she's female, and often overweight and mean.

McDaniel exaggerated the character to "grotesque" extremes, making her a clear object of ridicule. The all-Black crowds she played in front of got it right away, understanding clearly what McDaniel was doing, parodying the foolish, silly, and asexual caretaker Mammy.

"This stereotype, like other black images, was a by-product of white imaginations," Watts writes. "This audaciously comedic, yet forcefully serious performance won her admiration within Denver's black community. It was funny but it was also revolutionary, exposing white America's weaknesses and delusions."

It is profoundly ironic that McDaniel would gain notice for her clever subversion of Mammy in 1914, when she was just twenty-one, considering that she would become a target for image-conscious African Americans a quarter century later for playing so many obsequious servants in literally hundreds of Hollywood films.

The 1920s found McDaniel touring the country with an act she had honed that utilized her singing, dancing, and comedic talents. McDaniel billed herself as "the female Bert Williams," though she brought far more energy to the stage than the slow-moving Williams ever did. McDaniel worked the venues that were part of the Black vaudeville circuit known as the TOBA (Theatre Owners Booking Association) circuit, a nationwide chain of theaters offering Black acts to Black audiences. Organized by Black comedian Sherman Dudley in the 1910s, TOBA was crucially important to Black artists, giving them a slate of venues across the country where they could make money and keep eating—barely. At its peak in the 1920s, the circuit boasted more than forty theaters, including the Palace in Memphis, the Lyric in New Orleans, the Royal in Baltimore, the Howard in Washington, DC, the Regal and Monogram in Chicago, the Lincoln and Lafayette in Harlem. About a third of the theater owners were Black; the rest were white.

The TOBA tour was notoriously grueling, with performers playing three back-to-back shows a night, six days a week, for meager pay. Some of the owners were dishonest—and racist—and might refuse to pay an artist what they were promised. Actor Clarence Muse, the first African American to star in a Hollywood film, 1929's *Hearts in Dixie* with Stepin Fetchit, said of TOBA, "The actor who played this time usually ended up at the close of the season as broke as when he started."

What made the TOBA tour even more challenging was the fact that many of the theaters were located in the racist, segregated South. Theater owners didn't pay for travel, so artists were left to their own devices figuring out how to safely move from one town to the next.

"Engagements often required traveling hundreds of miles by bus through towns displaying signs that warned 'No Niggers Allowed!'" Watkins writes in *On the Real Side*. "Finding sleeping accommodations was always difficult; segregated restaurants and diners often meant traveling miles out of the way to eat, or worse, simply going hungry."

One of the worst theater owners was the nasty, unscrupulous racist Charles P. Bailey, owner of Atlanta's 81 Theatre on Decatur Street. According to Watkins, Bailey ran his theater like an antebellum plantation in the 1910s and '20s, when he was one of the most powerful men in Atlanta. He once beat Bessie Smith and had her thrown in jail. Ethel Waters had to flee the city after a heated argument with Bailey in which he told her, "No Yankee nigger bitch is telling me how to run my theater." She countered, "You and no other cracker sonofabitch can tell me what to do." She had to leave her fee and her costumes behind and take a horse and buggy to an out-of-the-way railroad station from which she could get out of Atlanta and evade Bailey's wrath.

To Black artists, TOBA stood for "Tough on Black Asses." But still, despite its many drawbacks, the circuit was exceedingly important to Black artists, giving all but the most famous their only opportunity to make a living as an entertainer. Watkins asserts that the TOBA years were one of the most important chapters in African-American entertainment history.

"It provided the principal stage for the transition from minstrelsy's rigidly maintained stereotypes to a performance style that more accurately reflected the majority tastes of the black community," Watkins writes. "Just as, later, Apollo Theater audiences were known to be demanding and impatient, TOBA circuit audiences were outspoken and inhospitable to acts that were either lackluster or strayed too far from preferred black performance style. . . . Audiences would greet unpopular acts with derisive catcalls, invective, and an occasional flying missile. That was usually enough to tighten up a performer's act."

Ma Rainey even sang about TOBA:

*You didn't ask me but I'm gonna tell you anyway
you might'ner . . . never heard old "Ma" sing them blues
if it wasn't for the T-O-B-A*

TOBA was a crucial step in the century-long progression for Black private humor, for the first time consistently putting it on display onstage for Black audiences—where it could also be seen and heard by whites (and stolen by white entertainers). It was still mostly shared in all-Black settings, but it was moving closer to its mainstream moment. The TOBA circuit was a source of embarrassment for many middle-class Blacks, who felt the humor was too crass and too close to the buffoonish characterizations they were trying to eradicate. As pointed out by Watkins, the humor on the TOBA circuit began to mature during the 1920s and early 1930s, moving closer to the style that would later be employed by comedians such as Slappy White, Redd Foxx, Nipsey Russell, Flip Wilson, and Richard Pryor.

With the onset of the Great Depression, as survival replaced the decadence of the Roaring Twenties, many vaudeville theaters shuttered their doors. Black entertainers were devastated by the crumbling of the TOBA network, whose owners also couldn't afford to stay open.

In the summer of 1926, McDaniel met a talented Black performer in Kansas City, Missouri, named Hartzell "Tiny" Parham, so nicknamed because of his enormous size (Black folk have always loved funny, ironic nicknames). A talented pianist and arranger who was a fixture in Kansas City's budding jazz and blues scene, Parham helped Black musicians by transcribing their original compositions into sheet music on paper. Joined by Parham, McDaniel recorded two blues songs she composed, "Quittin' My Man Today" and "Brown Skin Baby Doll." They had limited distribution, but they provided her with an entry into the music industry and allowed her to add *recording artist* and *songwriter* to her resume along with *comedian* and *blues singer*. In November of that year, she recorded two more original songs, "I Wish I Had Somebody" and "Boo Hoo Blues," this time for the national OKeh Race Records line, considered the apex for Black artists hoping to hit it big.

The blues became an important vehicle for McDaniel to express feelings and opinions that she would normally be barred from saying out loud, in this case laments about the male exploitation of women—an understandable topic for a woman who was regularly at the mercy of TOBA theater owners. Also, her marriage to Nym Lankfard had crumbled, certainly adding sauce to her blues.

"It must have been liberating for a woman who, confined by racism and sexism, found she had little power or control over much of her life," Watts writes. "Hattie McDaniel's was a constant struggle to claim control, to gain her independence. And with the blues, she was in a process of developing a persona that was brazen and insubordinate, a powerful, Black, feminist stage presence."

She continued to record throughout the 1920s, sometimes with Parham or other bandleaders like clarinetist Vance Dixon and vocalist Papa Charlie Jackson. After she moved to Chicago, she worked odd jobs to feed herself when gigs were scarce—at one point she was a restroom attendant at Sam Pick's Suburban Inn, waiting on white women using the toilet. When the venue was desperate for a singer, McDaniel stepped forward and thrilled the crowd with her rendition of W. C. Handy's "St. Louis Blues." She made $90 in tips and was offered a permanent gig, which she held for the next two years.

"I never had to go back to my maid's job," she would later recall.

But after the stock market crash in October 1929, the economy grew increasingly ugly, putting Americans on food lines across the country. By 1931, Sam Pick's Inn was forced to shutter. When Hattie's brother Sam beckoned her to Hollywood, where he had his own popular radio show on KNX called *Optimistic Do-Nuts*, she moved west. Sam was also doing a lot of work in the movies, where he was steadily getting parts, even some speaking roles. Their sister Etta, who worked as a live-in housekeeper for a wealthy Los Angeles family, also got work as a movie extra. At a time when Americans were searching for some form of subsistence, when theaters were shuttered, vaudeville was nearly defunct, the recording industry was in dire straits, and TOBA was gone, McDaniel looked to film as one of the few avenues for steady work as an entertainer.

One of the first stops McDaniel had to make if she was going to get a film career off the ground was to Charles Butler at Central Casting. He was the Black man hired by the Central Casting Corporation, which was run by the Motion Picture Producers Association, to head a division devoted to recruiting and casting Black performers for extras and bit parts. Butler would make two daily stops to the fourteen Hollywood studios to deliver news of casting calls to bit players, as well as to deliver their paychecks. According to Watts, Butler used his keen memory to recall the names and phone numbers of nearly all of the 1,500 Black actors registered with Central Casting in the early 1930s. But Butler was viewed with suspicion by many Black players because of his closeness to the studios, with some alleging that he played favorites and took money under the table to deliver choice roles.

When asked by the studio to deliver a "type," Butler would find actors who matched the physical ideal the studio was seeking. In some cases, he might have to gather as many as 500 people for a crowd scene. The Black players were nearly always cast as servants—mammies, maids, butlers, waiters, and porters—as the film industry had no interest in subverting racist stereotypes and white supremacist ideology. Dark-skinned and overweight—reportedly weighing close to 300 pounds, according to Bogle—McDaniel was a mammy the second she walked in the door.

"Black characters became props, manipulated by White filmmakers to signal specific messages regarding White social position and racial ideology," Watts writes. "Additionally, these images were often used as comic relief, expressed through distorted accents, large rolling eyes, wide minstrel-like grins, and dimwittedness."

White filmmakers wanted their Black servants to talk in such a broke-down, stereotypically ignorant-sounding dialect that studios would hire white speech coaches to teach them how to say their lines. While it was one thing to see minstrels onstage acting a fool, it was profoundly powerful and influential to see those images over and over on the big screen. Hollywood was shaping how America would view Black folks—ignorant and inferior—for generations to come.

McDaniel began working right away, earning $7.50 a day as a film extra beginning in May 1931. At the time, 6 million Americans were unable to find work, a number that would rise to 15 million by 1932. McDaniel could make more money working just six days in a month than in four full weeks as a domestic.

"A call from Charles Butler at Central Casting was like a letter [from] home," McDaniel wrote in a 1947 op-ed for *The Hollywood Reporter*.

To audition for her first speaking role, McDaniel said she had to borrow money to catch the streetcar to the studio. She got some timely advice from a friend, who told her, "Don't let anybody know you're down and out. Look breezy and people will think you are."

McDaniel got the part in *The Impatient Maiden*, in which she actually wasn't portraying a maid—she portrayed a woman hospitalized after winning a brawl against her husband.

McDaniel appeared in hundreds of films during her first three years in Hollywood, always playing some form of the stereotypical Mammy after her first role. But as Bogle contends, McDaniel was a talented performer who managed to bring more substance to her roles than the parts that appeared on paper.

"She played the fussy, boisterous, big-bosomed maid time and time again, using the stereotyped figure to display her remarkable talent and affinity for pure broad comedy," Bogle writes. "With her fiercely and distinctively American aggressiveness and her stupendous sonic boom of a voice, Hattie created rich, dazzling characterizations. . . . She emerged as the one servant of the era to speak her mind fully, and the world of her eccentric characters was a helter-skelter, topsy-turvy one in which the servant became the social equal, the mammy became the literal mother figure, the put-on carried to the forefront of the action, and the style of the servant overpowered the content of the script."

Watts contends that McDaniel brought to her parts the sassy personas she perfected onstage doing minstrel parodies and singing the blues, bringing a covert deceptiveness to her servants. In Watts's estimation, McDaniel was playing maids she knew would be fired in an instant in real life. Bogle critiques McDaniel's performances in his exhaustive work *Toms, Coons, Mulattoes, Mammies, & Bucks*, breaking down the ways that she brought something extra to the screen. He says that her breakout, "super-deluxe, grand-slam" performance came in *Alice Adams*, a film about a poor, small-town social climber played by Katharine Hepburn. McDaniel plays a cook hired by the Adams family to serve a meal during which Hepburn's character is pretending to come from a wealthy background. McDaniel makes clear from the start that she is lowering herself to serve the dinner, peppering her interactions with sassy backtalk and snide commentary as she smacks on a stick of gum.

"Used by director Stevens not only for comic relief but to point up the pretenses of the Adamses, McDaniel's maid repeatedly makes fun of the family's foolish attempts to put on airs," Bogle writes. "She makes her dining-room entrances and exits lethargically, as if she could not care less. Why should she hurry for these no-'count white folks? She carries her tray in the most off-hand fashion. When Alice speaks French to impress her guest, McDaniel is there to undercut the girl's airs with a monosyllabic grunt."

In this role, McDaniel solidifies for the audience that while she might be a servant, she isn't to be controlled. The audience is in on the joke—that this Black woman was only pretending to be subservient. It is a guise that McDaniel would hone in her film work, though she wasn't always given the freedom to imbue her characters with insubordinate sass. In *Saratoga* (1937) she appears opposite heartthrob Clark Gable, with whom she developed such an obvious rapport that audiences might forget they are supposed to be master and servant. Playing the maid of the notoriously short-tempered Jean Harlow's character, McDaniel comes off as more her equal than her servant. At one point McDaniel's character, obviously attracted to Clark Gable, says out loud, "If he was only the right color, I'd marry him." Such brazen talk was unheard of coming from a Black actress.

In the 1938 film *The Mad Miss Manton*, opposite Barbara Stanwyck, for whom McDaniel assumes a protective, motherly role, McDaniel "hurls verbal barbs with the speed and accuracy of an ace pitcher," according to Bogle.

"Just talking back was a triumph of sorts, and Hattie McDaniel was doing what every black maid in America must have wanted to do at one time or another," he writes. "McDaniel's flamboyant bossiness often can be read as a cover-up for deep hostility. Indeed, she seemed to time her lines to give her black audiences that impression."

In 1935, actor Clarence Muse began writing a regular column called "A-Talking to You" for LA's black weekly, the *California Eagle*, pushing for equality and racial justice, advocating for anti-lynching legislation, seeking desegregation. Muse also went after white Hollywood, self-publishing a pamphlet titled *The Dilemma of the Negro Actor*. He laid out the difficult choices that faced the Black actor because of Hollywood racism.

"There are two audiences in America to confront, the white audience with a definite desire for buffoonery and song, and the Negro audience with a desire to see the real elements of Negro life portrayed," he wrote.

Muse was establishing the quandary that has challenged Black comedians for the past 100 years, the tension between public and private Black humor. Do they play the clown for white folks in order to keep eating? Do they refrain from embarrassing material to appease Black folks seeking respectable representations? Do they keep the private stuff private?

"The challenge was for Hattie McDaniel to become even more subtle yet more subversive to conquer the dilemma posed by Muse," Watts writes. "With the enormous power and watchful racism of the white studios, McDaniel's job would be a hard one. Could she continue to successfully signify her indignation and still make a living?"

McDaniel didn't restrict herself to just the movies during the Depression years. Singing the blues onstage and performing in front of Black folk gave McDaniel a freedom to express herself that she didn't find in film. She worked for Los Angeles's risqué Follies Burlesque Theater. She joined a group called the Old Time Southern

Singers, which was founded by Sara Butler—the wife of the casting agent Charles Butler—to preserve Black spirituals; they performed in "plantation" clothes and romanticized the Old South. Her brother Sam got her a regular gig playing three different characters on his radio show, *Optimistic Do-Nuts*, allowing her to display her many talents and become so popular that KNX eventually gave McDaniel her own show, called *Hi Hat Hattie and Her Boys*. The name Hi Hat was teasingly given to her by the white announcer on Sam's program, who was having fun with her for appearing for her first show overdressed in an elegant evening gown. McDaniel mixed music with her sassy brand of comedy, as she teamed with the Los Angeles jazz band led by Sam McVea.

McDaniel brought all of her experience on-screen and onstage to a culminating role in the film that would stamp her name forever in the history books. Fittingly, it all started with a book. Written by Margaret Mitchell, who was born and raised in Atlanta, *Gone with the Wind* was a sprawling love story disguised as a meditation on the Civil War and Reconstruction. Though it was more than a thousand pages, the novel was wildly popular, selling over a million copies and winning the 1937 Pulitzer Prize for Fiction. Mitchell's conception of slavery didn't veer far from the grotesque perspective that mainstream white society favored—the South was a grand place before the war and the slaves were happy and content with their status, but the evil war came along and ruined everything. Film producer David O. Selznick immediately purchased the film rights, paying the unheard-of sum of $50,000—about $1.1 million in today's dollars. When the news broke that Selznick was preparing to bring the Civil War epic to the screen, the Black community reacted with alarm. Editorials in the Black press warned that the book contained so much racist propaganda and offensive material that it would be difficult to adapt it to a film that wouldn't be similarly offensive. Selznick pledged to the Black press that he would be careful with the material and would hire "the best possible cast."

When Hattie McDaniel dove into Mitchell's book, this was the first description of Mammy she came across:

A huge old woman, with the small, shrewd eyes of an elephant. She was shining black, pure African, devoted to her last drop of blood to the O'Haras.

Jill Watts writes that "Mitchell conceived of Mammy in the simplest terms—as an inferior who mimicked her owners and accepted her place, never aspiring to anything more than to lovingly serve white people. The loyal Mammy, never quite comprehending the standards she upheld, despised Yankees and those blacks who challenged traditional Southern social order. She existed to validate slavery and the fantasy of white superiority."

With dissension already swirling around Black actors like McDaniel for their stereotypical portrayals of Black servants, playing a character like Mammy without offending Black people would be quite a trick. Selznick launched a nationwide talent search to find the perfect actors to bring the story to life. This included a search for Black actors, something most Hollywood producers had heretofore not given a great deal of attention. The author Mitchell had white women visiting her to make a pitch for their Black maids; one white woman wanted to play Mammy in blackface; First Lady Eleanor Roosevelt wrote a letter of recommendation for her own personal maid, Elizabeth McDuffie, to be considered. Meanwhile, members of the Black press, including the *California Eagle*, endorsed McDaniel for Mammy. But McDaniel told friends that she believed she had played too many comic parts to win the role. However, when Selznick had McDaniel do a screen test with British actress Vivien Leigh, who was being considered for the role of Scarlett, the two of them showed an undeniable chemistry.

At age forty-five, McDaniel was offered the part. She signed a contract with Selznick for $450 a week (about $10,000 in today's dollars), helped in the negotiations by her white agent William Meiklejohn—one of the few white agents who took on Black clients. Before the film went into production, protests against the project continued, particularly from the NAACP and its executive secretary Walter White. White saw it as his job to challenge Hollywood's depictions of African Americans, so he wrote a letter to Selznick expressing his concerns about the film. He suggested that Selznick hire a consultant, "preferably a Negro," to make sure the picture wasn't offensive. Selznick hired a white expert on the Confederacy, but he never added a Black consultant. White also advised Selznick to read W. E. B. Du Bois's exhaustive tome *Black Reconstruction* to ensure historical accuracy. When Selznick passed White's advice on to the playwright Sidney Howard, Howard curtly responded that he had already read Du Bois's book.

"While Selznick believed he was sympathetic, his creative vision remained harnessed to the racism of his era," Watts writes. "He fundamentally lacked insight into the substantial problems that *Gone with the Wind* presented as a whole—that the core of the story and construction of black characters defended slavery and promoted notions of black inferiority."

Selznick even considered hiring D. W. Griffith, director of the profoundly offensive *Birth of a Nation*, which shows how blind he was to the racial implications of *Gone with the Wind*. The Black community's agitation with the coming film continued to grow. Hundreds of protest letters poured into the studio, demanding a halt to production. Earl Morris of the *Pittsburgh Courier* wrote that the movie would be worse than *Birth of a Nation* and revealed that the script still contained the word *nigger*. He pushed Black actors to reject roles in such films, specifically addressing his admonition to McDaniel.

"We feel proud over the fact that Hattie McDaniel won the coveted role of Mammy," he wrote. "It means about $2,000 for Miss McDaniel in individual advancement . . . [and] nothing in racial advancement."

Selznick courted the Black press, inviting journalists like Morris to the set to observe filming. After his visit, Morris assured Black readers the film wouldn't be offensive. Upon further discussion and consulting Black leaders, Selznick decided to remove the word *nigger* from the script.

For her part, McDaniel was content to do what the studio asked in promoting the film.

"McDaniel had continued her rise within the industry by being pleasant and compliant, collaborating with white racism to advance her career," Watts writes. "Even early on, McDaniel was not averse to doing whatever she could to promote herself with white Hollywood power brokers. . . . The disappointing reality was that McDaniel played to white racist expectations both in front of and behind the camera."

After filming was completed, Selznick looked through the footage and was astonished by McDaniel's performance, which then became fodder for the Hollywood gossip mill. Once the screenings began, the audience reaction was overwhelming for McDaniel. But when the studio decided to hold the film's big opening night in Atlanta, the Hollywood crew saw that Southern racism was still very much alive and well. City officials informed the studio that the Black cast members would not be welcome at the theater. Not only that, the officials insisted that McDaniel's picture couldn't even appear in the souvenir program alongside the other stars, which elicited Selznick's ire—though he eventually caved and removed her picture. For the opening, the studio held a big parade downtown, attended by three hundred thousand spectators, and a grand ball. At the theater, the master of ceremonies came out to address the crowd:

"We have all been thinking and talking a lot about the Old South lately. . . . Tonight we want to give you a glimpse into the past—and visit an old plantation on a warm, fragrant June evening. Can you smell the wisteria? Can't you hear those darkies singing? They're coming up to the Big House."

When the curtain opened, the crowd was greeted with an elaborate re-creation of the plantation in the film, Tara. The choir from Atlanta's prominent Ebenezer Baptist Church was singing spirituals dressed up as slaves. Watts notes a fascinating factoid—one of the teenagers in that choir was Martin Luther King Jr.

Bogle, the film historian, says one of the most remarkable things about *Gone with the Wind* was that the Black actors were able to present their characters as complex human beings with a humanity that had never been seen in a major Hollywood production. Bogle has particular praise for McDaniel: "McDaniel's Mammy becomes an all-seeing, all-hearing, all-knowing commentator and observer. She remarks. She annotates. She makes asides. She always opinionizes."

Watts notes that McDaniel wears a large expensive ring in the film and has exquisitely manicured nails, subtly signaling to the viewer that her character was just an act and not who she really was.

"Through the force of her own personality, McDaniel's character became free of the greatest burden that slavery—on-screen and off—inflicted on blacks: a sense of innate inferiority," writes Bogle. "Her Mammy has a self-righteous grandeur that glows. Even audiences unaware of what a fine performer McDaniel was sensed by her mammoth presence and her strong, hearty voice that here was an actress larger than her lines, bigger than her role."

Many Black viewers admired McDaniel's work in the film but condemned the production as a whole for showing an idealized, kindly version of slavery that was far from the truth. McDaniel told an interviewer that she based her performance not on Black servants but on legendary Black heroines like Sojourner Truth, Harriet Tubman, and Charity Still.

"This is an opportunity to glorify Negro womanhood," McDaniel said. "I am proud that I am a Negro woman because members of that class have given so much."

McDaniel was joined in the cast by another Black actor who drew ample praise and wonder at her performance, Butterfly McQueen. With her high-pitched squeaky voice and waiflike innocence, Butterfly seemed almost like a cartoon character. While providing important doses of comic relief to the film, she also did something else—she gave white audiences a view of a Black character that was vastly different than anything they had ever seen. By embodying a different kind of character—quirky, vulnerable, and emotionally expressive—McQueen introduced a new dimension to Black representation onscreen. In doing so, she challenged the narrow, one-note portrayals that had long dominated Hollywood's depictions of Black women. Even though her role was rooted in stereotype, her performance suggested that Black actresses could portray a wider emotional range and occupy more varied narrative space. However, McQueen herself had trouble finding substantial roles after *Gone with the Wind*. She was too singular and memorable a character to be slotted into just any clichéd servant role.

In the debate over how subservient and stereotypical Black actors should be, McQueen actually attacked her *Gone with the Wind* costar, alleging after the film's release that McDaniel was a sellout because she didn't fight back harder and she allowed the studio to run with the myth that McDaniel was so good because she was used to serving as a mammy in real life—a mammy playing a Mammy.

McDaniel was nominated for the best supporting actress award along with another star from the film, Olivia de Havilland. Overall, the film scored thirteen nominations. As she clutched her trophy onstage when she was presented with the award, McDaniel stepped to the mic and quickly revealed the essential tension that every Black performer battled, especially in white-controlled media like film.

"I sincerely hope that I shall always be a credit to my race and the motion-picture industry," she said.

It would be nearly a half century before Black actors could comfortably serve those two masters without shame or censure.

CHAPTER 5
AMOS 'N' ANDY

When commercial radio debuted in America on November 2, 1920, nobody had any idea that within a decade it would become the nation's most popular and influential cultural medium. By 1929, one in every three American homes had a radio. By 1939, every home had a radio, as did most cars. It was so much more intimate, immediate, and inexpensive than going to a theater for entertainment. By forcing listeners to use their imaginations to form a mental picture of what they were hearing, radio was more participatory than film or, later, television.

It may be hard to believe, but comedians initially resisted the lure of radio, thinking that joke-telling wouldn't work without an audience to react.

"It all seemed strange, talking into a microphone in a studio instead of playing in front of a real audience," Bob Hope said about appearing on singer Rudy Vallée's radio show, *Fleischmann Hour*. "I was nervous on those first radio shows and the Vallée engineers couldn't figure out why they heard a thumping noise when I did my routines until they found out I was kicking the mike after each joke."

But soon it became apparent that humor on the radio was a natural. First, it was the vaudeville acts, called "song and comedy patter" teams, transferring their stage routines to radio. Unsurprisingly, the medium was not welcoming to African Americans—at least their physical presence—except for prominent musicians like Fats Waller, Duke Ellington, Louis Armstrong, and Count Basie. But radio acts, just like minstrels onstage, were eager to use crass Black stereotypes in creating their shows, which was even easier than the stage because audiences couldn't see them as they imitated Blacks in what Watkins calls "racial ventriloquy." In this way, the minstrel acts who had begun falling out of favor in the 1920s were able to keep working in this new medium.

The top radio variety show in the country in 1932 was *Show Boat*, airing on NBC, which was the first national network. The rest of the NBC lineup included the *Sinclair Weiner Minstrels*, *Plantation Party*, *Molle Minstrels*, and *Minstrel Show*. It's quite clear to which audience NBC was catering.

"Racial ventriloquy, like the antics of blackface actors on stage and in silent movies, was crucial in establishing burlesque images that black performers would later be expected to emulate," Watkins writes. "They would linger for decades and, when authentic black comedians were finally allowed access to the medium, would continue to add an absurd and hauntingly ironic footnote to black radio comedy."

In 1928, a radio show debuted on WMAQ in Chicago that would have an enormous impact on the way the nation considered comedy. That show was *Amos 'n' Andy*, a situation comedy focusing on the antics of two Black men trying to navigate life in the big, bad city. The men were portrayed by two white performers, Freeman F. Gosden and Charles J. Correll, borrowing heavily from the methods of the white minstrels portraying and mocking Black people. But their antics weren't quite as offensive as the old-school minstrels that came before them, which could be considered progress of a sort. Many observers believe they stole their act from two Black performers, Flournoy Miller and Aubrey Lyles, who were a popular comedy team in the Chicago area. WGN, the powerful Chicago Tribune radio station, recruited Miller and Lyles to bring their act to the radio and even negotiated a contract with their agent. But when WGN presented the show to sponsors, they deemed it unacceptable when they found out the performers were actual Black men, rather than white men in blackface. Gosden and Correll claimed they independently came up with the idea on their own and brought it to WGN, though some believe the radio station brought the idea to them.

The situation comedy they created altered the face of broadcast radio, eventually becoming so popular that movies would be halted in the middle for fifteen minutes so the audience could hear the antics of Amos and Andy on the radio.

While the focus of this book is Black comedy, *Amos 'n' Andy* presented the audience with a version of Black characters so influential that it's hard to leave them out. So, Amos 'n' Andy are included with a bit of an asterisk—Black comedy, white comedians.

Of the duo, Gosden was the more talented at racial ventriloquy, having grown up in Richmond, Virginia, around Black people. He has said the character of Amos was based on his childhood friend Garrett Brown, nicknamed Snowball, with whom he staged impromptu minstrel shows when they were boys. Brown, an orphan, actually lived with Gosden's family for a decade as they were growing up. Both boys were skilled at mimicry, imitating the voices they heard around them in their Richmond neighborhood. When they put on impromptu shows for Gosden's father, who was ailing, they would be staged as minstrel shows, which of course was the dominant form of theatrical entertainment at the time.

In the summer of 1919, Gosden, who was twenty, met a twenty-nine-year-old pianist named Charlie Correll. Born in Peoria, Illinois, Correll had a big, ebullient personality that led friends and family to predict that he would have a career in show business. The men were drawn to each other right away, though they couldn't have been more different. Gosden was tall and thin, intense, and uncomfortable around strangers, while Correll was short and stocky and always calm and relaxed. They appeared together in minstrel shows, working for a producer named Joe Bren. The strength of their partnership was recognized by the manager of the WEBH radio station, who gave them a twice weekly show in 1925 called *Correll and Gosden, the Life of the Party*. One night when they sang "The Kinky Kids Parade," a song that was a big hit at the time, they added dialogue done in a Black dialect. They were called on to repeat that song over and over, which led Gosden to keep introducing more "Black" characters that he impersonated.

"The two performers had, quite casually, hit on a vital radio technique: through careful manipulation of the voice and by taking advantage of the directional properties of the microphone, two actors could create the impression of an entire group of people, using distinctive vocal traits to sketch out details of personality, and counting on the listener's imagination to fill in the rest," Elizabeth McLeod writes in *The Original Amos 'n' Andy: Freeman Gosden, Charles Correll and the 1928–1943 Radio Serial.*

The two men created a stage show that they presented at Chicago's McVicker's Theatre, performing five shows a day. They were offered staff positions at WGN, working as general utility men—but learning a great deal in the process about radio production and recording. They were approached by the station about creating a new show—station executives wanted something modeled after a popular syndicated cartoon strip called *The Gumps.* But Gosden and Correll didn't like that idea. They eventually came up with their own plan for a show, focused on a couple of characters doing jokes. They decided the characters would be Black.

"We chose black characters because blackface comics could tell funnier stories than whiteface comics," Gosden said in a 1981 newspaper story.

While the radio show relied on the Black stereotypes that had been gracing the stage for decades, the characters were given more depth and humanity than minstrels typically presented. The show was initially called *Sam 'n' Henry,* and it sounded different than anything else on the radio. The characters were Black, but the show didn't sound like a minstrel show. It premiered on January 12, 1926.

"The recognizable dialects provided easy identification of Sam Smith and Henry Johnson as rural Southern blacks," McLeod writes. "But listeners expecting typical blackface comedy would have been baffled by that evening's broadcast—for that initial script contained not a single real joke, not a single comic situation. Sam and Henry engaged in none of the usual snappy repartee associated with minstrel end men. Instead, they simply talked—not as flamboyant entertainers but as two ordinary people. And in the course of their conversation, their dialogue slowly and deliberately told a story."

While the early episodes did lean on Black stereotypes, the characters over time became more fully realized human beings grappling with the same challenges as many Americans, newly arrived Southern migrants trying to find gainful employment in the big city. The show was a hit in the Midwest, leading Gosden and Correll to come up with the idea of selling recordings of the show to other radio stations. This was a revolutionary concept, though there had been discussions in the radio community of distributing programs, which was dubbed syndication. But WGN was vociferously opposed to the idea, believing that the show should remain an exclusive feature on the most dominant station in the Midwest; offering it to other stations would have the station effectively competing with itself.

Gosden and Correll were upset at WGN's dismissal of their idea—one that would bring them more exposure and more money from personal appearances. They made $2,000 a week doing appearances for a local theater chain—the $100 a week they made at WGN looked quite paltry in comparison. They bided their time, waiting for their two-year contract with WGN to expire at the end of 1927. Gosden and Correll then brought the show to rival station WMAQ. But the title of the show was still owned by WGN, so they had to come up with a new name. As they worked on scripts for the new show, Gosden came across the name Andy in a dictionary list of common names. They added the name Amos and debuted *Amos 'n' Andy* on March 19, 1928. They were now able to pursue the syndication idea, which they called the "chainless chain," and even tried unsuccessfully to patent the concept. They sent recordings of the show to the other stations, accompanied by strict instructions—the stations had to air the recordings at the same time as the show was broadcast on WMAQ. The recorded program was leased to forty additional stations; the show was a hit.

In 1929, the show moved to NBC, sponsored by Pepsodent. Within another year, *Amos 'n' Andy* was a national phenomenon. It was the first-ever show to be syndicated. By the summer of 1930, the two men were making $11,000 a week. They sold *Amos 'n' Andy* merchandise—such as wind-up toys and a candy bar that was made of a vanilla-flavored wafer covered in chocolate (an obvious metaphor for the show). Some claim it was the most popular show ever broadcast on the radio—meaning that all of America identified with two "Black" characters, seeing the world through the eyes of these two men. That was a somewhat subversive concept in the 1930s. Watkins says Gosden and Correll "humorously mirrored the plight of the nation's common man, caught in the transformation from an agrarian society to a complex urban one." The two men would do a total of 170 different voice impersonations during the show's run.

While the show still trafficked in the same offensive Negro stereotypes, something was different. For one, the characters primarily existed in a Black world, so there were no white people from the mainstream with whom to contrast ignorant Black behavior, as was the case with most minstrels. Amos and Andy were presented as regular Americans, with the regular American goals of trying to figure out how to survive in challenging times—after all, it was the start of the Depression. In fact, the Depression came up often in the show's early years, such as this explanation of the stock market by one of the show's most entertaining characters, George Stevens, known as Kingfish, voiced by Gosden:

> Yo' see, a week ago Thursday, de big crash started. De bulls an' de bears was fightin' it out an' de bears chased de bulls.

When Amos was falsely accused of murder and put on trial on the show, the country was outraged, with threats of boycotts coming if Amos were to be convicted. Another show had Andy seemingly shot at his wedding, leading to a national controversy complete with lawyers around the country weighing in on whether he was legally married. For many fans, the show was an obsession. To capitalize on its popularity, newspapers even carried regular columns about the previous night's episode. Promoters learned to halt their theatrical shows for the fifteen minutes of *Amos 'n' Andy*, which would be played on the loudspeakers in the concert hall—and they even advertised that fact on flyers. An ad for the Dover Opera House in Dover, Maryland, stated the following:

Again Dover Opera House Leads!

For the convenience of our Patrons, we are presenting
AMOS 'N' ANDY
Every evening at 7 p.m., direct from WJZ via
PHILCO Balanced Unit RADIO
Be in your seat before seven and enjoy this
radio treat with the rest of your friends!

When making plans for an event, organizers would have to make sure it didn't conflict with the nightly show, during which the streets of America would clear out. All so the country could follow the lives of two "Black" men. In the summer of 1930, Gosden and Correll made their way to Hollywood to record an *Amos 'n' Andy* film, called *Check and Double Check*. But the film faced an immense looming question: How would the audience react to seeing their beloved Amos and Andy as white men in blackface?

They tried to use stylized movie makeup to turn them into Black men, rather than the over-the-top sloppiness of burnt cork. But they weren't fooling anyone—their features were so Caucasian that it was quite obvious they were white men in dark makeup.

"Neither performer appears comfortable before the camera, and they are further undercut by the plodding direction; dry, dead cinematography; and leaden pacing common to practically all early talking pictures," McLeod writes. "But even more damaging to the film is the script."

The film had a minstrel feel to it that wasn't present with the radio show. In addition, listeners had grown accustomed to crafting an image in their minds of Amos and Andy as Black men, so to see them on-screen as so obviously white was jarring to many. Gosden was so embarrassed, he didn't even let his children watch the film.

"Dad thought it was the worst film ever made," his son Freeman F. Gosden Jr., who was two when the film debuted, said in an interview. "He never let us see it. It wasn't until about ten years ago that I got my hands on a copy. After I finally saw it, I could see what he meant. He felt neither his acting nor the storyline was up to par."

"As soon as we put on blackface, we became just a couple of minstrels," Correll noted.

But the film still managed to do well at the box office, finishing the year as the film studio RKO's biggest hit of the season, grossing $1.7 million (about $32 million in today's dollars)—though the salaries of the performers, $250,000 plus a percentage of the gross, certainly ate into any profits. RKO, which was one of the biggest studios in the country, felt good enough about the picture to offer Gosden and Correll a multipicture deal. But they weren't interested. They just wanted to return to what they did well—radio.

In developing their show, Gosden and Correll wisely tempered the offensiveness of the characters, allowing the show to appeal to many Blacks as well as whites.

"Amos was neither as dense and gullible as the prototypical stage or screen Sambo portrayed by Aubrey Lyles or Charlie Mack, nor as much the quintessential darky as portrayed by Bert Williams," Watkins writes. "Although Amos was often duped by Andy's dim-witted schemes and was inevitably the straightman in their comic exchanges, in contrast to Andy's trickster image, he projected a mainstream, almost bourgeois sensibility. And although Andy was cast in the familiar image of the conniving stage dandy, he seldom displayed the rapacious venality and malevolence that quite often defined the type."

Amos 'n' Andy was responsible for the creation of a new radio genre, the serial comedy/drama, which eventually led to the invention of television situation comedies and soap operas—all fruit from the *Amos 'n' Andy* tree. McLeod goes to great lengths in *The Original Amos 'n' Andy*, which was published in 2005, to defend the content of the show. In pointing out that the show was also popular with African Americans, she suggests that Gosden and Correll's depiction of these Black characters couldn't be that bad if Black people were fans—though she wisely forms a distinction between the classes, noting that educated, middle-class Blacks were more likely to find offense.

Radio Digest magazine published a feature in 1930 examining the response to the program from African-American listeners. (It should be pointed out that less than 8 percent of Black families owned a radio in 1930.) Correspondent A. W. Clarke traveled to Harlem and to Hartford, Connecticut, to interview a cross section of Black residents about the show. Most of the respondents were middle-class. Supporters of the show felt it portrayed real-life characters in a sympathetic manner.

"Like everyone else in Harlem, I listen to *Amos 'n' Andy* every night," a woman who owned a rooming house on 134th Street in Harlem—the same neighborhood in which Amos and Andy live on the show—was quoted as saying. "Those white boys know how to play Negro parts better than any blackface comedians I have ever heard. For one thing, they do not belittle the Negro and I think their programs have done more to help the white people understand us than all the books ever written."

"If they were attacking the colored people, their entertainment would have died long ago," a man said in a Hartford barbershop, "but what they are saying is so humorous and free from the taint of prejudice I do not see how any person, white or colored, can take it in a personal way."

The man continued, "The modern Negro is too self-conscious. To give you an example of what I mean, I have a friend who owns a radio. He never misses *Amos 'n' Andy* when home among his family, but when in the presence of white people he just cannot stand to listen to them. I will listen to *Amos 'n' Andy* in any place among any crowd. *Amos 'n' Andy* have this race down pat, I am telling you."

A police officer who walked the streets of northeast Harlem told Clarke that most everyone he came into contact with were big fans of the show. But there were critics as well, though the criticism mostly centered around an embarrassment about the show airing dirty Black laundry—in other words, the depictions were *too* accurate. A Hartford attorney said, "Only the most illiterate type of Negro will speak as Amos 'n' Andy do—and that type is fast leaving us."

McLeod explores why she thinks *Amos 'n' Andy* was a significant break from the minstrels that came before it, claiming that the show did not traffic in stereotypes.

"If the essence of stereotyping is the use of unchanging, generic personality types, of cardboard figures with no inner motivation for their actions—then the characters of *Amos 'n' Andy* were not stereotypes," she writes. "A generic blackface character portrayed as 'lazy and shiftless' for no reason other than the fact that he is a blackface character is a stereotype. Andy Brown, a three-dimensional figure whose behavior grew out of deep and well-defined personal insecurities, is not. While it must be acknowledged that many of Andy's traits do overlap certain common stereotypes, it is equally important to note that his character flaws are consistently presented as the personal shortcomings of Andrew H. Brown, stemming from his own particular inner weaknesses and not from 'racial' traits."

However, her viewpoint seems somewhat idealistic, overlooking how often negative traits seen in one Black individual have historically been generalized to the entire race. And her argument reflects a debate that still rages in the Black community a century after *Amos 'n' Andy*'s debut—if Black people flock to a show, does that prove the show isn't offensive to Blacks? Creators like Tyler Perry have taken center stage in this debate: If it makes Black people laugh, is it by definition good for Black people?

"Correll and Gosden were entertainers producing their work for a mass audience, not social activists," McLeod writes. "It would have been easy, had they been so inclined, to simply follow the lead of a legion of blackface performers before them and to cling to the comfortable, shallow stereotypes. But instead, Correll and Gosden consciously encouraged their listeners to view the characters not as racial cartoons but as individuals whose color was merely one facet of their identity, and whose dreams, hopes, and fears were those of all people."

Watkins says Amos became a national symbol of "thrift and

responsibility" during the leanest years of the Depression, which was quite a statement in Jim Crow America. When the Depression ended, the show's focus changed to the deviousness of Kingfish, phasing out Amos. The amazing popularity of the show began to wane in the late 1930s as slicker new radio programs popped up. *Amos 'n' Andy* changed to a half-hour show in October 1943 with new supporting characters who were actually played by Black actors such as TOBA comedian Eddie Green and Ernestine Wade, who played Kingfish's wife, the infamous Sapphire—a name that for a generation became synonymous with the caricature of the loud, belligerent, domineering Black woman.

Amos and Andy were laughed at, not with, according to Watkins, which is an important distinction to make when talking about comedy with Black characters. It's perhaps the central question that Black comedians face in front of white audiences—other than whether or not they are funny. By the 1950s, the embarrassment of middle-class Blacks was a major factor in the decline of the show's popularity. With the emergence of the Civil Rights Movement, Black people no longer abided the stereotypes represented by the *Amos 'n' Andy* characters. The show's decline mirrored the decline of radio comedy, which was eclipsed by television. But there was another extremely popular radio show that survived the crossover to television: *The Jack Benny Show*.

Benny, more progressive than most about using Black actors on his show, introduced a character named Rochester, who was his valet. Played by Eddie Anderson, Rochester flipped the usual script and made Benny the butt of most of his jokes. Irreverent, vain, and pompous, Rochester would constantly poke fun at Benny and deflate his ego. This was considered a revolutionary advance in the 1930s, having a Black man challenge the authority of the white star. Rochester was a servant, but he often didn't act like one. With his gravelly baritone, his was a character that was hard to forget.

Anderson, born in 1906, hailed from a family of performers—his mother and father had a minstrel act and performed onstage and in the circus. He reportedly got his raspy voice from loudly hawking newspapers on the street when he was a teen. He and his brother developed a vaudeville act in the 1920s, singing and dancing. He appeared in Hollywood films, most notably playing Noah in *The Green Pastures*, before he won a part on Benny's show.

Rochester was one of the most outspoken Black servants to grace the radio airwaves, similar to Hattie McDaniel's Beulah. He was more friend and companion to Benny than servant, which was some measure of progress. But he was still a jive-talking servant, a fact that didn't sit well with many African Americans. Here's an exchange that typified the show's style of humor. Rochester has lost Benny's bicycle in a game of craps and Benny wants him to go get it back (Watkins 1994, 288):

BENNY: I want you to go to that garage and tell your friend to give you back my bicycle.
ROCHESTER: Without payin' for it?
BENNY: Yes, without payin' for it . . . Just grab it.
ROCHESTER: Now wait a minute, boss . . . That boy's got a razor that does everything but run out and get the mail.
BENNY: Well, Rochester, what are you scared of? . . . You carry a razor yourself.
ROCHESTER: Yeah, but it's only a Gillette and I'm out of blades.

THE NAACP AND other Blacks staged protests in response to an episode that saw Rochester partying and shooting craps in Harlem. Jack Benny was so upset by the uproar that he apologized. In the early 1950s, Benny brought the show to television as a biweekly that stayed on the air for another decade—even after the radio show ended in 1955 because of poor ratings. As Black people grew more impatient with the insulting clichéd Black characters that had populated entertainment for generations, the servant roles were mostly purged from radio and television (though the type would reemerge in some of the situation comedies of the '70s like *Benson* and *The Jeffersons*). But Rochester hung on, a testament to his cleverness and his evolution as a trusted member of the Benny household rather than as a painful stereotype. As Watkins notes, Rochester's role was to skewer Benny's bourgeois middle-class values with more down-to-earth Black sensibilities. "And since more blacks, unlike middle-class whites, were reluctant to have their idiosyncrasies publicly satirized, those comic episodes in which Rochester was portrayed as overly spirited and sensual (licentious) or fun-loving (irresponsible) called forth quick responses from the black community."

He was technically a servant, but Rochester represented an important step in the evolution of Black comedy. He was moving closer to a fully realized Black man with a life of his own, independent of the white star. After Anderson's Rochester, it was only a matter of time before a Black star would be given a chance to helm their own show.

An indication of how radical Rochester really was can be seen in the response of another population: white listeners, particularly from the South. When Rochester, helping Benny prepare for a boxing match against Fred Allen, accidentally hits Benny too hard and knocks him out, the network was flooded with letters complaining—though ironically Joe Louis was heavyweight champ at the time, having knocked out quite a few white men on his way to the title. Even as a joke, it was too much for white America to handle.

Besides playing Benny's sidekick, Anderson had a number of memorable appearances in Hollywood films, such as *Jezebel*, *Gone with the Wind*, and *Birth of the Blues*. He got to play Rochester in three Jack Benny films—*Man About Town*, *Buck Benny Rides Again*, and *The Meanest Man in the World*. He was also in the two all-Black classics *Stormy Weather* and *Cabin in the Sky*.

A contemporary of Anderson's with whom he was often compared was the comedian Mantan Moreland. Both were small men with big eyes that they used to comic effect. But whereas Anderson was calm and even understated in his humor, Moreland was closer to the over-the-top minstrel stereotypes of the past, with more buffoonish tendencies. Donald Bogle calls Moreland one of the "step-chillun" of Stepin Fetchit, the ultimate ignorant servant/sidekick. In Bogle's list of stereotypical Black parts, Moreland is the "coon." In fact, Watkins calls Moreland king of the coon servants.

"Before its death, the coon developed into the most blatantly degrading of all black stereotypes," Bogle explains. "The pure coons emerged as no-account niggers, those unreliable, crazy, lazy, subhuman creatures good for nothing more than eating watermelons, stealing chickens, shooting crap, or butchering the English language."

Born in Monroe, Louisiana, in 1902, Moreland had run away from home by the time he was twelve and tried to make it as a dancer. His first bit of notoriety came when he partnered in a comedy act with Tim Moore, the former professional boxer—he once fought Jack Johnson—who went on to great fame playing Kingfish when *Amos 'n' Andy* came to television and white actors in blackface would no longer be acceptable. They toured the club circuit for years until Moreland caught the eye of Hollywood in 1938, appearing as the faithful servant in films such as *Next Time I Marry* and *Irish Luck*.

Moreland had a frenetic energy on-screen, always accentuated by his expressive face and wide-eyed exaggerations. He became most famous playing Charlie Chan's chauffeur, Birmingham Brown, in a long list of Chan movies, such as *The Chinese Cat* (1944), *The Scarlet Clue* (1945), *The Jade Mask* (1945), *Shadow over Chinatown* (1946), *The Chinese Ring* (1947), and *Dark Alibi* (1946).

Moreland's Birmingham was a big reason for the success of the Charlie Chan series. Moreland's stock-in-trade was his skittish fearfulness, always running away when he is needed most.

"He was a fantastic cowardly lion with an uncanny command of stagecraft," Bogle writes. "In those films in which he was terr'fied of de ghosts, Moreland displayed an arsenal of gestures and grimaces that actors had traditionally used to steal scenes and develop characters. He was forever tripping over his own feet as he tried to make a hasty departure. He was notorious for his perfectly timed double takes. No other actor could widen his eyes like Moreland. Nor could any other manage his trick of running without actually moving at all."

Here's a typical exchange between Moreland, playing Birmingham, and one of Chan's sons (Watkins 1994, 246):

#1 SON: Confucius remind us, Birmingham, that he who fights and runs away . . .
MANTAN: I know . . . will live to run another day!
#1 SON: If you're scared, Birmingham, just keep saying to yourself, "I'm not afraid, I'm not afraid."
MANTAN: I'm not afraid. I'm not afraid. I'm not afraid.
#1 SON: How do you feel now?
MANTAN: I feel like a liar!

Moreland appeared in more than 300 films, an astounding number. With Moreland's stock phrase that became part of the American lexicon, "Feets, don't fail me now!" Bogle contends that Moreland's small stature helped increase his popularity, as it was easy for audiences to accept his cowardice. After Shemp Howard of the Three Stooges died in November 1955, his brother Moe approached Moreland and asked if he had an interest in becoming the third stooge, telling Moreland it was his late brother's wish. Moreland expressed his desire to take on the challenge, but Columbia Pictures intervened and stipulated that the role would be filled by a comedian already under contract—so Joe Besser, a white man, got the role.

Mantan Moreland's once-ubiquitous presence in Hollywood began to fade after World War II, as Black audiences grew increasingly vocal in their rejection of demeaning servant roles—and Hollywood, at long last, began to take notice.

Black Americans had fought valiantly in the war, helping secure victory abroad while facing discrimination at home. When they returned, many refused to accept the same second-class status in society—or on-screen. A growing movement pushed back against the familiar caricatures: the shuffling servant, the comic buffoon, the petty criminal. These portrayals rang especially hollow in light of the courage and sacrifice Black soldiers had shown on the battlefield. The postwar years marked a turning point, as demands for dignity, respect, and authentic representation reverberated through the entertainment industry.

The NAACP played a crucial role in organizing protests and

campaigns against films that featured negative portrayals of Black characters, and they lobbied entertainment studios to provide more dignified and varied roles for Black actors.

As one of Hollywood's best-known servants, Moreland was sitting in the crosshairs of the push for change. Moreland was forced to go back on the road to make a living, touring his act throughout the early 1950s with comedians such as Tim Moore, Redd Foxx, and Nipsey Russell. He scored a few more film roles, such as *The Comic* (1969) and *Watermelon Man* (1970), allowing him to play serious dramatic roles that had no traces of the buffoonish clown.

In a television special aired on ABC in 1967 called *A Time for Laughter: A Look at Negro Humor in America*, actor Sidney Poitier insightfully dissected the persistence of private humor in the Black community:

> There are few things that express the mood of the Negro better than his humor. Unlike his music, jazz, which has been able to break out and move freely through most of the societies of the world, Negro humor has stayed home. And through generations of fermentation, it has become a heady wine, rarely tasted by the outside world. For the most part, America has seen only a caricature of our humor.

CHAPTER 6
PIGMEAT MARKHAM

The career of Pigmeat Markham provides a fascinating case study in private Black humor eventually reaching the mainstream and becoming embraced by whites. Markham toiled for years in an all-Black realm, playing the Chitlin' Circuit theaters during the heyday of the TOBA venues—still donning the burnt cork way longer than most everybody else—appearing in the all-Black "race" films, recording raunchy comedy albums. Then he got an unexpected break that introduced him to the white world, courtesy of Sammy Davis Jr.

Dewey Markham was born in Durham, North Carolina, in April 1904, in a wooden house on Markham Street, named after his family. As he explained in his autobiography, *Here Come the Judge!*, it was common practice to name the street after the best-known people who lived there. "It wasn't exactly an honor, but if you wanted to tell somebody to go to our street, you told them 'Markham's street' and pretty soon that's how it got to be known." The young Dewey would build a tent in his backyard out of burlap sacks and preach "sermons" to the neighborhood kids—the family lived five blocks from the Baptist church where he attended Sunday school—or put on slideshows using a light bulb and old pictures projected onto a screen.

The people around him said he was going to be either a preacher or a minstrel man—since minstrel was the only real form of public performance available to a Black man in the early 1900s. At an early age, Dewey was traveling and performing in carnival minstrel shows with other young kids, mainly singing and dancing, wearing the burnt cork.

As he got older, he stayed on the road performing, joined now by a companion named Cecelia. At the end of one of his sketches, he yelled to the crowd on a whim, "My name is Sweet Poppa Pigmeat." Before long, he was known simply as Pigmeat Markham. By the late 1920s, Pigmeat had arrived in New York and gotten a steady gig at the Alhambra in Harlem, where he was required to liven up his act by putting in two new gags per week. That was a much more taxing regimen than touring on the road, where he could do the same act every night because he was in a new city.

Pigmeat's most famous character, the Judge, was born at the Alhambra in 1928. Pigmeat introduced a character who was a magistrate trying to help a mother figure out which of two men was the father of her child. He calls the three of them to the bench and announces that he's going to have the baby decide. But the baby doesn't respond to either man when the mother turns the baby toward them. When the mother turns back to Pigmeat, the baby howls, "Daddy!"

"The Negroes in the audience loved it—the whites, too, I guess—probably because the judge, the pompous oppressor of the Negro in so many Southern towns, was bein' brought down a peg by a Negro comedian," he wrote in his autobiography. "They made me play that sketch over many times, and finally I got the idea that I could turn the character into a full act. I added little bits and pieces down through the years—and new jokes all the time, but the format is always the same."

After Cecelia died, Pigmeat moved into burlesque, working with another comedian named Johnny Lee Long. One of the clubs they worked was Minsky's in Harlem, which eventually became a venue for Black performers called the Apollo in 1934, when it was purchased by Sidney Cohen and Morris Sussman. This was where Pigmeat really made his name. He would watch white comedians like Milton Berle, Henny Youngman, and Joey Adams sit in the front row with their assistants, who were taking notes, writing down the jokes so they could take them downtown to white audiences.

In 1935, while on the road at a spot on the East Coast called Dykes between Washington and Baltimore, Pigmeat came up with his first claim to fame. It was a dance he came up with as the guys were fooling around dancing to songs on the jukebox.

"I wasn't one to do much clownin' around in public," he wrote. "But it was a rainy night and there wasn't nobody else in the place, so finally I got out there and started doin' this step. They all laughed and said what was it, and I said I didn't know, that it'd just come to me. But just to show it wasn't no accident, I did it again."

The following Friday, as bandleader Don Redman led his group through "Honeysuckle Rose," Pigmeat suddenly burst onto the stage and debuted his new dance. He glided back and forth on each foot, wagging an index finger high in the air, full of attitude and swagger. The crowd went wild—so wild, in fact, that he had to come back for three, maybe four encores. After the show when he was asked what the dance was called, he said, "Oh, I was only just truckin' on down"—because he couldn't think of a name. He said the dance had already reached New York by the time he got back there, with waiters doing it in clubs for tips while they served their patrons.

"When I arrived at the Apollo and started doin' the original truck, it swept the whole *country*," he wrote. "I stayed at the Apollo and I had to do the truck every week for two years. If I didn't truck, the people wanted their money back!"

Here's how Bardu Ali, a jazz musician and promoter, described Pigmeat's act:

> Pigmeat would enter assuming a very important look in his long black judge's robe, wearing a cardboard hat with the tassel hanging in front of his face and carrying a telephone book.
>
> [In the other hand Pigmeat carried] a pig's bladder that he would have blown up like a balloon. He used this as a gavel, and whenever a defendant answered and Pigmeat didn't like the answer given, he would hit the prosecutor over the head with the bladder.
>
> [Pigmeat's] opening remark to the courtroom after first entering from his chambers was "Yes, I am here, and I'm going to give away a lot of time today!"

Then he would roll his eyes at the first defendant to walk up to the stand, almost always a super sexy chick (played by Vivian Harris), wearing a skin-tight dress. (Williams 1995, 23)

Pigmeat drove across the country to Hollywood with comedian Ralph Cooper in Cooper's big red Packard, which they jokingly called the "fire truck." Ralph had already been making low-budget Black movies, so Pigmeat made movies too. He bragged that while the other Black stars were playing servants in white movies, he and Ralph were doing something different.

"We were making all-Negro shows, written *for* Negroes, and showin' in Negro neighborhoods only," he wrote.

During World War II, he had a regular gig at the Lincoln Theater in Los Angeles, doing his act onstage and managing the place offstage. In 1943, right before he hit the Lincoln stage, he got a visit in his dressing room from several young Black men. They wanted to talk to him about the burnt cork he still slathered on his face.

"We had a real friendly talk and it turned out they wanted me to stop this blackface make-up thing," he wrote. "They said things was beginnin' to change with us, and me comin' out there in blackface caused a lot of unhappy memories, and it would be more dignified if I was to just go out there the way I was, in my own skin, instead of coverin' it up like I was ashamed of it. At first, I disagreed with them—not because I didn't like their way of thinkin' but because, to tell you the truth, I'd been workin' in blackface for so many years that I was scared to go on without it!"

Pigmeat told the young men that the people weren't laughing at the blackface, they were laughing because his jokes were funny.

"'You're just answering your own argument,' they finally said," according to Pigmeat. "'If it isn't the blackface that's getting the laughs, why can't you go on without it?' Well, I finally gave in and agreed to try it—but I warned 'em it was sure to be a flop."

Pigmeat walked out onstage feeling nervous without his mask. But he proceeded to do his act without it and of course got the same laughs he usually got. The point had been made. Pigmeat said he was right—it was the jokes that were funny, not the blackface. But the young guys were right too—he didn't need it. Pigmeat said those kids provided him with an enormous boost to his self-confidence.

"I was so happy, and so relieved, that I went back to the dressing room, threw the make-up in the wastebasket—and I've never gone onstage in blackface again," he wrote.

Through Leonard Chess, founder of Chess Records in Chicago, Pigmeat found his way onto vinyl in the 1960s. Established in 1950 by Jewish immigrant brothers Leonard and Phil Chess, the company became instrumental in the blues and R&B genres, producing legendary artists like Chuck Berry, Bo Diddley, and Muddy Waters before branching out into soul, gospel, and comedy records. Black humor had emerged on recordings with the blues, as artists often spiced their lyrics with sly, humorous sexual and racial references intended for Black audiences. Anybody who's ever listened to Bessie Smith sing, "I need a little sugar in my bowl, I need a little hot dog between my rolls" knows exactly what that humor was like. However, there was still some reserve, some self-censorship, exhibited on these records. Watkins calls it the "twilight zone" between the private Black humor that existed for generations and the freedom to go public that has come more recently.

"Knowing that their audience would be primarily black, performers could and did loosen many of their inhibitions," Watkins writes. "At least partially, they were able to abandon the pretense of 'coming dark' or acting out white fantasy and, occasionally, display some of the bawdier comic references to sex. Consequently, the recordings presented examples of authentic black humor that were seldom found in Hollywood films or on Broadway and radio."

Because they were seen as unrestricted forums for Black debauchery, these early race records—mostly banned from radio—were disdained by the Black middle-class as too low-down and embarrassing. Gradually, as Black music became more popular and influential, polite white society could no longer ignore it—not when it was the driving force behind such iconic white acts as Elvis Presley and Jerry Lee Lewis. But for comedy, the process of going mainstream was much longer and more complicated. They had the task of replacing the long-standing racist stereotypes that were historically associated with American comedy (from minstrels to *Amos 'n' Andy*) with more wholesome images of Black life—while at the same time honoring the often gut-bucket comedy that made Black people laugh in private. Pushing authentic Black comedy to the fore was considered a threat by many white Americans because it challenged the white supremacist narrative of Blackness.

By the 1950s, the recording industry was putting more risqué comics like Redd Foxx on vinyl, dramatically changing the types of humor that Black people could access on record. Foxx was raunchy, uninhibited, and extremely Black. His records might be hidden in the back of the album collection in most Black households—but Black folks, and some whites, certainly were buying them. Gradually, private humor was becoming more public, more accessible to the white mainstream, a transition that significantly benefited comedians like Pigmeat as he worked with Chess Records to crank out more material. He ultimately made sixteen albums with Chess.

Markham learned how to retrofit his humor to a white audience when he went on the *Ed Sullivan Show* in the 1950s. He and Ed actually sat down and went through his bits, with Ed picking out the ones he thought would go over best on his show. They were right—Pigmeat was a big hit. Pigmeat was there when Ed Sullivan got his first show sponsor, Emerson Radio. Everybody jumped around and cheered when they saw the big telegram plastered on the bulletin board. Regarding that sponsor, Ed impressed Pigmeat by how he responded when the Emerson salesmen, particularly those from the South, tried to tell him he should drop all the Negroes he had on the show. He had a bigger budget now, they told him, so he didn't need to book low-budget talent anymore—and besides, having Negroes on the show would hurt the company's business in the South. But Ed didn't listen to them.

"If I can't exercise complete freedom in selecting talent, I'll get the hell off," Ed reportedly said, according to Pigmeat. "I've never thought in terms of religion or color and I'm not going to start now. I'm looking for talent and, when I find it, it's going on the show. If *you* want to get the hell off, fine!"

Pigmeat's career got an enormous boost on March 25, 1968, when his comedy was introduced to mainstream America—though ironically Pigmeat wasn't even physically there at the time. During an appearance on the television show *Rowan & Martin's Laugh-In*, Sammy Davis Jr. was trying to think of a funny bit while onstage, and Pigmeat's "Here Comes the Judge" gag popped into his head. He started prancing around the stage, chanting, "Here comes the Judge." Somehow, the line really caught on. All of a sudden, to Pigmeat's shock, he became a hot commodity. His phone started ringing, and his asking price jumped to $4,000 a week. Pigmeat was sixty-three.

Laugh-In repeated the Sammy Davis Jr. episode two months later in May, and Pigmeat's popularity soared even higher.

"Little kids, who'd never heard of me, were runnin' around hollerin' 'Here come the Judge!' like it was something brand-new and beautiful," Pigmeat said in his autobiography.

Judge records, Judge sweatshirts—the public was snatching them up. Pigmeat was getting booked at venues that seated over 10,000 people and now earning as much as $7,000 a week. He even recorded a song called "Here Comes the Judge" that some view as the first-ever rap song. Pigmeat does his chortling patter on top of a seductive beat, sounding remarkably like the rap songs that would be created within the next decade.

> *Hear ye, hear ye*
> *This court is now in session*
> *His Honor, Judge Pigmeat Markham presidin'*
> *Hear ye, hear ye, the court of swing*
> *It's just about ready to do that thing*
> *I don't want no tears, I don't want no lies*
> *Above all, I don't want no alibis*
> *This Judge is hip, and that ain't all*

He'll give you time if you're big or small
All in line for this court is neat
Peace brother, here comes the Judge
Here comes the Judge

Sammy later told Pigmeat that after he taped the *Laugh-In* episode, he was talking backstage with George Schlatter, the show's executive producer. George asked Sammy if he knew where the "Here Comes the Judge" line came from, and Sammy said, "Sure, that's Pigmeat Markham's old skit." Sammy knew Pigmeat well—Pigmeat used to babysit Sammy backstage as an infant when Sammy's mother, a chorus girl, went out to perform, walking around with little Sammy in his arms.

George Schlatter wondered what ever happened to old Pigmeat and started making phone calls to casting directors. He eventually found his way to Dick Allen, Pigmeat's manager, and invited Pigmeat to come on the show. But Pigmeat was nervous about the white audience.

As he was headed to the studio to do the taping, he fretted over the script they had given him, which he said contained a lot of one-liner jokes. Pigmeat considered himself a "situation" man, meaning his humor derived from funny situations, not standing up and telling jokes, a style that still was considered innovative in 1968.

"I'm not much on one-liners or monologues like Bill Cosby or Dick Gregory or Flip Wilson or them," he wrote. "They are a new breed. I am the last of the old."

But what Pigmeat was most nervous about was whether white folks would "get" him. After all, he had spent more than four decades honing his comedic skills in front of Black people—in essence, saying the private Black humor out loud. Now he would have to relate to a white audience—most of whom had no idea who he was—in studio and across America. To make matters worse, he had never even seen *Laugh-In*.

"I was born and raised Black," he said. "I learned my comedy from Black comedians. The earliest skits and bits I did on a stage or under a tent were invented by Black men. The audiences I learned to please, all those years in small towns and in big cities, they were mostly Black too."

It is a crucial point he's making, about America's awkward introduction to authentic Black humor, as the country began to be exposed to the things that Black people laughed at when white people weren't around. This was the start of the long process of Black comedy going mainstream, initially acutely aware of the white audience—a preoccupation that would ebb over time.

"In fact, I've discovered that many white people aren't tuned to my act at all," Pigmeat continued. "When they hear it on records, just the way I do it onstage for Negroes, they don't dig the slang, they have trouble following my accent, they don't even get the point of some of the jokes. . . . My act is not history, it's comedy. It's not whiteman's comedy, it's Negro-born and Negro-popular."

When Pigmeat went on *Laugh-In*, at one point they put a wig on his head, handed him a guitar, and told him to sing "Way down upon the Swanee River" and "Tiptoe thru' the Tulips" in falsetto. After he was done, they told him it was a perfect send-up of Tiny Tim, the strange, white, curly-haired singer with the ukulele who had become a national phenomenon in the late 1960s. But Tiny Tim hadn't penetrated Pigmeat's Black world.

"Who is Tiny Tim?" Pigmeat asked.

CHAPTER 7
MOMS MABLEY

Alongside Pigmeat Markham, another comedic force was beginning to rise—one who would become one of the most influential figures in the history of Black comedy: Moms Mabley.

Born Loretta Mary Aiken in North Carolina in 1897, she witnessed—and helped shape—every major shift in American comedy across the twentieth century. Early in her career, she adopted the name "Mabley" to shield her family from the stigma of her being a "stage woman." But there was nothing shameful about what she built. In fact, she may have been the most subversive and brilliantly incisive Black comedian ever to take the American stage.

By her thirties, Mabley had crafted a strategy that would become her signature: She donned the costume of a harmless old woman—"Moms," a persona inspired by her grandmother. In tattered gingham dresses, floppy hats, and oversize shoes, she shuffled onstage like someone's dotty great-aunt. But once the act began, her comic timing and courage exploded: She unleashed sharp, fearless commentary on racism, sexism, sexuality, and the absurdities of both Black and white America. The audience knew it was an act—but they went along with it, because in that disguise, she said what others couldn't. And they laughed, loudly, because they knew she was telling the truth.

While the comedic acts that came before Moms typically consisted of two or more people onstage, using their interactions and conversations as the source of the humor, a vestige of the minstrel influence, Mabley was one of the first to stand in the middle of the stage and just do "monologue humor"—talking to the audience, chiding the audience, identifying with the audience, poking fun the whole time. She was the bridge between the hackneyed old minstrel and vaudeville acts of the late 1800s and early 1900s and the caustic topical humor of brilliant observers like Dick Gregory and Richard Pryor who came along in the 1960s and 1970s. But well into her seventies, Mabley was still a force, performing onstage and on film as a hilarious contemporary of Gregory and Pryor. It is a testament to her immense talent that she was able to thrive for so long, through so many different eras, in the fickle business of show.

Mabley first took the stage at the Apollo in 1939—and over the next three decades would appear there more than any other performer, earning $10,000 per week at the end of her career (she started at $85 a week in the 1930s). Mabley also became popular to white audiences, even playing Carnegie Hall in 1962 with Nancy Wilson and Cannonball Adderley. She was invited to the White House separately by President Kennedy and President Johnson. After visiting Georgia Governor Jimmy Carter in the governor's mansion in 1974, she predicted that he would one day be president—and he in turn invited her to the White House after he was elected. Her career is all the more remarkable considering that when Mabley broke into entertainment, women were not warmly welcomed in comedy.

"Even those women who did breach the gender line in mainstream stage comedy often had to endure public opprobrium; they were regularly shunted into stereotypical roles as mannish or dumb, or as virtual harlots," Mel Watkins writes in *On the Real Side*.

This is where Mabley's genius becomes apparent, as she devised a stage persona that would allow her to be more probing and confrontational than normally tolerated from a woman.

"She would do her famous shuffle, sing some comical parody of a popular song, tell stories, or just stand there, and the audience would howl," Watkins writes. "The stories most often focused on some folksy experience she shared with the audience or the obsessive quest for a young man, a gambit that became her trademark."

When Mabley—Loretta at the time—was young, her father, James P. Aiken, was one of the most powerful and prosperous Black entrepreneurs in Brevard, a town in Transylvania County, North Carolina.

Certainly, he was one of the most successful formerly enslaved people in the region, owning several business ventures—a bakery, the first barbershop for white people on Main Street, a drayage service to transport mail from the railroad depot to the post office, and a popular store-café that sold groceries and general merchandise. He also sold caskets, was a volunteer firefighter, and was a member of the committee that oversaw the first school for freed Blacks. Some said Jim Aiken owned half of Brevard. It was during his duty as a firefighter that he met an untimely death on August 25, 1908, when his fire engine rounded a curve, overturned, and exploded, killing him instantly. Loretta was eleven when she lost her father, which would unfortunately have a major effect on her life, as there was no one around to protect her. That same year, she was raped by an older Black man; two years later, she was raped by the white town sheriff. The young girl became pregnant with each rape. The babies were taken away from her; she reportedly didn't see them again until they were grown.

Her grandmother, Jane Aiken Hall—a former enslaved person who used to make gingerbread for her son Jim's restaurant and lived to be 104, honored by the *Transylvania Times* at the time of her death as the oldest woman in the state—had raised Loretta with a steady encouragement to go out in the world and make something of herself. When she was nearly fourteen, Loretta left Brevard to join a minstrel show. She changed her birthdate from 1897 to 1894 to make herself older and began performing on the TOBA circuit. Loretta never wanted to let people too close, because she offered different versions of her origin story at different times. At one point, she lived in a boarding house in Buffalo, New York, with other entertainers trying to make it in show business; her mother, Mary, sent her money every month to help with food and rent.

Loretta caught her first break in Houston. The popular husband-and-wife dance team known as Butterbeans and Susie saw her perform and persuaded her to join their act. Loretta was a pretty good dancer and singer, though these were never going to be the talents that brought her acclaim. She knew comedy was her ticket to fame, so she focused on creating a one-of-a-kind act. This was when "Moms" began to come to life.

Jack Mabley was the name of a young Canadian man she had met shortly after leaving home. She said, "He didn't want to live in the United States, and I didn't want to live in Canada, so no marriage occurred." She explained the name more cuttingly at a different time, saying that Jack Mabley took a lot from her, so at least she could take his name. But it was her granny whom Moms spoke of in the most glowing terms, acknowledging that it was Jane Aiken Hall who served as her muse.

"I had in mind a woman about 60 or 65 years. She's a good woman with an eye for shady dealings," she once said. "She was like my granny, the most beautiful woman I had ever known. She was the one who convinced me to go make something of myself. She was so gentle, but she kept her children in line, best believe that."

The early Black theater was an important source of work for Mabley, who performed in numerous singing-dancing-comedy shows called "revues." She appeared in *Bowman's Cotton Blossoms* in 1919; she wore blackface for the 1927 play *Look Who's Here* and also appeared that same year in *Miss Bandana*. She went out in blackface again in *The Joy Boat* in the 1930s, when she also worked in *Sidewalks of Harlem* and *Red Pastures*. In 1931, she joined forces with the renowned Harlem Renaissance writer Zora Neale Hurston on the elaborate Broadway play *Fast and Furious: A Colored Revue in 37 Scenes*; together they wrote some of the scenes and acted together in one skit as cheerleaders.

The show only lasted for seven performances, as reviewers weren't kind, calling it "mediocre." One critic asked for a Black show where the "humor will, on occasion, be humorous." When Mabley appeared with Pigmeat Markham, Tim Moore, Mantan Moreland, and Eddie Green in the Broadway musical *Blackberries* at the Liberty Theatre in 1932, the white Broadway audience was not pleased with the type of comedy that the performers offered—namely, the Black stuff they had been doing on the TOBA circuit. The white audience wasn't yet ready for any inkling of private Black humor. Mabley also got a small role as the madam of a brothel in Eugene O'Neill's film, *The Emperor Jones*, starring Paul Robeson. She was so disgusted by the script that she threw it away, though she did ultimately make the film (Williams 1995, 47).

"The people had written a thick book with all these lines," she said. "Now how can a white man write lines for a Harlem landlady? I saw it live. I knew what to be true, they didn't."

Overall, Mabley would appear in only four feature films, culminating with *Amazing Grace* in 1974, the year before she died. She took a star turn in 1948's *Boarding House Blues*, where she plays a character known as "Moms" who runs a boarding house for out-of-work entertainers. The setup reminded Mabley of her early days living in the theatrical boarding house in Buffalo.

"Show people live the way the rest of the world ought to live . . . always doing things for somebody else," she said.

There is an undeniable beauty in Mabley using the Moms persona as a vehicle for her comedy, elevating and celebrating the Black matriarch figure who is beloved in most Black families. The character gave Moms staying power, allowing her to survive for sixty years in an industry that could be cold and unforgiving, especially to women performers.

"In addition to bonding with her audience, assuming the maternal pose provided Mabley with a vehicle for boundary setting—for controlling the relationship between herself (the performer) and the audience," Elsie A. Williams writes in *The Humor of Jackie Moms Mabley: An African American Comedic Tradition*. "To stake out territory brought both protection and freedom since early vaudeville entertainers were often looked upon with suspicion and as loose women crossing the threshold of a man's world."

Williams points out other women who leaned into the Mom persona—Ma Rainey (Gertrude Pridgett), Big Memphis Ma Rainey (Lillie Mae Glover), Sweet Mama Stringbean (Ethel Waters). Though she didn't adopt the title of Mom, Phyllis Diller used her clothes, wigs, and glasses to create a Mom-like persona for her comedy. When she was offstage, Moms was likely to be caught wearing tailored slacks, silk blouses, Italian shoes, and stylish hats, especially to church. Religion was very important to Mabley. She maintained that God called her to become a performer when she was broke and pregnant in Buffalo. She once said she became an entertainer because she was very pretty and didn't want to become a prostitute.

"I got down on my knees and asked God to show me the way to make a living for me and his child, and then just as I've ever heard anyone talk, a voice came to me and said, 'Go onstage and I'll go with you,' and when I looked around and didn't see anybody, I knew it was God showing me the way" (Williams 1995, 70).

In assessing why comedy has been so challenging for women performers, writers like Karen Stoddard and Zita Dresner point to the aggression comedians typically bring to the stage. The roles characteristically granted to women, such as devoted wife and mother, always passive and submissive, don't leave room for antagonism, aggression, and levity. But in the view of Williams, Moms was a "womanist," a term Alice Walker introduced in *In Search of Our Mothers' Gardens* to describe audacious, courageous, grown women (Williams 1995, 72–73).

"Moms as feminist emerges as the controlling center and prime mover behind her comedic routines," Williams writes. "The womanist stance provided Mabley with the strength and character to perform aggressively and willfully, to define her persona and to establish herself as free to say what others of her gender, race, and time often had to suppress. Ignoring the prescribed notions of what was proper for the female, Mabley survived the male-dominated field of comedy by enlarging her Moms persona to incorporate multiple infrastructures: the woman of words, the trickster, and the fool."

As a woman of words, Moms used her tongue to signal to Black people that she was one of them, a member of the group—but one whose wit could cut you to the bone in a heartbeat. Especially if you were a man. She had a significant amount of material about male sexuality and libido—a place no other female comedian would dare go at the time. One of her jokes involves her asking her granny about sex when she was a girl:

One day she was sitting on the porch, and I said, "Granny, how old does a woman get before she don't want no more boyfriends?" She said, "I don't know, honey. You have to ask somebody older than me." She said, "A woman is a woman as long as she lives; there's a certain time in a man's life when he has to go to a place called 'over the hill.'"

She even performed a poem called "Over the Hill," which included the following:

> It's not the gray hair that makes a man old,
> Nor that faraway stare in his eyes, I am told.
> But when his mind makes a contract
> That his body can't fill, he is—over the hill, over the hill.

Donald Bogle said that Mabley "handled men as roughly as Bessie Smith sometimes did in song." (Bogle 2007, 160) This was a story she often told at the beginning of a set:

"Moms been accused of liking young men, and I'm guilty. Can't no old men do nothing for me (laughter), but bring me a message from a young man (laughter). Let me tell you girls something! George took me home last night and kissed me (laughter). My big toe shot up in the air just like!"

Various writers have described the trickster as a cultural hero whose job is to sabotage the system and topple the hierarchy. This is an apt description of Mabley's posturing onstage. Williams compares her to the griot in West Africa, who has the power to insult or verbally abuse other group members without impunity.

"As trickster, she could be her own person, redefine and reconstruct previously established truths, and shift loyalties as well," Williams writes. "From behind the trickster mask, Moms could revel in incongruities wherever she perceived them: among women, drug addicts, 'hipsters,' blacks, Chinese, gays, lesbians, bisexuals, transvestites, world leaders, white cultural heroes, sexual libertines, and topics such as race relations and integration."

As trickster, Mabley also told jokes that made fun of female attributes or excesses—just like male comedians. One of her jokes is focused on a female friend who has very large breasts. After Mabley attacked the friend for letting herself get fat and "not taking any of the weight off nor lifting some of it up"—referring to a bra for the large, hanging breasts—the friend decided she wanted to kill herself. So, Mabley crudely tells her how to do it:

"Get you a good .38 and be sure it's loaded all the way around; measure three inches below your left breast and pull the trigger."

Then Mabley adds: "Don't you know that fool went home and shot herself through the knee?"

While the trickster can be somewhat heroic for going after those in power, the fool is closer to the clown, giving the group license to laugh at their own people and their idiosyncrasies or failures. Mabley used the fool persona as a way of enforcing in-group control and deflating stereotypes. In one of her jokes, which she told at the white Playboy Club, Moms acts the fool as a way of puncturing the authority of white law enforcement and ridiculing Jim Crow. She describes what happens when she got pulled over by a police officer in a small town in South Carolina for running a red light.

"I saw all the white folks driving on the green light," she told the officer. "I thought the red light must have been for us."

Moms delighted in being seen as the truth teller. "I just tell folks the truth," she said. "If they don't want it, they don't come to Moms." In her truth telling, Moms began the excruciatingly slow—century-long—process of bringing private Black humor into the mainstream. Playing the fool, she gets away with it. Langston Hughes predicted the emergence of a Moms-like character in his 1926 essay, "The Negro Artist and the Racial Mountain," written during the Harlem Renaissance:

> We younger Negro artists who create now intend to express our individual dark-skinned selves without fear or shame. If white people are pleased, we are glad. If they are not, it doesn't matter. We know we are beautiful. And ugly too. The tom-tom cries and the tom-tom laughs. If colored people are

pleased, we are glad. If they are not, their displeasure doesn't matter either. We build our temples for tomorrow, strong as we know how, and we stand on top of the mountain, free within ourselves.

In this lewd joke, it is Moms's brother who is the fool: "My brother is dead because of one of those fairy tales. They kept telling him, 'Ding dong bell / pussy's in the well' and he got drowned like a fool!"

The following joke was a Moms favorite, again about one of her beloved topics—sex. The joke ostensibly is about how she liked to cause trouble as a little girl, focused on Easter:

"I had a whole lot of different colored eggs. We had an old setting hen around the house, and I went and took all the eggs from under her and put all these different colored eggs under her and she hatched them. Hatched out a whole lot of red, green, blue, purple, and orange chickens. The rooster came and saw all those different colored chickens. He got down on his knees, but he didn't hurt the hen though. But man, he went around the house and *damn* near killed that peacock."

Moms also loved to poke fun at class distinctions and make fun of "highbrow" culture such as the opera. She would do this by switching to standard English and singing a stylized aria that usually had a powerful message. Here's an excerpt from one she sang in 1962 about civil rights activist James Meredith and his fight to attend the University of Mississippi:

Now I ain't go'n sit in back of no bus.
And I'm goin' to the white folks' school.
I'm goin' praise the Lord in the white folks' church.
And I'm goin' swim in the white folks' pool!
I'm goin' vote and vote for whoever I please.
And I'll thumb my nose at the Klan.
And I'll double-dare 'em to come out from behind them sheets
and face me like a man.
They don't scare me with their bomb threats.

I'll say what I wanna say!
And ain't a damn thing they can do about it.
'Cause I ain't goin' down there no way!
And you know why?
Because it took a marshal, the Army too, JFK, and I don't know who!
Every law, and every rule
To try to get one boy in the Mississippi school.
School days, school days
Barnett said, "To hell with-the-congressional-rule days!"
Lead pipes and black jacks and pistols too!
Those are the books that they take to school!
They don't study science or history.
They study hate and bigotry.
They been scaring the heck out of you and me
Since we was a couple of kids.
What kind of school is this?
(What kind of fool am I?)
The school they call "Ole Miss"?

WHAT THIS "ARIA" demonstrates most of all is Moms's genius at finding clever ways to take swings at the white power structure without becoming a target herself for attack. Inside of an extended "joke" that allowed Moms to poke fun at high society by singing an aria, she delivers a devastating takedown of the ridiculousness of segregation protected by violence.

CHAPTER 8
REDD FOXX

It is a storyline straight out of Hollywood—that one of the crassest, crudest comedians ever to step on a stage could be transformed into the lovable Fred Sanford, America's irascible but bighearted soul. Redd Foxx's *Sanford and Son* was one of the most popular shows on television during a four-year run starting with its first season in 1972, each year sitting at number two in the ratings behind only *All in the Family*—and occasionally beating that show too. The show was so popular that it reportedly drove *The Brady Bunch* off the air in 1974. With its unmistakable, horn-driven melody, Quincy Jones's theme song "The Streetbeater" became an iconic part of American pop culture—blaring through televisions every Friday night as the opening credits rolled.

After a contract dispute over his salary, Redd Foxx secured a raise from $19,000 to $25,000 per episode—matching the pay of *All in the Family* star Carroll O'Connor. But Foxx came out ahead: He also negotiated 25 percent of the producers' net profits, a deal that underscored both his star power and business savvy. It was indeed a long, arduous, winding journey to the peak of Hollywood stardom for the sharp-witted, stubborn Foxx.

Born in St. Louis in his maternal grandmother's house on December 9, 1922, Jon Elroy Sanford was the second son of Fred Glenn Sanford and Mary Alma Hughes Sanford. His mother always made sure that everyone knew how to properly spell the name of her copper-complected, red-haired son: "Jon without the *h*." But most people added the *h* anyway.

Fred Sanford was an electrician by trade who worked odd jobs on the side to make ends meet—though often ends did not meet, and the family battled dire poverty, living in a tough neighborhood. Jon had a brother named Fred Jr. who was four years his senior and much bigger, burlier, and darker than Jon. While Jon had a boyish face and thick, curly red hair, resembling his mother's side of the family—the Hughes clan—Fred's features were less delicate and more pronounced.

Despite the age gap between them, the brothers were inseparable. Their bond was forged in part by loss—two sisters born between them had died in infancy—and strengthened by the need to look out for each other on the rough streets outside their home. Jon remembered Fred as a natural athlete, a standout in the neighborhood's pickup games played on patchy fields and garbage-strewn lots. Long before Jackie Robinson broke baseball's color barrier in 1947, Jon proudly watched his older brother play a mean first base.

When Jon was just four, their father walked out—an absence that would leave a lasting mark, especially on Jon's relationship with his mother. The only other time Jon ever saw him, he didn't even realize it. The man who bought him and Fred ice cream cones that day was a stranger. Only later did Jon learn he was their father.

"I remember an ice cream cone, two for a nickel. He bought my brother and I one," he would later recall. "That's all I remember about him." A neighbor told the boys that the generous stranger was actually their father. Since he never sent their mother money to help care for them, he didn't seem so generous after all—the cones were literally the least he could do.

Their mother, Mary, was struggling. Working as a domestic and with the family's main breadwinner gone, she was barely getting by. Desperate for better opportunities, she made the painful decision to leave the boys in the care of her mother—who lived several miles away in a run-down house on the other side of the city—and head to Chicago in search of work.

Jon never forgave her. He was only four, but even then, he knew something was wrong. He felt a mother wasn't supposed to leave her children behind to start over somewhere else. The hurt stayed with him. So did the sense of abandonment. Life wasn't so great with Grandma Hughes either—she was just as broke as her daughter, and she didn't appreciate young Jon wasting his time with his ear connected to his transistor radio, listening to comedian Fred Allen and dreaming of one day being an entertainer.

Jon and Fred finally got out of their grandmother's wooden shack in St. Louis when their mother enrolled them at St. Benedict the Moor Mission, a boarding school in Milwaukee—330 miles away. Jon was just six and a half, suddenly living in the dorms of an all-Black Catholic school founded in 1908 by Captain Lincoln Charles Valle and his wife, Julia, to provide quality religious education for Black children.

The school charged $20 a month for the boarding students, who made up about half of its 300-person enrollment. Despite the downsides of the distance from home and the strict religious setting, St. Benedict offered structure, education, and a chance to start fresh. One of Jon's classmates would later become a prominent figure in American politics: future Chicago mayor Harold Washington.

Jon lasted just two years at the boarding school; Fred stayed for three. Jon often acted up in class—cracking jokes, clowning around, unable to sit still. It frustrated the teachers but made him popular with his classmates. School officials, aware that he was a young boy far from home, missing his mother and with no father in the picture, occasionally showed compassion. But their patience had limits.

At night, Jon's fear revealed just how young he truly was. He wet the bed more than once—not from physical need, but from sheer terror. The shadows of tree branches outside his window took on monstrous shapes in his imagination, and he was too frightened to move. The school offered no comfort. Instead, the staff beat him for what they labeled as "accidents," treating his fear as disobedience.

Yet even in that difficult setting, something clicked for Jon—something that would shape his future. He noticed how much laughter, affection, and attention his older brother Fred earned by being the class clown. Jon wanted some of that too. In a place where warmth was scarce, humor became a kind of currency—and Jon was beginning to understand its power.

"I remember one time [Fred] came into the cafeteria and he was pulling an electric iron; he'd found an electric iron with the cord and that was his dog. He upset the whole dinner," Jon once said. "He'd say, 'Come on, Buster.' That was his dog's name. Everybody cracked up, and when I saw him do that and get all that audience participation from the kids in the Catholic home, I wanted to be a part of that thing."

When he was eight, Jon left St. Benedict's, taking the bus back to his grandmother's house in St. Louis. She enrolled him in Banneker Elementary School, where his behavior continued to be a problem for his teachers. This was not uncommon for future comedians—the classroom as an early stage.

"School meant nothing to me," Jon later said. "Knowing that George Washington crossed the Delaware—how was that going to help me in a brick fight in Saint Louis?"

We got the benefit of one of his classmates' takes on young Redd in school—LaWanda Page, the comedian who would later costar in *Sanford and Son*, was a classmate at Banneker.

"Sometimes if the teacher would get on him about something, he would try to jive," she recalled. "I remember he said, 'Miss Blue'—that was the teacher's name—'Miss Blue, I love you.'"

Jon spent a lot of time on the streets, hanging with his buddies on corners, hustling for a buck. He would dig around at the market for discarded fruit and vegetables to sell. He also sold newspapers and donuts—anything he could get his hands on. He got expelled from fifth grade in 1932 for throwing a book at a teacher—though Jon had a different take, saying he was throwing the book back at the teacher who threw it at him, trying to protect himself. Jon clearly had a problem with authority figures. Fred, at fifteen, rarely went to school at all, spending his time on the streets with his buddies. Exhausted, Grandma Hughes sent Jon to Chicago to be reunited with his mother. He moved into her small one-bedroom apartment on the South Side.

Though they were now in the same space, the proximity didn't lead to any strengthening of the mother-son bond. He was still punishing her for abandoning him. He also was upset that they were so broke.

"I was so raggedy I was too ashamed to go and pick up my diploma when I got out [of Banneker]," he said. "They mailed it to me."

Jon enrolled at Chicago's DuSable High School soon after it opened in 1935. Named after "The Father of Chicago," Jean Baptiste Pointe du Sable, the Haitian fur trader who was the first non-Indigenous person to settle in Chicago, the school saw an influx of Black students originally from the South. Because of his deft humor and perpetual smile, Jon quickly acquired the nickname Smiley. One of his friends said, "Every word he said was funny."

Jon also joined the 58th Street Gang, which mostly spent its time playing the dozens outside the local drugstore and causing trouble in the neighborhoods around Fifty-Eighth Street. The gang soon learned that you didn't want to go up against Smiley in a game of the dozens. (For the unfamiliar: The dozens is a competitive verbal sparring match rooted in Black culture, where people exchange witty, often biting insults—usually about each other's families, especially their mothers. It is as much about creativity and delivery as it is about cutting humor, and winning means earning respect.) He used his wit to take guys down in a heartbeat—a skill that would later serve him well taking down hecklers in nightclubs.

One of his DuSable classmates, Dempsey Travis, described him in this way: "He could talk about you, your mother, and other members of your family in derogatory language that would make you want to fight, run, or simply just cry. He had a split personality like Dr. Jekyll and Mr. Hyde. Because during the day at school he was a very jolly person, whereas after school in the company of the 58th Street Gang he turned into a reincarnated devil."

Jon was drawn to the celebrated music program at DuSable High School, led by the legendary Captain Walter Dyett. The program had an extraordinary track record, producing stars like Bo Diddley, Nat King Cole, Dinah Washington, and pianist Dorothy Donegan—who happened to be there at the same time as Jon.

Jon had always loved music. He grew up crooning along to the smooth harmonies of the Ink Spots and the Mills Brothers on the radio. At DuSable, that love turned into something more. He and three classmates decided to start a band—but there was just one problem: They couldn't afford instruments. So, they improvised, forming a low-budget washtub group they called The Four Bon Bons. One boy strummed a beat-up guitar, another pounded rhythms on an old washtub, while Jon and a friend sang, danced, and cracked jokes.

They played on street corners around Fifty-Eighth Street, passing the hat after each performance. It wasn't much, but it was their first taste of showbiz—and for Jon, the thrill of making people laugh and clap would prove irresistible.

Jon did so poorly in the classroom at DuSable that he lasted just two semesters before dropping out after turning sixteen. Jon and his bandmates did a show at DuSable—Dyett let Jon perform even though he had dropped out—that was considered a rousing success. They decided it was time to hit the road, to escape the confines of the Windy City. On the night of July 5, 1939, Jon's brother Fred drove them to the train station, where their plan was to hop a freight car that would take them to New York. Jon's relationship with his mother, Mary, was so strained that he left without even saying goodbye to her. In his later years, after he became Redd Foxx, he would tell the story of how they found themselves in a freight car full of onions and "cried all the way there."

They made it to Buffalo first—where they stole some loaves of bread and cans of pork and beans—before they hopped on another freight car. This time they got all the way to Weehawken, New Jersey, just across the Hudson River from Manhattan. With the lights of the big city beckoning in the distance, they got chased by several police detectives. Two of the guys got caught, but the police couldn't catch Jon. The two were held in the county jail for a month, falsely accused of breaking into a nearby nursing home. Jon ran toward the river and jumped into a small tugboat that was heading toward Manhattan. In fact, the boat was traveling straight for Harlem. It docked at 125th

Street, serendipitously making Harlem the place where he first set foot in New York.

Jon arrived in Harlem in the summer of 1939, just as the glow of the Harlem Renaissance was beginning to fade. He came alone, expecting to reunite with his crew at an apartment building on West 138th Street—but when he got there, no one was waiting. Suddenly, Jon was on his own in a new city, with no money, no connections, and no place to stay.

His first priority was survival: food and shelter. He never spoke in detail about those first few days, but the stories that trickled out hinted at desperation. He likely slept on rooftops, using newspapers for warmth, stole bottles of milk and loaves of bread, and skipped out on dinner checks at local diners—where he figured he could blend in and disappear before anyone caught on.

It was a rough landing, but Jon was determined to make something of himself. Harlem, even in its twilight, still held promise. He just had to find his way to it.

His friends Steve and Lamont—finally released from jail—reunited with Jon and immediately went to work. They recruited three more guys from the neighborhood and changed the group's name to the Jump Swinging Six. They were still the same basic washtub band, but now they had the New York City subway as a stage, busking on platforms and outside stations, playing for donations. Jon later said they would sometimes make as much as $50 a night each, which would mean a total of $300. The Jump Swinging Six would soon win a coveted slot on a nationally syndicated radio show called the *Major Bowes' Original Amateur Hour*, which reached 27 million listeners.

This enormously popular show, the *American Idol* of its day, would feature musical guests competing against each other with the national audience phoning in to pick a winner. More than ten thousand people applied each week to be on the show, but only fifteen would be chosen to appear on the air. A few years earlier, Frank Sinatra and his group, the Hoboken Four, performed several weeks in a row without getting the gong from Major Bowes, who would bang it if he didn't like an act. The show was considered a major launching pad. Alas, Jon's group finished second from the bottom that night, receiving just 137 votes—the winning act got almost 4,500 votes.

Jon loved to explore Harlem's nightlife, adopting the Savoy Ballroom as his favorite spot. "The Savoy was very important because I found such great relief in dancing, and I danced pretty good. I would hustle all day long, so I could get to the Savoy, meet some chicks and hear all the best bands."

Costing just 50 cents to get in, the Savoy offered nonstop dancing to some of the best music of the time. "There was never anything like the Savoy before or since," Redd Foxx later said. "Just imagine two thousand people dancing to that same beat—it was wild! Sometimes I'd be downstairs at the pool hall right under the ballroom, and you could see the floor sinking with the rhythm. Most of my life then was wrapped around the Savoy."

After the Japanese bombed Pearl Harbor on December 7, 1941, the Jump Swinging Six were effectively over. One the members, Steve Trimble, enlisted in the service while another went back to Chicago. For his part, Jon tried to devise a scheme to avoid the draft. His new nickname was Foxy, an allusion to his sharp dress and way with the ladies. He had no interest in walking away from all of that to fight foreigners overseas, so he found a way to trick the draft board with fake heart trouble.

"I went to a draft board in Harlem," he explained. "The doctor decided I had a heart condition, so I was rejected. I had eaten a half bar of Octagon soap, which causes heart palpitations."

The next few years found Sanford struggling to stay afloat. He wheeled around dresses in the garment district in midtown; he worked as a busboy at a restaurant in Greenwich Village. Without steady work, he was forced to turn to crime, this time more serious than stealing milk. He was arrested for suspicion of armed robbery and got an extended stay in the Tombs jail complex in lower Manhattan—though he claimed it was mistaken identity. He spent five days in Rikers for drinking people's milk deliveries, getting caught by a cop with an empty bottle in his hand. He was sent to jail for marijuana possession. He had started using drugs—marijuana and later cocaine, which was more expensive. He was invited to shoot up heroin by two friends, but when he went to their place after playing pool, he found them dead of an overdose.

"From then on that was enough for me not to mess with no heroin. I can still see those two cats laying there backwards on the bed with their knees bent. If I'd of [sic] finished that pool game ten minutes sooner, I would have been just as dead as they was."

Foxy Sanford got a job washing dishes at a Harlem joint called Jimmy's Chicken Shack, which was a favorite spot for music celebrities. Iconic jazz pianist Art Tatum used Jimmy's as his headquarters, while artists like Hazel Scott and Billie Holiday sat in on jam sessions at Jimmy's, which was owned by bandleader Andy Kirk. Jimmy's was an important stop for Sanford, because that's where he became close friends with a teenager named Malcolm Little—later to become famous as Malcolm X. Foxx biographer Michael Seth Starr described them as "inseparable." These two light-skinned Black men with reddish hair, both stylish dressers and favorites with the ladies, spent so much time together that their nicknames recognized their closeness: Sanford became "Chicago Red" and Malcolm became "Detroit Red," monikers used to distinguish them from each other.

"He was a beautiful guy," Foxx said. "Malcolm was about the same color as me. You could hardly tell us apart. We both had those conks and our hair was red with a high pompadour and we had the zoot pants—just like the 'high drape pants' Billie Holiday used to sing about in her blues."

At the time, Malcolm was the only person he trusted. He knew no matter what kind of scrape he might stumble into, Malcolm always had his back. Malcolm would even join Sanford sleeping sometimes on the St. Nicholas Avenue rooftops, piles of newspapers keeping them warm. The two slid into a life of petty crime. In one instance, a young woman who had a thing for Sanford "accidentally" left open a window to the dry cleaners where she worked, allowing Jon and Malcolm to slip in and steal about a hundred suits. They used the rooftop as their base of operation and sold one or two suits a day until they were gone. They also sold weed to the musicians playing the nightclubs of Harlem, establishing a rep as the go-to weed dealers.

"They were hustlers," remembers John Williams, husband of jazz pianist and composer Mary Lou Williams. "Redd Foxx was more of a hustler than Malcolm X. He was something! He was down trying to sell marijuana to us. A lot of us used it."

Redd Foxx later told the story of what happened when he and Malcolm joined the Communist Party for the food and girls—the closest Malcolm got to politics at the time. At a meeting on St. Nicholas Avenue, they signed some papers and were given a pile of party literature to read.

"You'd dance with the chicks, smell the perfume, and eat the sandwiches," Redd said. "You just couldn't avoid being part of things like that because there was food, man—stacked-high cake and lemonade, even baloney you could put in your pocket. I'd have joined the Ku Klux Klan if they'd had some sandwiches."

The dynamic duo began to experience tension when Malcolm's forays into crime got more serious. Jon was more interested in fun than crime, so he drifted away from Malcolm, whose criminal activity seriously intensified, including dealing hardcore drugs. The world came to know Malcolm's story when he was finally sent to prison and underwent a religious transformation, joining the Nation of Islam and becoming Malcolm X. After that, they would reunite only once, nearly twenty years later in Harlem in the early 1960s.

In his book, *The Redd Foxx Encyclopedia of Black Humor*, Redd says he even helped Malcolm with his speechifying.

"Malcolm X was a friend of mine and he was having a hard time getting people to listen to him," Redd says. "So I suggested that he try telling people a funny incident. Before you get down to the nitty-gritty, get them to laugh first. Then, when you've got their attention, drop your spiel on them. He tried it and it worked."

After his time with Malcolm, Jon got more serious about show business as he tried to get a fresh start. He was still thinking he'd become a professional singer, so he first needed a catchy name that would pop, something that would look good on marquees. He used the "Red" from his nickname and combined it with "Fox," since he had also been known as Foxy. He didn't like his name to be so clearly a color, so he added a D. To change his last name from identification with the wild animal, he added an X.

"I figured 'Redd Foxx' looked better on a marquee than 'Red Fox,'" he said.

He caught a break when he got hired as an emcee at a Chitlin' Circuit club in Baltimore called Gamby's. Facing the tough crowds in Baltimore was where he learned how to work a room and how to deal with hecklers. The singer Jimmy Scott, who became close friends with Foxx, observed the effect he had on the patrons at the club.

"He was telling jokes and everybody was crazy about him," Scott remembered decades later. "That was just his natural way. He would crack up the house. And he was cool with the women. They were crazy about him. He had a good set of ladies that ran after him."

In September 1946, Redd caught a break when Herman Lubinsky, who ran Savoy Records, brought him into his recording studio in Newark. In one session, Redd recorded five blues songs for Lubinsky—who had gained a reputation for grossly underpaying his artists, including Charlie Parker, Billy Eckstine, and Sarah Vaughan. He was joined at the session by his bandmates from the Jump Swinging Six, plus a few Savoy studio musicians. The result was songs that felt like the blues, but had a humorous flavor, talking about subjects like beautiful women and infidelity. In "Lucky Guy," he sings about how his woman will never cheat on him.

> *I'm a lucky guy and I ain't gonna sing no blues.*
> *My baby's got bad teeth bad feet can't even wear no shoes.*

The songs failed to catch on. They weren't reviewed in *Billboard* or *Variety*, nor did they do much in sales. But what Redd did get around this time was a new wife—just five days after he met her.

One night, a musician friend brought a woman named Evelyn Killebrew to Redd's Harlem apartment. What she didn't know—and what Redd quickly discovered—was that the friend had brought her there with a horrific plan in mind: to sexually assault her.

"We had a big fight, I put him out, and she stayed there with me for protection, more or less, but five days later we were married," Redd would later recall.

Evelyn's father wanted his daughter to be comfortable, and he wanted to keep an eye on Redd, so he moved the couple into his big house in Newark, where he ran a successful dry-cleaning business. Redd initially liked the stability of his new middle-class lifestyle, something that was foreign to him at the time. But show business was still his love. He played a few clubs in Newark and did some more emceeing. His raunchy brand of humor led to a new nickname: Filthy Mouth. He traveled down to Baltimore and played some of the clubs there, where the club owners hadn't forgotten him. He also came up with a new scheme to make money—growing his own marijuana. With the assistance of his wife, Redd dug his hands into the earth and nurtured crops of weed in the backyard of his father-in-law's house, unbeknownst to the father-in-law. Things did not end well. Somebody ratted them out to police, and Redd got busted, which was reported in the *Baltimore Afro-American*:

> Fellow entertainers often wondered how Jon Elroy Sanford, a small-time comedian, could afford to drive a Cadillac. Last week they got their answer. Sanford, better known as Redd Foxx, was growing marijuana in his Newark, New Jersey, backyard. Federal agents found a quantity of reefers in his coat pocket and also in the Cadillac. Both he and his wife, Evelyn, are under $5,000 bail. (Starr 2011)

Evelyn's father bailed them out and paid the fine so they wouldn't have to do any jail time. But Newark was now a place to flee for Redd. In one of his frequent trips to Harlem, he met a man who would become an important partner for him: comedian Melvin "Slappy" White. White, who was married to singer Pearl Bailey, was a year older than Redd and even more experienced at telling jokes onstage.

White, born in Baltimore, had spent years working the Chitlin' Circuit. His jokes leaned on clever setups with a bit of social commentary.

A Slappy joke: *We was so poor my uncle invented the limbo by slipping under the pay toilet.*

Or: *Just remember, if Adam had been born black, there'd be no woman. Can you imagine someone taking a rib from a black?*

Slappy's partnership with Redd developed in 1947 just as Slappy was breaking up with Pearl. As a result, Pearl blamed Redd for the problems in her marriage, which grew into a long-standing feud between the two. As for Redd's own marriage, he would stay out for days at a time with Slappy without checking in with his wife. Divorce eventually followed.

Slappy and Redd formed an act that featured Slappy as the straight man setting up the quick-witted but prickly Foxx. After bombing in their first appearance at the Palace Theatre on Broadway, they went out on the Chitlin' Circuit to hone their routine. Redd claimed they were "as good as Dean Martin and Jerry Lewis."

Working the Chitlin' Circuit was not a launching pad to the mainstream for the comic duo. They couldn't break through the Jim Crow stubbornness of the white clubs.

"The white public's concept of Black comedy was two white guys in plaid suits, shuffling about with a broom, and doing an act in blackface," Foxx said. "A Black stand-up comic couldn't find a job."

In 1952, the great jazz singer Dinah Washington asked Redd and Slappy to be her opening act. Washington, already a big star at twenty-seven, offered them $1,000 a week to open for her in Los Angeles. But a month into their gig with Dinah, the two broke up after Dinah invited Slappy to travel back east with her and not Redd. Redd's ego was crushed, particularly when Slappy accepted her offer. He was stuck in LA, a city that he found as racist as the South, with no money and no prospects. But he loved the weather in LA and couldn't see himself returning to the cold. He got a job in the kitchen of a jazz joint called Club Alabam but was soon moved onto the stage as an emcee when management saw how funny he was.

Biographer Starr notes in *Black and Blue* that Redd's style was different from his comic counterparts' in the 1950s, whose material consisted of standard jokes and celebrity impersonations. Not so with Foxx.

"Redd was a different comic beast," Starr writes. "Many of his friends were jazz musicians, and he'd spent his years in clubs grooving to jazz riffs and immersing himself in their weed-scented lifestyle. What he did now was to cut and paste jazz's freeform vibe to his stage act, infusing his onstage patter and pacing with an almost anything-goes attitude. It pushed him toward a style that seemed leisurely and off-the-cuff as he strung together a loose mélange of comic stories, riffing on whatever seemed to pop into his head. And he used the language of the streets, since he felt that made him more identifiable and accessible to his Black audience."

Redd's reputation as a "blue" comedian continued to grow, though commentators have noted that it was more his subject matter than his language that earned him the rep. Redd's act drew the notice of a businessman named Dootsie Williams, who had started Dooto Records, which focused on R&B and "novelty" records. When he saw Redd's act, Dootsie saw dollar signs.

"He wasn't really obscene, just naughty by those standards," Williams said. "But then, he was so outrageous in such a way that nobody would ever think of putting him on record. But I thought, 'This guy can sell.' If he could shock and make such an impression that people would fall out in the aisles on him, I said, 'This will sell.'"

Williams turned out to be quite prescient. Though Redd himself didn't think it would work, he did sell. In early 1956, Dooto Records released an album of Redd's comedy called *Laff of the Party, Volume 1*, which was a collection of bits during his performances at the Oasis Club in LA. Though Redd had established a reputation as a blue comic, the album contained no profanity, just sexually suggestive clever wordplay and double entendres.

Around this time, Redd fell in love again. Betty Jean Harris was part of the Harris Sisters, a singing group from Oklahoma that had scored a minor hit with the song "Kissin' Bug" and was booked at the Oasis Club, when Redd became smitten at first sight. They got married in Las Vegas after just a week of dating. Redd adopted Betty Jean's daughter, Debraca, who came to live with them in Los Angeles. The newly minted couple hit the road in a 1936 Plymouth, searching for gigs as a team—she sang, and he told jokes. Redd's comedy album was selling, which helped him get booked into clubs. But he faced severe racism. The mid-1950s was a time when big-name acts like Sammy Davis Jr., Louis Armstrong, and Nat King Cole couldn't even stay in the fancy Vegas hotels where they performed, having instead to enter through a side entrance or the kitchen. Redd's album *Laff of the Party* became all the rage on college campuses, as students reveled in the rebelliousness of Redd's comedy. In record stores, the album would be stashed out of sight because of its raunchy theme, but its grassroots popularity was spreading by word of mouth. The Black press began to call Redd "the King of the Party Records" because the album was so popular at Black parties.

"Everybody bought the records," singer/actress Della Reese remembered. "And a really good, fun night in the Black community, and the White community, too, was, 'Come over, I have some Redd Foxx records and we'll listen and we'll laugh.' And he made you laugh."

Dooto Records kept cranking out the Foxx party records to keep up with the growing demand. Redd was becoming more popular to white audiences due to his fame on white college campuses. Between 1956 and 1958, Dooto released about twenty-five Foxx records of varying length and production quality. In March 1958, Dootsie Williams presented Redd with a gold record for selling one million albums.

Because he refused to tone down his act to appease the mainstream, Redd became a hero of sorts in the Black community. The singer Tony Orlando tells a story about when the DJ Ernie Durham pointed out Redd at a club in Detroit.

"I remember I was sixteen years old and I was coming out the door and [DJ] Frantic Ernie says, 'You know who that is over there, man? It's the great Redd Foxx.' And there was Redd, walking into this room, and you would think, even in 1961, amongst African

Americans, this was a god. He walked into that place and you would think Elvis walked in. I'll never forget that."

While Redd was still having a difficult time getting booked at the larger clubs because he was viewed as too blue, he watched younger comedians like Dick Gregory and Godfrey Cambridge, with their more intellectual approach, get the bookings that were denied him. Yet he still refused to change his act.

"Working clean doesn't pay anything," he explained. "If I do clean material, I'm just another Negro comedian. My forte is nightclubs. That's what I love, and they pay as much as anything else, maybe more. If I clean up I could do a couple of TV shows and then it's over. It's not easy out there."

In May 1961, Redd filed a lawsuit against Dooto Records, claiming that Dootsie Williams owed him $350,000 in back royalties. He also wanted to be released from his contract and to take possession of all his masters. He claimed that he had been paid just $11,000 in royalties since the first *Laff of the Party*—and there were at least thirty-four more that were released by Dooto. Williams countered that he had paid Redd more than $70,000 in royalties over the previous five years. Finally, in September 1963, more than two years later, the case was resolved with a judge ruling that Redd had not been underpaid. In fact, the judge determined that Dooto overpaid Redd, and that he owed the company $11,000.

Redd's act in Vegas was caught by legend Frank Sinatra, who took a liking to him. Sinatra bought out Redd's contract with Dooto and signed him to Loma Records, which was the R&B offshoot of Sinatra's Reprise Records, both owned by Warner Brothers.

"Frank Sinatra changed my whole recording scene," Redd said. "He saw me working one time and he actually rolled on the floor laughing. He said, 'I want to sign you up.' I told him I was all tied up, but he said, 'Don't you worry. I'll take care of it.' I don't know what happened, but somehow or other, a couple of days later I was free."

Sinatra's mob ties were well known, so Redd didn't need details on how Sinatra got him released from Dooto. Now that he was part of the Sinatra team, things opened up a bit for Redd. He got better bookings and made more money; his first Sinatra record, *The Both Sides of Redd Foxx*, sold 15,000 copies in thirty days. It was the first time many white people had ever heard Foxx. He also got a boost from appearing on the ABC special *100 Years of Laughter* that was narrated by Sidney Poitier and from being the subject of a five-page feature in *Ebony* magazine. His deal with Sinatra allowed him to issue records on his own label, so he formed the labels Alma Records, named after his mother's maiden name, and M.F. Records, the profane meaning of which was quite clear.

In 1967, Redd fulfilled a long-held dream by opening his own club in LA called the Redd Foxx Club. It was a huge move for him. He put down $40,000 of his own savings to buy the small club on La Cienega that used to be called the Slate Brothers Club—where Sinatra had discovered Don Rickles.

"After working in so many dumps over the years, Redd's dream was to own his own place, where he wouldn't have to shake down the owner to get paid (in cash) or worry about someone skipping out with that night's take from the door," Starr writes in *Black and Blue*. "He wanted a place where he could get up onstage and do his stand-up when he wanted to, with no language or content restrictions placed on him. He wanted a place where he could give other performers—not just comics—a place to work in an intimate, comfortable setting. He wanted a place where he could indulge his cocaine habit with fellow performers like Richard Pryor—and no one telling him he couldn't do otherwise."

Unfortunately, Redd wasn't a particularly astute businessman, and the club struggled from day one. The club was rather small, holding about 150 people and seventy-five tables, so that meant it had to be jam-packed every night in order to make money. But the bartenders and other employees were skimming money from the till and even stealing merchandise. Redd was gone too frequently to keep tabs on everything that was going on.

"Los Angeles is a rotten town for nightlife," Redd said. "Everybody knows that. Everybody knew it in 1967, too, when I bought the joint. Everybody, that is, except me."

Nevertheless, the club became a hang spot for comedians, who enjoyed watching Redd work the room. Richard Pryor, Flip Wilson, Bill Cosby, they all came through, as did Sinatra. Redd—or The Boss, as everyone called him—would frequently sit in front of the club and hold court with young comics.

"I hung around there often," Pryor said. "I loved it. I loved watching [Redd]. I loved getting on that stage and just tripping—ad-libbing new routines and so on."

Cosby said Pryor was so good, and his approach was so fresh, that he would blow all the other comedians away. In fact, Pryor, who had been a fairly tame act when he first entered the business, credited Redd with giving him the courage to step onstage and be himself. At the end of 1967, Redd made an appearance on *The Joey Bishop Show* and used the platform to plead with the audience to help his club. He actually started crying on the air as he talked about his club's financial troubles.

The tears worked. In just twenty-four hours, the club booked Billy Eckstine, Sammy Davis Jr., Bill Cosby, and Lou Rawls, who all volunteered their services. A long line of celebrities started showing up—Marlon Brando, Slim Pickens, Eartha Kitt, Hazel Scott. George Burns sat in the front row with two women every night. Cosby decided to go even further, buying a percentage stake in the club—in the process upgrading the sound system and increasing the cover charge from a dollar fifty to five dollars. But the club continued to struggle. Cosby booked artists like Sarah Vaughan, Dizzy Gillespie, Carmen McRae, and Esther Phillips, but it wasn't working.

"I think many people took a look at the marquee out front and, seeing the names, said to themselves, 'It must be a joke, and I'm not going to go in there,'" Cosby said.

Cosby saw firsthand how the employees were stealing from the club—though Redd's sister-in-law, who worked at the club, claimed that it was in fact Redd who would regularly dip into the cash register when he was there and pocket wads of cash.

"I remember one night we took in around $2,300. I was very happy about that, and I decided that I was going to go buy some liquor. But before I could get to the bank, over half of it was gone," Cosby said. "It got to be very, very strange."

When Cosby one night decided to clean up, he stumbled upon dozens of unpaid bills stashed under the cushions of the sofa in Redd's office. Cosby and Redd parted ways amicably, though Cosby felt guilty about it, like he was abandoning his friend.

In December 1970, fate stepped in to resolve the club's bad fortunes. A cigarette had been left smoldering on that same couch in Redd's office, sending the building up in flames. The club burned to the ground. But despite the seeming misfortune, Redd's star was about to ascend quite dramatically.

Redd's manager, Bardu Ali, approached Redd in 1969 about playing a small role in a movie called *Cotton Comes to Harlem*, but Redd didn't like the paycheck attached, saying he refused to work for pennies. The film was the directorial debut of actor Ossie Davis, the man who performed the eulogy for Redd's buddy Malcolm X when he was killed in 1965. Fortunately for Redd, he finally decided to take the part, playing a fast-talking Harlem junk dealer named Booker Washington Sims, known as Uncle Budd, who lives in a shack on the East River.

"He was cast because he *was* Uncle Budd," said producer Samuel Goldwyn Jr. "I mean that seriously. He was perfect. I didn't know him, quite frankly, but when we were casting, Ossie said, 'There is only one person to play this because he is Uncle Budd, and that's Redd Foxx.' And everyone agreed. . . . My introduction to Redd Foxx was on the set. I turned my back and there was this loud noise and clapping. It was Redd showing up for his first day of work, and the whole cast, as one, felt they were meeting a great celebrity."

Redd, forty-six at the time, grew a scraggly beard that was tinted gray, along with his hair, to make him look older. Redd has several memorable appearances in the film, including the final scene that serves as a punch line for the entire somewhat implausible film about hustlers searching for $87,000 that was hidden in a bale of cotton—based on a novel by Chester Himes, who launched his writing career after serving eight years in prison for armed robbery. While the film got mediocre reviews, it was warmly embraced by the Black community, excited that it was actually filmed in Harlem. Seen through the prism of history, *Cotton Comes to Harlem* was one of the films that launched the blaxploitation movies of the 1970s.

Though the Civil Rights Movement had brought about major changes to American society, those advances had yet to reach Hollywood. Breakthroughs were hard to come by. There was Bill Cosby, starring in *I Spy* from 1965 to 1968. Diahann Carroll was single mom *Julia* in 1968. And in 1970, there was *The Flip Wilson Show*. Flip was a friend and mentee of sorts of Redd Foxx, who was eleven years older and whom Flip idolized. Flip began working as a stand-up after being discharged from the service in 1954, frequently headlining at the Apollo Theater by the mid-1960s. Flip spent many hours watching Redd onstage, taking notes from the master at work. In fact, Redd was responsible for one of Flip's early show business breaks.

During an appearance on *The Tonight Show* in 1965, Redd was asked by Johnny Carson who he thought was the funniest comedian in the business. Without hesitation, Redd said, "Flip Wilson." Carson proceeded to book Flip on *The Tonight Show*, which led to other television appearances and better nightclub gigs. His 1968 comedy album, *Flip Wilson, You Devil You*, won a Grammy Award. In 1970, NBC gave Flip his own show, the first network variety show to be hosted by an African American. The show was a big hit—the second-most-watched television show in America in 1970 and 1971. Americans from all walks of life were walking around repeating Flip's catchphrases, "What you see is what you get!" and "The Devil made me do it!" Flip brought his friend Redd on his show numerous times during its four years on the air.

With the cancellation of old-school variety programs like *The Ed Sullivan Show* and *The Jackie Gleason Show*, the networks were looking for edgier fare. Producer Norman Lear came along to answer the call, first with the lovable racist Archie Bunker in *All in the Family*. Next, Lear wanted to adapt the British comedy *Steptoe and Son*, about a junk man and his son and their bickering relationship. The son wants a better life for himself, but he can't abandon his father, though they spend most of their time arguing. With his producing partner Bud Yorkin, Lear set out to find the American actors who could bring the characters to life in an American version. They set out initially looking for Italian or Jewish actors, since most of the junk men in New York were of that background. But that idea wasn't working out. When they approached the Black actor Cleavon Little to play the role of the son, he said he wasn't available, but he recommended Redd Foxx for the cantankerous father.

"We auditioned a lot of good actors, but they just weren't built for that character," Yorkin said. "And then I caught *Cotton Comes to Harlem* and right away I said, 'There's the guy: Redd Foxx.'"

His voice had been rendered hard and gravelly by all the years of smoking, and he had the movements and mannerisms of a man much older than his forty-eight—the character was supposed to be sixty-five.

When they asked Redd if he was up to playing the role, he said, "I'll do anything; I'll take my teeth out if you want me to."

They also found twenty-four-year-old Demond Wilson, a Vietnam vet from Valdosta, Georgia, who had worked on Broadway and in a few small roles on television and the movies. When he and Cleavon Little appeared in an episode of *All in the Family* as burglars who break into Archie Bunker's house, Lear and Yorkin thought they might have their son.

Wilson flew to Las Vegas to meet with Redd. He went to Redd's house with Bardu Ali and Redd cooked dinner for everybody.

"We read the script and we just sort of hit it off in the very beginning," Redd said. "Some people, you meet them and shake hands with them and from then on it's a lifelong thing. You get that sort of communication. That's the kind of personality he had," Redd said of Wilson.

After CBS passed on the pilot, Yorkin approached executives at NBC. He even convinced them to sneak into the CBS studios to watch Redd and Wilson tape a scene, just across the hall from where the *All in the Family* cast was rehearsing. Yorkin decided to have the entire *All in the Family* cast watch Redd and Wilson's scene; Redd and Wilson had only met four days earlier.

"The *All in the Family* cast fell on the floor," Yorkin said. "I've never heard guys laughing like that. It went on and on. So we finish this thing and Herb [Schlosser, NBC exec] comes over and says, 'It was great, it was funny,' and he takes me over to the corner and says, 'You're on the air January 18th. I'll give you seventeen shows to start with.' And that's how it started."

For the show's new American name, the producers found out from Redd that his original name was Jon Sanford. The show would be called *Sanford and Son,* and the main character would be Fred Sanford, in honor of Redd's real-life older brother, Fred, who had died years earlier. Naming the character after him was a deeply personal tribute.

Redd also came up with the name Lamont for his son, in honor of his old friend Lamont, the bandmate who rode the rails with him to Weehawken.

To Redd, it looked like perhaps he had finally made it. He was going to lead his own television show. All the years of struggle were coming to fruition. Redd said at the time that he had been waiting for an "honest" Black comedy for thirty-five years, since he started in show business. During an appearance on a local LA television show, Demond Wilson probed the tension that had long existed in Black comedy: He said what would set *Sanford and Son* apart was that it would have "Black people acting and talking like Black people really do. They'll be saying things the way Black people normally say them. Like on some TV shows you might hear a Black person saying, for instance, 'I am not going to do that.' Instead, he'd say it like this, 'I ain't gonna do dat. Not me!'"

When *Sanford and Son* premiered, it drew rave reviews. Cecil Smith of the *Los Angeles Times* called it "richly, humanly, roaringly funny"—the funniest series since *All in the Family.*

Still, the show wasn't without early controversy. Some Black viewers felt the son, Lamont, was too harsh toward his father, clashing with norms of Black familial respect. Redd and Demond Wilson shared similar concerns, and the writers responded by softening the dynamic between Fred and Lamont. That course correction only strengthened the show's staying power.

The breakthrough success of *Sanford and Son* signaled to network executives that Black-led sitcoms could draw big audiences—and paved the way for a wave of Black-centered shows in the 1970s that expanded the scope of representation on prime-time TV. Chief among them were *Good Times* and *The Jeffersons*, both of which also came from Norman Lear's prolific creative engine.

Good Times, which premiered in 1974, was a spin-off of *Maude*—itself a spin-off of *All in the Family*. Built around Florida and James Evans, a working-class couple raising their children in a Chicago housing project, it marked the first sitcom to portray a two-parent Black household. Esther Rolle, who played Florida, had originally appeared on *Maude* as a domestic worker, but she insisted that if she were to headline her own show, she would do so as the matriarch of a full Black family, not a stereotype. She got her wish.

The result was a show that resonated deeply with Black audiences, capturing the dignity and struggles of a family trying to stay afloat with humor, faith, and perseverance. J.J. Evans, played by Jimmie Walker, quickly became a cultural sensation thanks to his animated delivery and the unforgettable catchphrase "Dy-no-mite!" But the spotlight on J.J.'s antics created tension behind the scenes. Both Rolle and John Amos, who played James, felt the character was veering into caricature, undercutting the more serious themes the show aimed to explore. Amos was eventually written out of the series and his character killed off, but the clash underscored a broader tension—between comic relief and social realism, between visibility and dignity.

Still, *Good Times* marked a critical shift. It was a show about a poor Black family surviving America's economic and racial systems—not a fantasy, not a punch line, but a complex reflection of real life.

If *Good Times* showed Black life at the bottom of the economic ladder, *The Jeffersons* showed what it could look like at the top. Spun off from *All in the Family*, the series followed George and Louise Jefferson, a wealthy Black couple who had "moved on up" from Queens to Manhattan's Upper East Side. George, played by Sherman Hemsley, was fiery, opinionated, and unafraid to speak his mind—often to the discomfort of the white neighbors around him.

Louise, played by Isabel Sanford, served as his grounded, graceful counterbalance.

Premiering in 1975, *The Jeffersons* broke barriers by centering a successful Black family in prime-time—and by featuring one of television's first interracial couples, Tom and Helen Willis, without apology or fanfare. The show blended broad laughs with pointed commentary on race, class, and the uneasy compromises of assimilation. Over eleven seasons and more than 250 episodes, *The Jeffersons* not only remained a ratings success—it redefined what was possible for Black characters on television.

These shows—*Sanford and Son*, *Good Times*, and *The Jeffersons*—reimagined the contours of American television. They showcased the full range of Black life, from struggle to success, from grief to joy, from the front stoop to the penthouse.

And at the center of it all was Redd Foxx, now a household name. He and Betty Jean moved into a lavish home in North Hollywood. His face appeared on the covers of *Jet* and *Ebony*—both published by his former classmate from DuSable High School, John Johnson—and he was profiled in the *New York Times*. Even as Fred Sanford became a beloved character in white households across America, Redd refused to water down his nightclub act to match his TV persona. Fans expecting Fred got Redd—and if they were offended, that was their problem.

He said adults should know better coming to a Redd Foxx show expecting to see Fred Sanford. He had people walk out of his shows—including an NBC executive and his children—because they were expecting Fred Sanford and got old Redd Foxx.

"Fuck that. I been Redd Foxx for over 50 years. I've only been Fred Sanford for two," Redd said.

Redd won a Golden Globe Award, got nominated for an Emmy, and the show ended its first season with an average of nearly 16 million viewers per show, which was astonishing for a midseason replacement. *All in the Family* averaged over 21 million viewers. The crowning achievement in terms of media splash was the cover of *Time* magazine, with the headline "The New TV Season, Toppling Old

Taboos," featuring photos of Redd, Carroll O'Connor, and Bea Arthur from *Maude*.

But there were also voices of discontent, particularly in the Black community. In an opinion piece in the *New York Times*, professor and author Eugenia Collier wrote that the show was a white creation that pandered to the worst Black stereotypes and called it "dangerous." Created by white men, Sanford and Lamont were not strong Black men but rather "merely two more American child-men." While most of the shows were written by white writers Aaron Ruben and Gene Farmer, the third episode of the second season was actually written by Richard Pryor and his writing partner Paul Mooney. However, sensitive to the criticism, Ruben hired actor and playwright Ilunga Adell (previously known as Adell Stevenson) as the first full-time Black writer.

"The writers are beginning to learn that Black is another language," Redd said.

In the first season, Redd actually used the word *nigger* in an episode—the first time the word was ever said on network television. That was part of his ongoing efforts to make the show feel "real." Redd pushed Ruben to hire a Black director, so they turned to a young Stan Lathan, a veteran television director who was working on *Sesame Street* at the time and had directed Moms Mabley in the movie *Amazing Grace* shortly before she died.

"It was a big deal that Redd had gotten them to hire a Black director, and they all admired him [on the set] for that and appreciated him for that because it was a very symbolic move," Lathan said. "They would come around and watch rehearsals, and the first time I walked into the [NBC] commissary there was a huge stir among the Black employees. I was immediately welcomed and made to feel it was something special. It was a huge event for the show's crew and staff, the experience of suddenly dealing with a Black director who was under thirty and very skilled and aware of what he was doing."

Television producer Ilunga Adell called Redd "the funniest motherfucker I ever met."

"You know how some people are always 'on'? He wasn't 'on.' He was just naturally funny," Adell said. "It was like he had a funny computer in his head and stuff just came out funny. And Redd Foxx was very intelligent. I really think he would have been a good dramatic actor."

RCA released an album that contained bits of dialogue from the show and the Quincy Jones theme song; it sold millions of copies. *Sanford and Son* was an enormous hit, one that crushed the competition every week. CBS programming director Fred Silverman, who passed on *Sanford and Son*, much to his undying regret, put up every kind of show he could think of opposite Redd Foxx and Demond Wilson, from detective shows to a *Planet of the Apes* series. They all flamed out. Fred Sanford was now a cultural icon. It was a remarkable development in the history of Black comedy in the US, that a Black show helmed by one of the most unapologetically raunchy comedians in the land could become a national phenomenon.

"We probably don't have more than a couple of clowns in a century and Redd Foxx was a clown," Norman Lear said. "I know he was considered a comedian. But the difference between a comedian and a clown, in my estimation, is that every square inch of a clown is funny. His knuckles are funny, his earlobes are funny; Redd could walk into a room and announce that your mother had died and get a laugh from you. He was inherently, innately funny in every part of his being. So we fell in love with that."

When Silverman moved from CBS to ABC, he tried to steal Redd away from NBC. Redd was upset that NBC still hadn't given him his own variety show—something that even sportscaster Howard Cosell had gotten. Silverman offered him that and more—such as a production deal that would allow him to develop shows for ABC. Redd did have a financial piece of the *Sanford and Son* spin-off called *Grady*, starring his friend on the show Whitman Mayo, but the show failed to find viewers and was canceled after twelve episodes. In April 1976, ABC announced that it had signed Foxx to a "multimillion-dollar contract" as a performer and producer. Redd said publicly that NBC didn't show him respect because of racism.

Around this time, Redd starred in the low-budget comedy

Norman . . . Is That You? with Pearl Bailey—with whom he was still feuding over conflicts from decades earlier when he partnered with Slappy White, her ex-husband—but the movie did miserably at the box office.

The final episode of *Sanford and Son* aired on March 25, 1977, in its sixth season. The show had fallen so far in the ratings that it was twenty-seventh out of the top thirty prime-time shows, just ahead of *Good Times*. To promote his upcoming variety show on ABC, *The Redd Foxx Comedy Hour*, Redd appeared on *The Barbara Walters Special* in May 1977, which gave viewers an up-close look at Redd's lavish lifestyle—including a wall in his bedroom that was a glass enclosure containing live macaque monkeys. Walters interviewed Redd and his new wife, Joi, a Korean cocktail waitress he had met in Vegas.

As he worked on his new variety show, producers were worried because Redd was stoned all day—he'd do marijuana to relax and coke to get back up, in a never-ending cycle. Yet observers said the drugs never affected his performances. After the show premiered, it was praised by critics but failed to find an audience, slipping to fifty-second place in the ratings by November, two months after its September debut. The show was canceled in February 1978; Redd was fifty-five years old.

Fred Silverman moved to NBC and wanted to recapture some of the *Sanford and Son* magic, so he offered Redd a chance to helm a show called, simply, *Sanford*, with a white redneck played by Dennis Burkley as his overweight live-in sidekick at the junkyard. The show was canceled in January 1981, four episodes into its second season.

Redd filed for bankruptcy in 1983, three months after his sixtieth birthday, citing $1.6 million he owed the IRS and more than $800,000 he owed other creditors. In addition, the state of California said he owed another $400,000, plus $600,000 he owed in alimony payments (he was now divorced from Joi) to his ex-wives. Redd spent money as soon as he made it—a habit exacerbated by his drug habit and his addiction to the game keno in Vegas, where he regularly dropped huge sums.

In early 1988, Eddie Murphy reached out to Redd to star in a movie he was developing called *Harlem Nights*. It was considered a vanity project for Murphy, coming on the heels of his huge successes with *48 Hrs.*, *Trading Places*, *Beverly Hills Cop* and *Beverly Hills Cop II*, and *Coming to America*. Murphy was starring in the $40 million movie, in addition to coproducing, writing the screenplay, and directing. Murphy assembled a comedy dream team—him, Richard Pryor, and Redd Foxx, in addition to Della Reese. The hilarious banter between Redd and Della on the set inspired Murphy so much that he reportedly went into his trailer and took just thirty minutes to write a treatment for a show that would have Redd and Della playing husband and wife.

"We were just playfully going at it during a break," Reese said. "Richard Pryor was sitting on the side. When I got a good line in on Redd, he said, 'I wouldn't let no woman talk to me like that.' And then, Redd would get one in on me. He [Pryor] kept instigating and we kept signifying with each other. Eddie Murphy was standing on the side and he was cracking up. The whole cast came in and everybody was laughing. We stopped production. Eddie said, 'This is a television series.' And he began to write it."

Though the movie did well at the box office when it opened, critics panned it for weak writing, primarily setting the blame at Murphy's feet. The dream team wasn't fully utilized, they said. As Redd continued to battle with the IRS—he told someone he wasn't going to pay his taxes until the country elected a Black president—he did an extended run at the Hacienda Hotel in Vegas for $20,000 a week. One night in 1989 a young comedian approached him and told Redd he was from Chicago and was a huge fan. He told Redd his name: Bernie Mac.

"I was rambling on, and he just shut me up real quick: 'You want to go on?'" Mac said.

When he did his thing onstage, Mac said he "had this feeling in my heart and the back of my mind that I held my own." When Redd came out and told the audience, "'That's a funny motherfucker,' that gave me the heart and gave me the confidence I needed to not second-place myself to anything and anybody."

On November 28, 1989, IRS agents descended on Redd's house

and took most everything he owned, from the diamond-encrusted watch from Elvis he was wearing on his wrist to a picture on the wall of Lena Horne kissing him. Redd stood on the street in his underwear, cursing. The whole thing was witnessed not only by neighbors but also television news cameras, broadcasting Redd's humiliation to the world. His attorneys eventually worked out a payment plan to get the IRS off his back and save many of his possessions, including his house.

Meanwhile, Eddie Murphy followed through on his idea to produce a Redd Foxx–Della Reese television show. It was called *The Royal Family* and would premiere on CBS in the fall of 1991. According to the president of CBS, it was the best-testing comedy CBS had seen in years. The show debuted to tepid praise from critics but solid ratings. Reese said she was so happy for Redd's sake that the show was a hit.

But on October 11, 1991, Redd had a heart attack on the set—right after he recorded an interview with the show *Lifestyles of the Rich and Famous*. He died that night at the age of sixty-eight. His death was national news, with the *New York Times* devoting an entire half page to his obit, headlined "Cantankerous Master of Bawdy Humor." On his headstone at Palm Valley View Memorial Park in Las Vegas is a chiseled head of a red fox; the fox is winking back at us.

Once the highest-paid Black entertainer in the country, Billy Kersands thrilled audiences with his physical comedy and exaggerated contortions on the minstrel stage.
Harvard University Library

Bert Williams rose to become the most successful African-American vaudeville star of his era. Despite the indignity of performing in blackface, he brought depth and humanity to roles written to demean.
Schomburg Center for Research in Black Culture, Photographs and Prints Division, The New York Public Library

Lincoln Perry, better known as Stepin Fetchit, became Hollywood's first Black movie star. His "laziest man in the world" persona cemented his fame but also embodied the era's most damaging stereotypes.
Publicity photograph, 1959

Bert Williams in blackface
Library of Congress, Prints and Photographs Division

Gone with the Wind premiere
Hattie McDaniel (event images) / Atlanta History Center

From left to right:
Hattie McDaniel with Olivia de Havilland and Vivien Leigh
Gone with the Wind *(MGM, 1939)*

The first African-American Academy Award winner, honored for her role as Mammy in *Gone with the Wind*. Her career reflected both the breakthroughs and limits of opportunity for Black actors of her time.
Publicity still, 1951

Jackie "Moms" Mabley, one of the first women in stand-up, built a legendary career on the Black vaudeville circuit and later broke into mainstream comedy with sharp, sly humor disguised in grandmotherly charm.
"Jackie 'Moms' Mabley," NYPL Digital Collections (1940–59)

Alvin Childress (*right*) and Spencer Williams Jr. (*left*) starred in the TV version of *Amos 'n' Andy*, a show rooted in blackface minstrelsy but later performed by Black actors.
Publicity still, CBS Television, 1952

Comedic legend Pigmeat Markham (*left*) and saxophonist Benny Carter (*right*) sharing the stage, blending humor with harmony.
Digital Public Library of America

Two vaudeville veterans, Mantan Moreland (*left*) and Pigmeat Markham (*right*), whose careers spanned stage, film, and early television.
Schomburg Center for Research in Black Culture, The New York Public Library

Known as "The King of the Party Records," Redd Foxx built a bold, uncensored comedy career before finding mainstream fame.
Bettmann Archive

Dick Gregory used stand-up as both comedy and protest, becoming one of the first comedians to openly fuse humor with civil rights activism.
Courtesy of the artist's estate

Redd Foxx and Demond Wilson in *Sanford and Son*, the Norman Lear sitcom that brought Foxx's sharp humor to primetime.
NBC Television, 1972

Flip Wilson was one of the first Black comedians to host a network variety show.
Publicity still, 1971, courtesy of NBC Television

Wilson's most famous character, Geraldine, became a pop culture sensation of the 1970s.
NBC publicity still, 1971

Before *The Cosby Show*, Bill Cosby was already a star stand-up, known for clean, family-centered storytelling.
Publicity photograph

The Huxtables
NBC Television

The Cosby Show redefined Black sitcoms in the 1980s, offering a vision of Black middle-class success and relatability. *NBC Television*

Eddie Murphy in *Raw*—the *SNL* breakout delivered a seminal performance that made stand-up feel like rock 'n' roll.
Paramount Pictures

Richard Pryor revolutionized comedy with raw, fearless storytelling about race, poverty, and American contradictions.
Publicity still, courtesy of the estate of Richard Pryor

A spin-off from *The Cosby Show*, *A Different World* spotlighted HBCU life and became a cultural touchstone.
Getty Images / NBCU Photo Bank

The Wayans family's sketch show, *In Living Color*, launched stars like Jim Carrey, Jamie Foxx, and Jennifer Lopez. *FOX Television, 1990*

Damon Wayans and David Alan Grier's recurring sketch pushed boundaries of representation and parody. *FOX Television*

In Living Color's dance troupe, the Fly Girls, broke new ground for hip-hop dance on TV. *FOX Television*

Wayans's iconic character skewered authority with the refrain, "Homey don't play that!" *FOX Television*

Will Smith turned sitcom stardom into global superstardom, blending comedy with emotional depth. *NBC Television*

Best remembered for Jaleel White's Steve Urkel, *Family Matters* mixed family comedy with sitcom absurdity.
ABC Television, 1989

Martin Lawrence's *Martin* became a definitive sitcom of the 1990s, full of outrageous characters and quotable moments.
FOX Television, 1992

Created by Yvette Lee Bowser, *Living Single* captured the lives of six friends navigating careers and relationships in Brooklyn.
FOX Television, 1993

The first Black woman to create a primetime sitcom, Bowser reshaped TV comedy from behind the scenes.
Courtesy of Yvette Lee Bowser

Bowser with her writing staff, who helped craft a show that balanced laughs with cultural resonance.
Courtesy of Yvette Lee Bowser

The 2000 "Kings of Comedy" tour and Spike Lee film, featuring (*left to right*) Steve Harvey, Cedric the Entertainer, Bernie Mac, and D. L. Hughley, redefined arena comedy.
Paramount Pictures

Dave Chappelle's groundbreaking sketch series, *Chappelle's Show*, became a cultural catalyst through its fearless, unflinching satire.
John Bauld via Wikimedia Commons

CHAPTER 9
DICK GREGORY

As Black people began to aggressively fight for equal treatment across all aspects of American society in the 1950s, the comedy that Black America produced had to shift to reflect the times and the national mood. America was ready for a smart, worldly comic who could point out the silly contradictions of racial prejudice in a way that whites would find palatable. Enter Dick Gregory.

Though he eventually became known almost exclusively for his extreme activism and for his diet powder, Dick Gregory was the first Black comedian to cross over and achieve massive mainstream success. If the evolution of Black comedy in America is a steady march toward fearlessness, toward feeling no anxiety about saying the private out loud, Gregory was a groundbreaking figure—one of the most important in American history. In some ways, Gregory was the Jackie Robinson of comedy: After he stepped onto the stage, American comedy would never be the same.

Darryl Littleton, author of *Black Comedians on Black Comedy*, told NPR in 2009 that Gregory made history simply by sitting down: "Dick Gregory is the first to be recognized—and he'll say it—the first Black comedian to be able to stand flat-footed, and just delivered comedy. You had other comedians back then but they always had to do a little song or a dance or whatever. Sammy Davis had to dance and sing, and then tell jokes. Same with Pearl Bailey and some of the other comedians. But Dick Gregory was able to go on television, sit down on the Jack Paar show—and sit on the couch and actually have a discussion, and that had never happened in the history of television."

Gregory took advantage of a change in the white American public's willingness to be chided about its hypocrisy—a public whose hand was being forced by the burgeoning Civil Rights Movement. With a surgeon's eye, Gregory studied white comedians and white audiences, crafting routines based on his investigation of what white America would allow. The country was ripe for racial satire, which was a way to acknowledge the ugliness of Jim Crow in a lower-stakes environment. He saw that they would accept his acerbic takedowns of American bigotry—as long as he delivered it with a healthy dollop of humor.

"When I left St. Louis, I was making five dollars a night. Now I get five thousand dollars a week for saying the same thing out loud I used to say under my breath," Gregory once noted.

Gregory wasn't trying to integrate white people's neighborhoods or have his children sit next to theirs in kindergarten. All they had to decide was whether or not to laugh. But it was an enormous advance for Black comedy—artists could now at least acknowledge the American stain when performing for a white audience. Ironically, it was two groundbreaking white comedians who opened the door for Gregory's cerebral style—Mort Sahl and Lenny Bruce.

Gregory entered the world in St. Louis, Missouri, on October 12, 1932, the second of six children of Presley and Lucille Gregory—though Presley was mostly absent. His mother struggled to keep her children fed working as a domestic for a white family. As Lucille taught her children, "we ain't poor, we just broke," Gregory wrote in his first autobiography (Gregory 1964, 25). "Poor is a state of mind you never get out of, but being broke is just a temporary condition." In his early years, Gregory used humor to deflect the aggressive teasing of peers over his family circumstances.

This is a typical exchange with a kid on the block that Gregory shared:

> Hey Gregory, where's your daddy these days?
> Sure glad that motherfucker's out the house, got a little peace and quiet. Not like your house, York.

What you say?

Yeah, man, what a free show I had last night, better than the [movie theater], laying in bed with the window open, listening to your Daddy whop your Mommy. That was your Daddy, York, wasn't it?

His childhood poverty became a rich source of humor for him later on. But that's not to say those years weren't scarring to him. He tells one particularly ugly story about witnessing his father beat his mother:

> He beat her all through the house, every room, swinging his belt and whopping her with his hand and cussing her and kicking her and knocking her down and telling her all about his women.
>
> "Think you're so goddamn good, bitch," said my Daddy, cracking my Momma across her back with his belt. She whimpered and fell against a little table, knocking over a lamp from the white folks. She bent over to pick up the lamp and Big Prez kicked her in the backside and she fell forward on the linoleum floor. She lay there, her face pressed against the linoleum, sobbing.
>
> He grabbed her hair and pulled her up to her knees. Momma looked up at him, tears running down her cheeks. Slap. Right across her face. "I got bitches, women like you never seen, proud to walk down the street with Big Prez." Slap. Momma fell down on her face again. (Frierson 2020, 11)

There was no humor there. Just brutality that Gregory surely never forgot.

But Gregory laced the retelling of other childhood moments with considerable humor, such as his recounting of what happened when his mother got a visit from neighbors. Dick and his siblings often moved around the neighborhood with old and stained clothes, since the family didn't have money for new clothes. The parents of other children in the neighborhood came to the Gregory house to inform Lucille that her children weren't proper playmates for the other children. In response, a shamed Lucille told her kids that they had to stay in the house until she could afford better clothes. To make sure they complied, she hid their clothes so they wouldn't have anything to wear. The kids were not to be deterred—they put on the only clothes they could find: their mother's dresses, gifts to her from the rich white folks.

"The people laughed at us when we went outside in dresses, pointed and slapped their legs. We never played so good as we played that summer, with all those people watching us."

While a student at St. Louis's Sumner High School, Gregory realized that he could shower every evening at school if he joined the track team. On the way to the shower, Gregory discovered he was a talented runner—in fact, one of the best distance runners in the state. When Sumner began participating in integrated meets, Gregory continued his prowess, becoming state champion and finishing second in a fifteen-mile race against college boys. It was actually his desire for public acknowledgment of his running talents that led to his first bit of activism. He had been outraged when his name was omitted from Missouri's annual track-and-field book, though he had finished first in the one-mile race for African-American runners. At a PTA meeting in 1951 where Black parents marched outside to protest overcrowded classrooms, Gregory went to the mic to complain about his omission and took his first public stand for change.

Gregory's high school coach was an alumnus of Southern Illinois University in Carbondale, and he helped Gregory enroll at the school, where he continued his running prowess and broke a state record in the half mile; as a sophomore in 1953, Gregory won the school's Outstanding Athlete award.

Gregory was also a leader off the track, and he told the story of an incident that led to him integrating the Varsity movie theater in Carbondale when he and a date were told they couldn't sit in the orchestra section. When he refused to move, the manager called the police, prompting Gregory to leave with his date, who was in tears.

"Be sure and get your money back," the manager told him.

"Keep it. I'll be back," Gregory said.

When he returned the next day by himself, they let him sit in the orchestra. When he started showing up with other Black students, the theater let them sit in the orchestra too. In effect, the theater was now integrated. One day the manager asked Gregory for a favor: A big Hollywood film called *The Robe*, about ancient Romans and the early followers of Jesus, would be premiering, and he had paid a great deal for the rights to show it—but he would go bankrupt if the white customers were scared away by the idea of sitting next to Black customers. If Gregory and the other Black students agreed to stay away from the orchestra during *The Robe*, they could sit anywhere they wanted afterward. Reluctantly, Gregory agreed.

Gregory was drafted into the army and served from 1954 to 1956. During his time in the service, he developed his fondness for performing onstage—under duress. He had done a few amateur shows at SIU and in the army, but the stakes were raised after a colonel discovered him asleep inside an enormous pot in the kitchen, where he was on kitchen patrol.

"You are either a great comedian or a goddamned malingerer," the colonel said. "There is an open talent show at the service club tonight. You will go down there, and you will win it."

Gregory did as he was ordered—he won.

After the service, Gregory had lost his motivation to finish college. He dropped out of school and moved to Chicago, where his older brother lived. His idea was that he would somehow make it as a performer and comedian, so he actually paid for his first gigs—paying the emcee $5 for stage time. He did well enough that he did the same thing the following week at a different club. The owner offered Gregory a salary of $10 a night to be the weekend emcee. And a career was born.

Gregory said he wasn't funny at first. But he was willing and anxious to learn. Hard work would always be his trademark. He studied comedy albums, books, magazines, TV shows, on the constant lookout for material. He even tried out his routines on the older couple who rented him a room, utilizing their feedback to get better, funnier. He gained enough of a following to ask for a raise, buoyed by the club advertising a Fourth of July event "starring the hilarious Dick Gregory and His All-Review."

"I told them if they didn't give me a two dollar raise I'd quit on them," he said. "They didn't give me a raise." So he quit.

Gregory bounced around doing shows here and there, until he heard about a former nightclub fifteen miles south of Chicago that sat vacant. Gregory convinced the building's owner to let him take over the lease, and he became manager of the Apex Club.

"In Dick Gregory the Apex boasts one of the best young comics of the season," the *Chicago Defender* said in March 1959. "His antics are of the side cracking variety and always fresh material."

As with Redd Foxx, Gregory discovered that running a club was more than a notion; the finances proved to be too daunting. By July 1959, it was over for him at Apex—just seven months after it began. Now with a wife and an infant daughter to support, Gregory scrambled to find work in Chicago, taking odd jobs to add to his wife's salary as a secretary at the University of Chicago. When he performed at auditions hosted by the American Guild of Variety Artists, the white nightclub owners wanted to know if he could sing or dance. History couldn't be escaped.

"I'm a comedian, sir," he told them.

Gregory's research into the keys to joke-telling unearthed fascinating findings about race that he employed throughout his career. He discovered that the demeanor of a Black comedian mattered greatly, after Americans had spent much of the past century with explicit expectations for how Black performers were supposed to act. He concluded that white audiences either hated Black comics or felt sorry for them because they were Black. He said the former were not reachable and the latter were not reliable. In order to dispel the pity, Black comics had to step onto the stage with enough confidence and poise that the audience would immediately forget about its perceived superiority and view the comics as equals.

"It was not necessary that they told racial jokes or focused on social satire, but it was essential that they dislodge all traces of the minstrel image of the servile, slow-witted Sambo, which had hounded them like a shadow for over a century," writes Mel Watkins in *On the Real Side*.

Watkins points out that while comedians like Timmie Rogers, Slappy White, and Nipsey Russell had stepped away from the stereotypical images promoted by a century of minstrels, they weren't entirely free of the demeanor that came with the stereotypes.

"Most retained some subtle residual mannerisms: a passively slumped shoulder while delivering a punch line, an overly exaggerated widening of the eyes, or an apprehensive glance in search of approval from non-black crowds" (Watkins 1994, 501).

Commentators began to compare Gregory to white satirists Mort Sahl and Lenny Bruce, who used a swaggering, blistering cockiness to take on American hypocrisy and injustice. Here's how Gregory responded to hecklers who threw the word *nigger* at him:

> You know, my contract reads that every time I hear that word, I get fifty dollars more a night. I'm only making ten dollars a night, and I'd like to put the owner out of business. Will everybody in the room please stand up and yell nigger? (Frierson 2020, 28)

For the first time, a Black comedian was standing in front of a room full of white people and talking about race with no fear. It was a major advance for Black comedy.

"You gotta say this for whites, their self-confidence knows no bounds. Who else could go to a small island in the South Pacific, where there's no crime, poverty, unemployment, war, or worry—and call it a 'primitive society,'" he said in one of his stand-up appearances.

Gregory's first big break came in 1961. He got a call that Hugh Hefner, America's burgeoning titan of smut as head of *Playboy* magazine, wanted him to perform as a fill-in at the Playboy Club in Chicago. A notable story about what happened when he arrived at the club displays the cleverness of Gregory. The stage manager reportedly decided that it was best to postpone Gregory's stage debut because the Playboy Club had been rented out by a group of Southern white men in Chicago for a frozen-food convention. But Gregory responded that he would go on anyway, knowing the enormity of the risk. What he did when he walked out on that stage changed the arc of his career and announced the arrival of a trailblazing new talent.

> Good evening, ladies and gentlemen. I understand there are a good many Southerners in the room tonight. I know the South very well—I spent twenty years there one night.
> Last time I was down South I walked into this restaurant, and this white waitress came up to me and said: "We don't serve colored people here."
> I said, "That's alright, I don't eat colored people. Bring me a whole fried chicken."
> About that time these three cousins come in—you know the ones I mean, Klu, Klux, and Klan. And they say, "Boy, we're givin' you fair warnin': Anything you do to that chicken, we're gonna do to you." About then the waitress brought me my chicken. "Remember, boy, anything you do to that chicken, we're gonna do to you." So I put down my knife and fork, and I picked up that chicken, and I kissed it. (Watkins 1994, 497)

The reaction to Gregory was quick and intense. Hefner extended his contract from a few weeks to three years, at $50 a night. An article in *Time* magazine helped his star soar, leading to appearances on the Jack Paar and David Susskind talk shows. However, he initially refused to appear on Paar's show because Black performers never got invited over to the couch; when Paar personally called him to promise that would change, Gregory relented. It was an early marker of his commitment to fight for racial equality, no matter the stakes.

Newsweek declared in December 1962, "From the moment he was booked into the Playboy Club . . . Jim Crow was dead in the joke world."

Watkins argues that Gregory was actually helped by his inexperience working the Black Chitlin' Circuit because he had never adopted the subtle mannerisms of subservience and deference in front of white people. From a professional standpoint, 1961 and 1962 were two of the most successful years a Black comedian had ever had in crossing over to the mainstream. "Within a year of his debut, he was a national celebrity.... Gregory had vaulted ahead of a large field of more experienced African American comedians and become the first black comic superstar since Bert Williams and Stepin Fetchit" (Watkins 1994, 497).

Many older Black comedians didn't see anything particularly original about Gregory's early material and wondered what all the fuss was about. Gregory was simply repeating many of the jokes and stories Black folks had said amongst themselves for years. Gregory was just saying it out loud, in front of white people. A report by writer Nat Hentoff claimed that Timmie Rogers, Slappy White, and Nipsey Russell showed up to a Gregory set at New York's Blue Angel in 1961 and sat in the front row armed with a tape recorder and "undisguised disdain." Slappy White wrote to Gregory, "We wanted to find out which of our material not to use anymore."

In many ways, Gregory's rapid ascent was a result of timing. The country was finally ready for a smart Black man to tell America about itself, using the filter of humor.

> Gregory had devised a stand-up persona that cast him as a patient, self-assured ironist, capable of dispensing witticisms about racial relationships with cool detachment.... Sophisticated, aloof, and seemingly observing from a viewpoint of amused neutrality, he was able to introduce into integrated settings a racial satire that, while more aggressive than that of his predecessors, was clearly more palatable to white Americans. (Watkins 1994, 498)

While his joke-telling was placing him in spaces no Black comedian had ever occupied, Gregory was becoming increasingly focused on fighting for Black liberation. He accepted a fall 1962 invitation from civil rights activist Medgar Evers to speak at voter registration rallies in Jackson, Mississippi. Gregory fell in love with Mississippi; the plight of Black people in the Delta became an obsession that would stay with him throughout the rest of his life. He began to cancel bookings so that he could stay on the front lines of the Civil Rights Movement's efforts in the South.

"It seemed no matter where the Movement took me," he wrote, "I always end up back in Mississippi, where it all began for me" (Frierson 2020, 72).

Dick Gregory was the most popular, highest-paid African-American comedian in the country in the early 1960s. He received a $25,000 advance ($260,000 in today's dollars) from Colpix Records to make two comedy albums—the first album, *In Living Black & White*, was a top seller. By his fourth album, *My Brother's Keeper*, released in 1963, Gregory decided to employ the work as an instrument to help the freedom struggle in Mississippi—using his own funds to produce and distribute the album and sending the $37,000 in profits to Sunflower and Leflore Counties in the Delta, where residents were facing starvation conditions. Gregory led a Food for Freedom drive and delivered 20,000 pounds of food to the Delta.

"Mississippi is part of the United States, you know," he said. "They don't know it yet, but they will pretty soon."

He shook the nation in 1964 with the release of his first autobiography, *nigger: An Autobiography*—the lowercase "n" intentional—co-written with journalist Robert Lipsyte.

In an interview with NPR, Gregory explained his bold choice of title: "So this word 'nigger' was one of the most well-used words in America, particularly among black folks. And I said, 'Well, let's pull it out the closet. Let's lay it out here. Let's deal with it. Let's dissect it.' Now the problem I have today is people call it the N-word. It should never be called the N-word. You see, how do you talk about a swastika by using another term?"

Gregory was a fearless fighter for Black people in the US and abroad, getting arrested more than 100 times during the 1960s and

'70s. He was shot in the leg in Watts, a neighborhood in Los Angeles, in 1965 while acting as mediator during a standoff between police and a rioting crowd. He started using fasting as a method of political action, calling attention to causes he cared about deeply.

"This is my fourteenth month of not eating solid food to protest the war in Vietnam and the reason I mention that now is because I'm hungry," he once said.

The fasting was paired with his intense interest in health and nutrition, which he considered an issue of utmost importance to African Americans. By the early 1970s, Gregory became a fixture on college campuses, connecting with the rebel spirit of young people as he riled them up with impassioned lectures. He once estimated that he spoke at 300 colleges a year, "sometimes two per day." In 1973, he announced that he was retiring from stand-up comedy—though admittedly he wasn't even doing stand-up anymore, devoting his time to activism for a dizzying number of causes. In 1974 he ran from Chicago to Washington, DC, to publicize his war against poverty and hunger—using his personally developed nutrition drink as his sustenance.

"I thought about Momma as I ran from city to city, state to state," he wrote in his autobiography *Callus on My Soul*. "Sometimes I would run all day without seeing a tree, a house, or even a bird, just open lonely highways. I wondered if she could see me on those lonely roads. Almost all of her life, Momma had walked the streets of St. Louis trying to feed her babies. There I was, twenty-two years later, running across America for all the poor children like me. I understood the sound of hunger coming from their little stomachs; I understood Momma."

Gregory, who died on August 19, 2017, at age eighty-four, carved out his own form of direct action that should be viewed as another method of resistance against American bigotry, transforming the comic stage into a forum for protest.

CHAPTER 10
FLIP WILSON

While Dick Gregory was riding high atop the comedy mountain in the early 1960s, he was being closely watched by another smart young comic who would become a transformative figure himself a decade later. Flip Wilson was the perfect bridge between the mid-century Black comedians who were relegated to the Chitlin' Circuit to put food on the table, with their crass but hilarious takes on Black life, and the cerebral Black jokesters who came along and crossed over to the mainstream with more intellectual, less aggressively ethnic comedy. Before there was Eddie Murphy clowning across the screen on *Saturday Night Live*, there was Flip. Before Tyler Perry donned a dress and became Madea, there was Flip as Geraldine. Flip's fame hit full speed so fast, the first car he ever owned was a Rolls-Royce.

Clerow Wilson Jr. was born in the midst of the Depression on December 8, 1933, in Jersey City, New Jersey, a gritty city whose primary claim to fame is its proximity to Manhattan just on the other side of the Hudson River. Like so many other Black families in The Hill, one of the poorest and blackest sections of a city where poverty reigned, Clerow's family was desperately poor. Clerow Sr. was a janitor and handyman who had a dozen children with his wife, Cornelia. Clerow Jr. was the tenth child and the darkest of the brood, which was meaningful in the 1930s. "You're black as burnt toast; black as a bad banana," his father told him. "I ought to throw you out with the garbage."

When he was about seven, he got rejected by a girl from one of the "good families" on the block—who said he had skin so dark it was "almost blue"—because he was a "ragamuffin." Her name?

Geraldine—which he would later turn into one of the most famous names in America.

"Then she said she might be my girl if I got her some fake fingernails at Woolworth's," he said. He stole a pair of nails, but they turned out to be the wrong size. When he went back to do it again, he got caught.

"Then Geraldine wouldn't talk to me because I was a criminal," he said (Cook 2013, 9).

Young Clerow's life changed dramatically one day when he came home to discover that his mother had run off with another man, taking her baby boy, all the family's furniture, and all of Clerow Sr.'s money. She had brought a fake death certificate to the bank and emptied his account. Clerow's dad lost his apartment when he couldn't make the rent. The family bounced around, first sleeping in a coal shed, and then everybody fending for themselves as Clerow Sr. slept in various basements. Sometimes when restaurants gave him unsold fruits and vegetables at the end of the day, Clerow Sr. would share the bounty with Clerow Jr., dividing up items like apples, bananas, cabbage—eating whatever wasn't already spoiled. Clerow would introduce his boy to patrons at the bars he frequented, bragging about his namesake.

While some of his siblings wound up in foster homes, Clerow went to live with his sister Eleanor, who was married to a long-haul trucker and had three kids. Neither Eleanor nor her kids wanted him there, which the kids demonstrated by torturing him with food.

"They always ate first. I had to wait. I got what their kids didn't eat, and they resented me being there, so they'd slop their food around and play with it, just to show me who was who."

Clerow also didn't grow up with the healthiest view of the opposite sex: He'd watch his sister cheat on her husband with other men when he was on the road with his truck. His father was so broke that he would drift around The Hill, looking for any work he could find that would pay a buck. Eventually, Eleanor let Clerow Jr. in on the secret—his real father was a man named Leroy Taylor, an ex-boyfriend of Cornelia's who drank at many of the same bars as Clerow Sr.

"Come here, my boy," Leroy would call out to him inside one of the dives in The Hill. "You working hard in school? You got enough to eat?"

Leroy would give the boy money and take him on drives in his Model T Ford to the zoo, the circus, and one day to a stage show in nearby Newark. The show was at the palatial Mosque Theater, where the boy saw Count Basie and His Barons of Rhythm. As Clerow sat wide-eyed, a man in blackface came onstage wearing a top hat, white gloves, and spats. He proceeded to do a routine called "Open the Door, Richard," which was later made famous by Pigmeat Markham. The boy witnessed the animated reaction of the crowd and was mesmerized.

"I thought, 'Wow, they all *love* that guy. That's what I want to do. That's what I want to be.'"

Clerow had a lot of festering anger over the abandonment by his mother, something he never really moved past. When he found out about his biological father, he was horrified at what she had done.

"What a dirty trick—this woman has a son by her boyfriend and names it Clerow. Her husband's name!" he said. "And then she leaves us, but she takes my baby brother with her. Why not take me too?" (Cook 2013, 12).

As Kevin Cook points out, his hatred of his mother gave him an advantage when playing the dozens game with his neighborhood buddies in Jersey City. Since so much of the insult battle rested on guys' feelings about their mothers, Clerow was inoculated from the worst insults because he didn't care what anybody said about her.

"I always won," he said. "I could beat anybody talking that shit because they couldn't hurt my feelings about my momma. I hated the bitch."

When Clerow was in elementary school at PS 14 in Jersey City, he gamely offered to step in when the little white girl playing Civil War nurse Clara Barton in the school play got a debilitating case of stage fright. Fidgety little Clerow already had a bit part in the play as a wounded soldier, with no lines. But he told the teacher, Mrs. Davis, who was acting as director, that he had memorized the whole play lying on his stretcher for rehearsal after rehearsal. They tracked down a blond wig, put Clerow in Clara's white smock, bonnet, and high button shoes. The crowd roared when he walked out onto the stage; little Clerow ate the applause up. As he pranced around that stage in the dress, the audience might have been tickled to know they were witnessing the debut of a man who would later become the nation's most popular cross-dresser.

As the neighbors filed complaints about the unruly Wilson kids, Clerow and his siblings got shipped off to various foster homes. Living with a Black family in Bayonne, a blue-collar town south of Jersey City, eight-year-old Clerow was so nervous and homesick that he began wetting the bed. The woman of the house thought she knew how to get him to stop: beat him. That didn't work. Clerow wound up running away eight times that year. They kept transferring him to different foster homes. If they didn't provide Clerow with a stable family life, they at least gave him material he would later mine for his comedy—such as the loud-talking, Cadillac-driving preacher who would become one of Flip's most famous characters.

By the time he was eight and a half, he was shipped off to the New Jersey Reform School at Jamesburg, about forty miles from Jersey City. Though the notorious place was surrounded by barbed-wire fences, Clerow loved it there, living with about 400 boys seen as too unruly for foster care. He had a white teacher who supplied him with comic books, and he had a white night watchman who would wake him in the middle of the night to pee so he wouldn't wet the bed. The teacher, Mrs. Jones, and the watchman, Mr. Herman, sang him "Happy Birthday" when he turned nine and gave him a can of shoe polish and a box of Cracker Jacks, which he said were the first birthday presents he ever received.

"It's my happiest memory of childhood," he said (Cook 2013, 15).

As a teen, Clerow moved back to Jersey City to live with his father and his Uncle Lemuel, a brother of his mother. He attended Henry Snyder High School and worked at a bowling alley, resetting pins. When he was seventeen, in June 1950, Clerow joined the Air Force—nine days before the start of the Korean War. He was the only Black airman in the barracks among 300 men at Hamilton Air Force Base in San Rafael, California. Up to that point, his interaction with white people in racially segregated Jersey City had been limited. The two white people he had grown closest to, the teacher and the watchman, were kind to him. But he would quickly find out they were the exceptions.

"Nigger, step out of line once, and you're going to the guardhouse," a military police officer at Hamilton told him when he arrived, by way of a greeting.

He got stationed at a typewriter, working as a clerk, eventually learning to type fifty words a minute and earning a promotion to corporal. He worked at base headquarters for the director of personnel, becoming a valuable advisor and helping him make personnel recommendations—until he got busted back down to airman when he was accused of stealing a shirt he said he had borrowed from another man's locker. After he got stationed in Guam, Clerow had a flash of inspiration that allowed him to put his comedic skills to use. He asked his captain if he could give a "speech" at the monthly Troop Information Meeting. The men tried to avoid the meetings like a disease, but Clerow thought he could improve attendance if the men were entertained. He had been doing casual reading on the sexual habits of animals native to Guam. He came up with a killer routine about coconut crabs and stapled fliers all over base announcing his speech: "Sex and the Coconut Crab." More than 400 men attended, eager for anything that would serve as entertainment. The audience loved the routine. And they loved him, pounding him on the back and repeating his funniest lines back to him.

His captain arranged for him to do the routine at the army and the navy compounds all over Guam. He kept adding more material, always studying, establishing his comic chops by constantly reading, observing, taking notes. He would soon take to using yellow legal pads for his notes and observations, something he would continue throughout his career. He even adapted material from Shakespeare's *Julius Caesar*, throwing out a bunch of phrases like "choweth downeth." As he was leaving the stage to the sound of thunderous applause, one of the airmen, picking up the Shakespearean theme, shouted, "He flippeth his lid!" And that was that—his nickname Flip was born.

After being honorably discharged in January 1954, Flip—now twenty—set out to make it as a comedian. But he had a hard time catching a break, so he took whatever jobs he could find. Along with his discharge papers, he carried a letter from his captain praising Airman Wilson as a popular entertainer, a skilled typist, and a credit to his race. His first stop was in San Francisco, where he snagged a gig at the Manor Plaza as a bellhop during the day, then as a clerk in the evening because of his typing skills. In the downstairs showroom of the Manor, Flip got to watch the sets of one of the biggest music stars on the scene in the 1950s, the saxophonist Louis Jordan. There was a very small number of bandleaders who were guaranteed draws at the time—Duke Ellington, Count Basie, and Louis Jordan. Jordan had dominated the *Billboard* magazine race charts—launched in the 1940s to track the popularity of music by African-American artists, primarily in the genres of blues, jazz, and gospel—with Louis Jordan and the Tympany Five scoring eighteen number one singles and fifty-four top-ten hits. On the club scene, Jordan's five-piece band was much cheaper to hire than the popular sixteen-piece big bands, meaning Jordan was gobbling up gigs that might have gone to Basie and Ellington. Jordan, lauded as the "King of the Jukebox," earned a previously unheard-of $70,000 (almost a million in today's dollars) for playing two weeks at the Golden Gate Theatre in San Francisco in 1948. Music historians credit Jordan as being the bridge between big bands and the smaller, more nimble rock and roll bands that came later in the 1960s.

Flip would sit downstairs in the Manor's showroom during his rare breaks, nursing a glass of wine, listening to the seductive sounds of Jordan and the Tympany Five. Flip saw that when the band finished a set, the crowd grew bored during the lull. Some couples left and didn't come back. Flip went up to the manager, a cheap man in an expensive suit named Willie McCoy (Cook 2013, 36).

"Let me go on during the break," Flip said.

"Go on and do what?" McCoy asked.

"Talk."

"Talk?" McCoy laughed. "Talk's not an act. *I* can talk."

"You'll sell more drinks," Flip said. "Give me five minutes."

The next day Flip decided he needed more of an act, so he risked his few coins on a big floppy stovepipe hat and a tuxedo from Salvation Army. He thought back to that first comedian he ever saw in Newark at the Mosque Theater, doing the "Open the Door, Richard" routine, and figured everybody loves a drunk.

While Jordan and his band finished their first set, Clerow sipped white port wine with a dash of lemon juice, the Fillmore District drink of the moment. When Jordan bowed and led his Tympany Five off the bandstand, Clerow counted to ten. *No hurry*, he thought. Let it happen. With no introduction, he stepped into the spotlight. Shielding his eyes, he said, "Bad day. I had a bad day today." Pause. "Almost as bad as you all look."

That got the patrons' attention. As bad as *they* looked? They weren't sure if this rumpled fellow was part of the show or just a lush on his way to the bathroom. He bumped into a drum set; customers smiled and pointed. Despite the wine buzz, his mind raced, turning over which lines he might say next. At the same time, he felt his gorge rise like he might throw up. Eyes on him, people snickering—it turned his stomach. Would they love him? Hate him? He avoided their eyes by looking at the stage lights. There was a safety there, a clean white like the spotlight on Clara Barton at PS 14, and for the first time he could remember, he felt at home.

"Had cornflakes for breakfast," he said suddenly, "but I ran out of milk. What's worse than that? Do you eat a little half bowl with a normal milk level, or one big soggy bowl with dry flakes up the sides?"

Scattered laughs.

"This chick I'm going out with, we're rockin' and rollin', you know what I mean, and she yells out, 'Oh, Ray, I loves you!'" He looked miserable. "Ray's my brother. Bad day."

More laughter. Laughs from paying customers, not joke-starved servicemen. Now flying on more than wine, he dropped the drunk act and spoke as himself, riffing on what he'd seen riding the bus around town—the fog, the cable cars, the drunken sailors, the junkies and bums. "I was so turned on," he remembered years later. "I couldn't wait for them to shut up laughing so I could say the next thing" (Cook 2013, 38).

Flip pushed his luck when Louis Jordan returned with his bandmates for the next set. Flip refused to leave the stage, ignoring them for ten more minutes as he continued to enthrall the crowd, which was into him. McCoy, the manager, waved his arms and pointed at Jordan, who was pissed off. McCoy finally marched onto the stage and dragged Flip off.

"Watch who you're grabbin'!" Flip yelled.

"Watch who you're upstagin'," McCoy said. He gestured toward Jordan. "That's ten thousand dollars a week." As the customers patted Flip on the back and congratulated him, McCoy told him, "They like you. But pull more shit like that and you're done here."

The headstrong Flip responded, "You can't 'done here' me. I quit."

But he was back outside the next day, pacing in front of the club. McCoy pulled up. "People are asking after you," McCoy said. "You can do the break every night. Ten minutes, all yours."

"Fifteen," Flip responded, and walked away.

As much as any comedian who came before him, Wilson studied the dynamics of joke-telling, dissecting the bones of a joke to determine why some audiences laughed and some didn't. He read and reread Max Eastman's book *Enjoyment of Laughter*, underlining pieces of advice on nearly every page. "There is a science to humor," Eastman wrote. Flip bought a yellow legal pad and began writing down his observations on comedy and the leading comedians of the time. He saw that avoiding overtly sexual material would probably take him further, so he stayed away from it, which already differentiated him from most of his Black contemporaries at the time. That made it easier for him when he began to be embraced by the white mainstream. But that's not to say his style wasn't Black, because it definitely was. For instance, his delivery and material were Blacker than Gregory's. He began to develop characters, like the flamboyant Reverend Leroy and the sassy Geraldine—whose signature line, "The devil made me do it," entered American lexicon almost as soon as Flip debuted her.

They struck a powerful chord with Black audiences—and found resonance among white audiences too. Wilson was the first Black comedian to introduce a decidedly Black voice to the mainstream. With Flip's emergence, the steady march toward unleashing the private Black voice took a major step forward.

> His easier access in the late sixties was facilitated by the older comedians who had struggled to break down barriers. Rogers, White, Russell, Gregory, Foxx, and Mabley had made tremendous inroads; Cosby and Cambridge had demonstrated that comedy could be essentially colorless. The public was, quite simply, beginning to become accustomed to black comics. Still, Wilson's enthusiastic celebration of black style was unique when he emerged; in one sense it was a throwback to the old ethnic comedy of the Negro stage clown, but Wilson managed to present it in a new, more dignified and assertive style, giving it universal appeal. Timing, an un-self-conscious affection for African-American mannerisms and culture, a meticulous, studious approach to comedy, and a captivating personality were all, in part, responsible for his success. (Watkins 1994, 520)

When Flip was out on the road with a piano player, Charles Calloway, with whom he had developed a two-man act, he discovered how much people loved seeing a man in a dress. Calloway would play and sing a blues song about a woman who done him wrong—and Flip would bounce on the stage in the guise of that woman, wearing a blond wig and tight skirt. When Calloway sang that his girl left him for a man with a bigger bankroll, Flip bumped the piano with his hip.

"Wasn't just his bankroll was bigger, honey!" he said, to the uproarious laughter of the crowd.

The act went over so well that Flip was concerned about being labeled as a drag queen. So, he developed another character, the loud-mouthed preacher modeled after his former foster father.

Flip eventually split from Calloway and spent years crisscrossing the West, looking for work, sometimes getting a shot at clubs on the unforgiving Chitlin' Circuit. His goal was to always have at least a hundred dollars in his pocket, since Greyhound had a deal where you could ride anywhere in the country for ninety-nine dollars; that way, he'd never be stranded—the bane of any traveling entertainer's existence. In 1958, Flip determined that if he wasn't famous in fifteen years, by 1973, he would hang up his joke book. "Meanwhile he intended to outthink and outwork all the guys who just liked to get high and make people laugh."

One day somewhere in the Midwest, Flip watched a Black soldier step off the Greyhound to greet his very ecstatic family. The soldier's sister exclaimed, "Mama, here come Willie back from the army! Show Mama how you march, Willie. *Hup*, two, three, four!" Flip loved the tone of the girl's voice and practiced imitating it. He soon incorporated it into his act whenever he needed a female voice; it went over extremely well with audiences, who couldn't get enough of her. It was this voice, inspired by a nameless sister of a soldier, that would one day become beloved by America as the voice of Flip's most popular character, Geraldine.

As Flip sat and watched *The Tonight Show* one night in 1964, he was upset that a competitor, Redd Foxx, was appearing on such a distinguished platform when Flip seemingly couldn't buy a laugh. In other words, he was feeling sorry for himself. Redd finished his set and sat down next to Carson's desk. Flip fumed. After a bit of banter, Carson asked, "Redd, who's the funniest comedian out there right now?"

"Flip Wilson," Redd said without hesitation. And just like that, Flip's life changed overnight.

It didn't take long for the phone call to come: "Johnny wants you to be on the show."

On two separate occasions, Flip waited impatiently in the studio before someone on Carson's staff told him Johnny had spoken to the more famous guests too long and had run out of time. His third booking came while Watts was in flames during the riots in August 1965. Flip thought there was little chance the show would bring out a Black man to tell jokes—but he nonetheless got his break. During Flip's routine, Carson said "Funny!" out loud, a major sign of approval from his eminence.

He was back on a month later. This time he told a joke that had an even more dramatic effect on Carson. It was about a woman who took her newborn baby on the train. Another passenger whistled and said, "That's an ugly baby!" The mother reported the incident to the train conductor, who swore that such disrespect would not be tolerated on the Pennsylvania Railroad. As an act of apology, the conductor offered the mother "a free meal in our dining car—and maybe we'll find a banana for your monkey" (Cook 2013, 93).

Carson laughed for almost a half minute and pounded the desk. As Carson shook Flip's hand, America's comedy impresario said, "That is one of the funniest things I've ever heard in my life!" Over the next two years, Flip would appear on Carson's show twenty-six times, even being chosen as one of the guest hosts who stepped in for Johnny when he took time off.

Flip's bookings and asking price soared because of Carson. He soon played the Sahara in Vegas in 1966, opening for crooner Bobby Darin. When the Sahara changed its mind about Flip, deciding that he would no longer go on, Darin stepped in and said he would tear up his contract if they didn't hire Flip—a move quite similar to those made by Darin's rival Frank Sinatra. Darin eventually became one of Flip's closest friends—though Flip also hung out quite a bit with Sinatra and the rest of the infamous Rat Pack.

Flip hired Monte Kay, a well-known manager whose roster included jazz greats like Stan Getz and Sonny Rollins—and who, at the time, was married to the actress Diahann Carroll.

"Flip, you can rise above color," Kay told him. "With the right management you can be bigger than Redd Foxx, bigger than Red Skelton."

"How about Bill Cosby?" Flip asked him.

"Bill who?" Kay jokingly responded.

Flip excised profanity from his act. As Cook points out, he was becoming more like Cosby, less like Foxx. He and Kay launched a plan for him to have his own network television show by 1970. The first step was to do more network television. Flip became a regular on a show called *The Kraft Summer Music Hall*, which was replacing Andy Williams's prime-time show. Flip grew close to two restless young writers on the show who were too talented for the corny fare they were being asked to write. Their names? George Carlin and Richard Pryor. Both were tightly wound and neurotic, spending much of their time smoking weed and making fun of *The Kraft Summer Music Hall*. They were still mourning the death of their idol, Lenny Bruce, who had just overdosed in August 1966. Flip also added another lucrative gig to his roster, as a regular on the prime-time *Ed Sullivan Show*.

It was a tempestuous time in America, which made it a challenging time to make a living telling jokes. Flip didn't avoid racial material, but he was sure not to make it the centerpiece of his act. When he appeared before an integrated crowd right after race riots in 1967, he said he was wearing his "riot outfit."

"Got it in Detroit—right out of the window," he said, adding that he liked to do his shopping in the summer when prices went down—all the way down to zero.

That year, the *New York Times* recognized the fine line he was trying to walk: "Mr. Wilson is a Negro, and his material touches on matters that the average nightclub patron could not be expected to find amusing—race riots, looting, police brutality. But, hold, it is all in fun."

Richard Pryor famously told Flip, "You're the only performer that I've ever seen who goes onstage and the audience hopes that *you* like them."

Flip's first album, 1967's *Cowboys and Colored People*, was a hit, and even got nominated for a Grammy—though it lost to Cosby's *Revenge*. Wanting a bigger cut beyond the industry standard, Flip started his own label called Little David Records with the help of

Monte Kay. A subsidiary of Atlantic, it debuted with Flip and George Carlin as its first two acts. Noting Flip's growing national popularity, NBC came with an offer—a lucrative five-year development deal that would include his own series and a payment of $40,000 to do an hour-long pilot. To signify his arrival, Flip bought himself a blue Rolls-Royce convertible—the first car he ever owned. But Flip was smart with his money. He told Kay and his financial advisors that for every investment opportunity they brought him, they would have to match his investment. "If I go broke," he said, "you motherfuckers going with me." Flip never went broke.

One of NBC's initial ideas for Flip was to team him up with Stepin Fetchit (Lincoln Perry) to form a sassy comic duo. But that idea was squashed after Fetchit, now sixty-six, was thoroughly disgraced in the 1968 documentary *Of Black America* narrated by Cosby. Cosby and the documentary framed Stepin Fetchit's screen persona as emblematic of harmful stereotypes created and perpetuated by Hollywood. The documentary aired at the height of the Civil Rights Movement, and Fetchit's persona was viewed as being in direct conflict with the movement's goals.

As he worked on his own show, Flip kept up his guest appearances on other shows, particularly Carson. But network execs were torn on whether he should have a sitcom, a variety show, or maybe an all-Black talk show.

Finally, six weeks after Neil Armstrong took his giant leap for mankind on the moon, *The Flip Wilson Special* aired on NBC. Almost immediately it was a huge hit. In his opening sketch, the Reverend Leroy and his wife are talking about her addiction to shopping, with her shouting "The devil made me buy this dress!" The next day that phrase was heard on schoolyards and in break rooms across America. And then there was Geraldine. Geraldine J-O-N-E-S, as she was quick to spell it for you.

> Here was the coming-out of a character that would dominate Flip's act and much of the rest of his life. He named her after the real Geraldine, the prettiest girl in The Hill

neighborhood of Depression-era Jersey City, who'd duped little Clerow into shoplifting fake fingernails for her. . . . While Geraldine's hip-rolling walk might have come straight from burlesque, her attitude—"Don't you touch me!"—suggested women's lib. Her catchphrase was a deeply ironic assertion of self that owed much of its punch to the fact that it came from a man in a skirt: "What you see is what you get!" . . . Geraldine was the right girl at the right moment, and Flip knew it. (Cook 2013, 114)

Flip was so popular that his special drew 42 percent of the viewers in its time slot, making it the eighth-highest-rated show that week. But even after the success of the special, the network execs were afraid of the variety-hour format; there were so many celebrities with variety shows—Doris Day, Red Skelton, Bill Cosby, Carol Burnett, Dean Martin, and Johnny Cash included. So, NBC floated the idea of a sitcom to Flip instead.

"I'm not up for that," Flip told them. "I've got a great deal of experience emceeing and performing in nightclubs. I know I can carry a variety show" (Cook 2013, 116).

When they eventually offered him a variety show on the Thursday-night lineup, with the customary Hollywood deal of NBC owning the show—with Flip earning up to a million a year—he told them it wasn't good enough. He wanted to *own* the show. It's what Lucille Ball and Desi Arnaz had done with *I Love Lucy* and what Jerry Seinfeld would do with *Seinfeld*—claiming an ownership stake in a program and, by default, making millions more. It was a gamble that would pay off only if the show stuck around for a while—as most shows did not. The execs relented to Flip: He would be his own producer, taking less money up front in exchange for ownership.

Flip's first episode aired on September 17, 1970, kicking off the decade with the bold announcement of a new American superstar. With nods to police brutality, over-the-top preachers, James Brown singing, Flip dancing with Big Bird, and the debut of Geraldine Jones, the show destroyed the competition. It was the top new program in

1970, drawing almost as many viewers as the Super Bowl and consistently beating *The Mod Squad*, *Laugh-In*, and *Bonanza*. Newspapers called it "Flip Fever."

"Everybody watched it. It was appointment TV," recalled Whoopi Goldberg, who at the time was fourteen-year-old Caryn Johnson, living in Manhattan's Chelsea-Elliott housing projects. "I'd go to my Catholic school the next day and kids were all doing Geraldine, saying, 'What you see is what you get, honey!' Even the nuns! You'd hear the nuns say, 'The devil made me do it,' and they'd giggle."

The show's format implemented what Flip called a "fruit salad"—pairing guests from vastly different backgrounds—B.B. King performing with Sid Caesar, Andy Griffith with Curtis Mayfield—on the show each night. He brought on older Black comedians like Moms Mabley. Even Cosby—his biggest competitor—was a guest. Flip insisted on paying guests $7,500 (over $60,000 in current dollars), far more than his competitors. He wanted to have Redd Foxx on the show, and he wouldn't relent when the network pushed back, afraid of Redd's vulgar mouth. Foxx went on the show, and boosted ratings.

"Flip was a transitional figure. He was so lovable and cute he charmed middle America into accepting a Black TV star," said comedian Lily Tomlin, whose relatives drove all the way from Kentucky to Burbank to attend the taping of Flip's show in which she appeared. "My aunt and uncle were *not* enlightened, but when I took them to meet Flip, they almost knocked me down going into his dressing room. 'Oh, Flip, you're our favorite comedian—after Lily, of course!'"

In *Life* magazine, white critic John Leonard said Flip was more authentically Black than Bill Cosby. "He has not sanitized his blackness for home consumption." This signaled a major development: The nation had now reached the point where white people could sense which comedians were telling them things Black people previously only spoke of in private. They sensed that Flip did it—and they loved him for it; Cosby did not.

Flip won a Grammy for his 1971 album *The Devil Made Me Buy This Dress*. He added a pair of Emmys to his trophy case in 1971 when he won for comedy writing over Carol Burnett's team and for

Outstanding Variety Series over *Laugh-In* and *The Carol Burnett Show*. There was no doubt about it: Flip Wilson was America's favorite comedian. The host of the Emmys that year, Johnny Carson, joked onstage that "Flip's done a lot for the Black man. He put him in a dress."

Carson's joke pointed out one of the most profound criticisms leveled at Flip: that Geraldine was an emasculating figure for Black men, and an insulting figure to Black women—similar to the Sapphire character on *Amos 'n' Andy* years earlier. It was an attack that would resound over the succeeding years, directed at artists from Eddie Murphy to Martin Lawrence to Tyler Perry. But Flip didn't slow down a bit. He appeared on the cover of the January 31, 1972, issue of *Time* magazine with the headline "TV's First Black Superstar."

Richard Pryor joined Flip's show in 1973 as a writer and occasional talent—announcing his own arrival with the declaration "Super Nigger is here!" Pryor had already appeared as Diana Ross's (Billie Holiday's) piano player in *Lady Sings the Blues* and had co-written the hit film *Blazing Saddles* with Mel Brooks—though Pryor was devastated when the studio wouldn't let him play the lead because of his drug-addled history and chose Cleavon Little instead. Flip and Pryor had great respect for each other, but there was also considerable tension in their relationship. Part of it stemmed from the fact that, though Flip was only seven years older than the thirty-two-year-old Pryor, Flip had cut his comic teeth on the hard-nosed Chitlin' Circuit and had a more compromising attitude toward the white people he now heavily depended on. Pryor had not traveled that route and called Flip "NBC's house Negro," to which Flip replied by chiding Pryor that on prime-time TV his primary role is to sell Rice Krispies. "If you think this is going to be the H. Rap Brown show or the Richard Pryor show, you can turn in your jacket."

"Flip's tight ship got loose when Richard was on," said white comic actor Tim Conway. "*Extremely* loose. Richard would barely look at the script. Flip went along and we improvised. That was one of Flip's strengths, making use of everybody's ammunition" (Cook 2013, 155).

By Flip's third season, his numbers were starting to slip. He had dropped down to the twelfth-highest-rated show. He had enough episodes to hit syndication, which meant millions more for Clerow Productions. But NBC decided it wouldn't renew the show for a fifth season.

When Flip exited the studio lot in 1974 for the last time in his Rolls-Royce, he could speed away knowing he had just spent four years as perhaps the biggest star on television. He was forty years old and worth between $12 and $15 million, not counting the syndication money. More importantly, he had burst into network television and demonstrated that a Black man could become a beloved figure in a predominantly white land. Flip's comic heirs would quickly take full advantage.

The Black comedians who broke into the mainstream during the 1950s and '60s changed the game by bringing a sharp, satirical edge to African-American comedy—an element that had mostly been shared within the Black community until then. But in doing so, whether to distance themselves from harmful stereotypes or because of their own comedic styles, many of them dialed down or left behind the raw, street-style humor that shaped them.

Flip Wilson was different. While he used satire too, his lively characters and joyful energy brought back the flair, the rhythm, the unmistakable sound of Black comedic tradition. His playful approach didn't just entertain—it helped reopen the door to more authentic expressions of Black humor.

CHAPTER 11
BILL COSBY

When Bill Cosby strode onto the set of *The Tonight Show* in August 1963, his first big show business break, he looked out over a comedic landscape that was slowly starting to reflect the changing fortunes of African Americans. Pigmeat Markham had hooked up with Chess Records and was being introduced to a much wider audience on vinyl than he ever had on the Chitlin' Circuit. Moms Mabley was finally discovered by white people, playing at the prestigious Carnegie Hall in 1962. Redd Foxx was establishing himself as King of the Party Records, selling more than a million albums and finding his way into homes all across America—though his records would sometimes be stashed out of sight because of their raunchy content.

Dick Gregory, the most successful Black comedian in history up to that point, stood atop the Black comedy mountain, widely embraced and celebrated for his cerebral style. Gregory opened the door for brainy comedians like Cosby to avoid race in sets that focused more on the humor of our common humanity. Flip Wilson was still relatively unknown, honing his act, on the road donning his Geraldine dresses, waiting for his break. Richard Pryor was searching for his comedy sea legs, trying out different personas—including one that he stole straight from Cosby, as a clean storyteller—until one felt right.

But before he found his comedic voice, Cosby's act was a carbon copy of Gregory's in approach and demeanor. At first, Cosby didn't mind telling jokes about race.

"The biting, witty kind about the Negro role in America," Cosby said, recalling his early material. "But pretty soon critics regarded me as a sort of hip Nipsey Russell or Philadelphia Dick Gregory" (Frierson 2020, 33).

He joked at the time, "Some people call me 'the Philadelphia Dick Gregory,' but that's silly. I'm taller—and better looking." Cosby noted that he felt like he was in Gregory's shadow with everything he did in those early years. So, he decided he would be the anti–Dick Gregory—though Frierson pointed out that Cosby, in excising race from his act, might also have been influenced by a June 1962 profile of Gregory in New York's *Amsterdam News*, arguably the nation's most important Black newspaper, that said Gregory wasn't focusing on race and was poised to make a half million that year.

"Rather than trying to bring the races together by talking about difference, why not bring them together by talking about all the similarities?" Cosby said. "I want to reach all the people."

It's a question that every Black creative has to face at some point: How "Black" do I want to be? Because of the unique challenges African Americans have endured, observers are often uncomfortable when Black artists seem to ignore race altogether. Even athletes can face that question—Michael Jordan caused a huge uproar over a comment he made while joking with Chicago Bulls teammates Scottie Pippen and Horace Grant that he didn't want to publicly support Black Senate candidate Harvey Gantt in his 1990 campaign against well-known racist Senator Jesse Helms because "Republicans buy sneakers too."

As Cosby was coming up, Black artists were increasingly turning to television to advance their careers, hoping to take advantage of the enormous audiences—and rather large paychecks—now available to them in television. But in the early '60s their appearances generally were as occasional guests on white shows. The Black community was clamoring for an African-American entertainer to get their own show. The New York Society for Ethical Culture did an investigation in which it had about 100 of its members watch television for two weeks, noting when African Americans appeared. Their finding? Not very often. The NYSEC released its report in 1962, criticizing the television industry for failing to include Blacks in regular daily programs. (Nat King Cole had had his own show in 1956, but it only lasted a year because it couldn't secure a national sponsor. "Madison Avenue is afraid of the dark," Cole famously said of his inability to find sponsors.)

On his way to eventually becoming perhaps the most famous Black man in America, Cosby did a masterful job of crafting a public image of education, class, and refinement that was far different than his actual story of desperate poverty, horrible grades, and dropping out of high school—and college. Fans of *The Cosby Show*, viewing the lovely, art-filled home of Cliff and Clair Huxtable every week, and noting Cosby's doctoral degree and focus on education and historically Black colleges and universities (HBCUs), could be excused for believing that Bill Cosby's actual upbringing wasn't that far off from Cliff's on the show. In fact, much of that was an image he had carefully curated. It was actually his wife, Camille, who grew up like the Huxtables. As a child, Bill would have barely been aware that families like that of Camille Hanks even existed.

William Henry Cosby Jr. was born in the midst of the Great Depression on July 12, 1937, to Anna and William Cosby in a section of North Philadelphia known as Germantown after its founding by German Quaker abolitionists. But by the time young Bill came along, the area had become predominantly Black—though there were still racial dangers: By the late 1920s, a total of twenty Ku Klux Klan klaverns had formed around Philadelphia, making it the group's largest outpost in the Northeast.

William and Anna lived with their young son on Beechwood Street; two houses down was another Black couple, the Gaines family, who had been childhood friends of Anna and Bill Sr. They had a little boy named Johnny who would become Bill's best friend. The two boys were both keen on finding mischief, embarking each morning on a new adventure—like climbing the neighbor's fence and letting her dog out of the yard, then pretending to "rescue" the dog and return it to its distraught and grateful owner.

Little Bill sought the outdoors or Johnny's house to escape the tensions in his own home—increasingly because Bill Sr. drank heavily as he tried to support his growing family, which now included a sickly second child named James. He would beat Anna as she harangued him for spending his factory worker's paycheck at the local bar instead of bringing it home to her. When Bill was five, the family could no longer afford the rent at its place on Beechwood and had to move five miles away to a cheaper place on Stewart Street that had no hot water and no tub in the bathroom—Anna bathed her boys by heating water on the stove and sponging them down. Bill had to say goodbye to Johnny, who called it the saddest day of his life.

"When he moved," Johnny said, "I thought the world had ended" (Whitaker 2014, 29).

Bill looked forward to spending time with his grandparents to get away from the darkness in his own house. His grandmother Martha (Anna's mother) would sometimes pretend to be asleep on the couch, then she would abruptly sit up and spit her false teeth out of her mouth at Bill, causing him to scream in mock terror and run away. He said those scenes with Grandma were "the greatest laughs I ever had."

After the US entered World War II, Bill Cosby Sr. decided to enlist, inspired by the story of the Black cook Dorie Miller, who bravely manned an antiaircraft gun and started firing at the Japanese planes overhead after his ship, the USS *West Virginia*, was struck at Pearl Harbor. Bill Sr. saw it as a way to escape his rocky home life while making some money for his family. He spent the next fifteen years at sea, serving three tours of duty, though he managed to come home on leave often enough to father two more sons. Around the time that Bill Sr. enlisted, the Cosby family made a move that would prove providential for young Bill. They got an apartment in a new public housing project in North Philly called the Richard Allen Homes, which housed more than a thousand families and offered Bill a vast new collection of playmates. Decades later, a few of them made their way onto Bill's children's show, *Fat Albert and the Cosby Kids*, though most of the *Fat Albert* characters came from Bill's imagination or were composites of several kids. The apartment was actually smaller than the house they had just left, but it had hot water and a bathroom with a tub, plus new appliances and a reasonable rent of $46 a month.

The Allen Homes is where Bill discovered he had a talent to make people laugh. Like a lot of comics in their youth, Bill used this talent to avoid being the target of the violence that swirled through the projects—though he wasn't afraid to fight if he had to. When the hoodlums descended on young Bill and his elementary school friends to steal their pocket money, Bill would make them laugh; so, they let Bill and his friends pass by with their pockets and pride intact. Bill found out that he was really good at imitating people and sounds. When they snuck into the movie theater on Fairmount Avenue and spent the afternoon mesmerized, Bill—who went by the nickname Shorty, given to him by the older hoodlums—would later entertain his friends with his impersonations of the characters on-screen.

The family's continuing financial troubles left a mark on Bill. When his mother was late with the rent—which happened several times before she figured out she could have her husband's navy pay sent directly to her—they nailed eviction notices on the apartment's front door. Though most of the other kids likely weren't much better off, that didn't stop them from cruelly mocking Bill.

"If your father sold all that wine he drank, you could pay your rent!" one of the kids once joked when another eviction notice was posted at the Cosby home.

Bill was close with his brother Russell, seven years his junior, though they also got on each other's nerves. "At the kitchen table, they alternated between clowning and bickering. On some days Bill made Russell giggle by squirting food coloring in his eggs. On others they fought over helpings of scrapple, the mixture of pork scraps and cornmeal that Anna fried up in a cast-iron skillet. If one of the brothers thought the other had been served a better piece of scrapple, he would spit on it" (Whitaker 2014, 41).

Bill's sickly younger brother James died in 1946 at the age of seven from rheumatic fever, just before Bill's ninth birthday.

Undoubtedly mourning the loss, Bill held a chronic disinterest in school, consistently bringing home bad grades. School bored him; he was more interested in being the class clown. His academic record was redeemed a bit in sixth grade by a new teacher, Ms. Forchic, a Russian woman who Bill didn't know had been his mother's closest childhood friend. She assured Anna she would turn him around.

In fifth grade, Bill had taken an IQ test—a new policy had just been implemented, testing students to see who had advanced learning potential—that identified him as the smartest kid in the entire school. He thought it was pretty cool, until his friends started teasing him about it. His fifth-grade teacher, Mrs. McKinney, transferred him to her advanced class, but he spent much of his time there pining to be with his boys in the "dumb class" because they got to play outside or take field trips to the zoo and planetarium, while Bill had to stay in school for extra work with the other advanced kids.

Mrs. McKinney decided that if she couldn't fight her bright-but-bored young student's joking nature, she would work with it. She asked him if he wanted to tell jokes at the front of the class. It was a critical moment—one that seemingly has occurred in the early lives of many comedians. Bill didn't know what to do, so he stuck out his butt and imitated the jiggling walk of the older women in the projects. His classmates loved it. He then told them funny stories about sharing a bed with his brother.

"The laughs grew even louder, and Bill felt like a surge of electricity was running through his body. Later, he would recall it as his first experience of the adrenaline rush that comes with performing before a live audience" (Whitaker 2014, 43).

When it came time for high school, despite his bad grades Bill passed the entrance exam for Central High, the city's most prestigious high school and the all-male counterpart to Girls' High, where his mother had gone. Bill still had little interest in academics. His mind was preoccupied with three things: jazz, sports, and the "Down Cats," the group of friends he'd spend the majority of his time with. Bill's obsession with jazz would remain throughout his life, revealing itself in myriad ways. He was particularly drawn to Miles Davis, whose cool jazz sound was starting to change the face of bebop. Cosby decided he was going to transform himself into a jazz drummer, like one of his idols, Philly Joe Jones. Using money he had saved from part-time jobs, he purchased a used drum set and occasionally took lessons at the Wurlitzer's Music Store when he had the $2.50 fee. But mostly he practiced on his own. One weekend, a local musician named Groove Holmes asked Cosby if he could fill in for his missing drummer. This was how the gig went down:

As soon as he got on the bandstand, he started dropping bombs like his hero Philly Joe. But Groove wanted a simple backbeat: "Come on, man," he kept hissing, until Cosby calmed down and started hitting the drums "on the two and the four."

"That's it!" Groove called out. "Leave it right there!"

But Cosby couldn't resist showing off, and soon he was back trying to play like Philly Joe or Art Blakey.

When the first set was over, Holmes handed him sixteen dollars and told him to go home.

Cosby was eager to play football for his new school, but his grandfather Samuel (his father's father) was against it, telling him he shouldn't be playing football before age twenty-one because his bones weren't set. Cosby didn't listen—and proceeded to break his left shoulder during the first game when he fell trying to avoid a tackle. While waiting for his shoulder to heal, Cosby's eyes drifted over to the track-and-field facility. His best event became the high jump, but he also did hurdles and middle-distance relay.

At Central, Cosby had curated a group of friends who shared his passion for jazz. They spent most of their time together listening to jazz albums and cruising in cars, looking for parties. Cosby came up with the name Down Cats and even printed membership cards with the group's logo. While people were smoking marijuana around him, Cosby declined to indulge. The Down Cats hung out as much as they could at a jazz club on Lombard Street called the Showboat, located in the Douglass Hotel. Cosby would paint a mustache on his lip to pass for twenty-one so he could get in the club, where he would nurse his Coke for two hours during the jazz matinee in the afternoon. One afternoon in 1954 when Cosby was seventeen, he met his hero, the epitome of everything cool, Miles Davis. Miles was playing the matinee with his band, and he was resting on the stairs during a break. Cosby sat next to him but had no idea what to say to break the ice with the famously aloof star.

"Everything going all right, is it?" he finally said.

"Yeah," Miles answered.

Cosby couldn't think of what to say next. He kicked himself as they sat in silence. Cosby finally stood and said, "I'll see you later, Miles."

"All right," Miles said.

That was it. But Cosby lied to his friends, who were watching and figured that he was too scared to say anything. "He told me everything was fine and asked me where I lived. He told me he might come up and visit me sometime!"

The move to Central failed to spur Cosby's interest in his academics; he constantly struggled to keep up his grades. He failed so many classes that he had to repeat a semester, and then repeat a whole year when that didn't work. In 1954, he transferred to Germantown High School, though he didn't fare any better there. While Central had been less than ten percent Black, Germantown was more than half Black. Cosby's athletic prowess led him to become captain of the football and the track teams. But by 1955, at age eighteen, he saw no future in school, especially since his friends were graduating. He realized he could be in his twenties by the time he graduated. So, he dropped out. He got a full-time job at a shoe repair store and a part-time job at an auto body shop. He enrolled in night school for his mother's benefit, but he didn't last long there either. Cosby was adrift. Jazz music and sports were the only fields Cosby saw where a Black person without money or family connections could become a big success, but he now knew he didn't have enough talent in either to make it.

Cosby saw the armed services as his only way out, so he decided to enlist in the navy because he thought drowning in the ocean was the least unpleasant way to die compared to getting shot in a foxhole or out of the air. Besides, that was what his father had done—and he remembered his mom saying how handsome the white navy uniforms were.

"So, you want to join the navy to see the world?" the recruiter asked him.

"No, I just want to get off my block," he responded.

He wasn't a bad recruit once he accepted his circumstances—he was stuck in the navy for the foreseeable future. The navy saw his leadership ability and appointed him recruit chief petty officer, in charge of keeping his fellow sailors in line. Cosby joined the Hospital Corps, which was in charge of medical care for the soldiers. He found out that hospital corpsmen wore special badges that prohibited the enemy from firing on them, as per an edict of the Geneva Convention negotiated after World War II. That was a regulation he wholeheartedly endorsed. In addition, Cosby wanted to one-up his old man, who had been just a mess worker during his navy years.

His first deployment was in a remote place called Argentia, on the coast of an island off the far eastern shore of Canada. There, he befriended a Black pilot named Ronald Crockett who loved jazz just as much as he did. The two became inseparable, spending hours talking about sports, racism, and their favorite jazz cuts.

Crockett, who went by the nickname Stymie because he resembled the character in *The Little Rascals*, was amazed by how much Cosby got away with because he was so funny. "Cosby would sneak up on white sailors as they were napping and pull their feet: They would snap awake angrily, and then smile when they saw who it was. 'Oh, Cos!' they said with a smile."

Cosby was ecstatic when he found out he could play sports in the military, participating on the navy's basketball and track teams and playing football with the Marines. In track and field, he had impressive personal bests: 6'5" in the high jump, 46'8" in the long jump, and 10.2 seconds in the hundred-yard dash. After he injured his left shoulder again, this time a dislocation requiring surgery, Cosby had to do physical therapy. He really liked the woman who ran the unit, Lt. Jean Lamb, and asked if he could be transferred there since he had experience working with patients.

Cosby used the unit as a stage to entertain the patients with his funny stories. Lamb brought her frisky miniature schnauzer Chipper to work with her, delighting the patients. With Cosby and the dog, the physical therapy ward became the most popular wing in the hospital. He would make up dazzling stories that featured Chipper as the hero—Lamb worried that her stroke victims might have another one from laughing so hard. In many of his stories, he pretended Chipper could talk.

Nearing the end of his four-year commitment, Cosby told Lamb he wanted to be a teacher so he could help kids who were growing up like he did in North Philly. He thought he could get a degree in physical education and become a gym teacher and coach at a junior high school, when the kids were still young enough to reach. Cosby came up with a plan to attend Temple University in North Philly and get the school to pay his way. At a track meet at Villanova University, where he would be running for the navy, Cosby introduced himself to the Temple coach and told him he wanted a track scholarship. The coach had seen how gifted an athlete he was, so he told Cosby he could secure a scholarship—but first he had to take the SAT.

> As Cosby sat in a school auditorium in Philadelphia and gazed at the booklet full of multiple-choice questions on the SAT exam, he felt as if his entire wasted school career were passing before his eyes. His high IQ wasn't going to help him remember the vocabulary he needed to answer the reading comprehension questions and the formulas required to solve the math problems. *So, this was what Mrs. McKinney was talking about!* he thought, remembering all the clowning and daydreaming he had done in fifth grade. Cosby was tempted to put down his pencil and walk away, but that would be the end of his new life plan. So he imagined himself playing poker in the navy and did his best to bluff his way through the exam. (Whitaker 2014, 75)

He got a terrible score of 500 points on the exam—which was just half the average American student score in 1960. But the recommendation letter from Lamb and the coach's recruiting report were enough to get him a seat in the class of 1964; he was going to be a twenty-three-year-old college freshman. Cosby set his mind on finishing school this time. He told himself he couldn't afford to waste this chance.

Cosby pledged the Temple chapter of the Black fraternity Omega Psi Phi—the country's oldest Black fraternity. He played on Temple's freshman football squad and helped lead them to an undefeated season. "He loved to hit people," said his coach, Gavin White (Whitaker 2014, 77).

In addition to dishing out punishment, Cosby could also take a hit. After a violent tackle had him laid out on the field, what Cosby called feeling like "caterpillar fuzz," Coach White and the team's trainer ran onto the field to tend to him.

"Ask his name!" the trainer said.

"Rumpelstiltskin!" Cosby responded.

"He's all right!" White said as he shook his head and smiled.

Cosby called Coach White an "abolitionist," a term he used to describe white people who went overboard to help him when he needed it—people such as his sixth-grade teacher Miss Forchic or Lt. Lamb in the navy.

Cosby was still keen on trying to make it as a jazz drummer. He hung out in Philly at the places where drummers congregated and jammed together. He was asked to fill in with trumpeter Charlie Chisholm's band when drummer Jimmy Griffin left. He played around the city with Chisholm and began to imagine that perhaps a jazz career was possible. But with sports and school, he was having a hard time making it to practice and gigs on time, annoying Chisholm—who also thought Cosby joked around too much onstage. Chisholm eventually had enough and fired Cosby.

His interest in comedy took shape around this time, in part due to the teacher in his Remedial English class, which he was forced to take because of his abysmally low SAT scores. In response to a prompt to write about a "first experience," Cosby wrote about the first time he lost a tooth and wondered if the Tooth Fairy would be able to find him in the Richard Allen Homes. He wanted to write a good paper to impress the teacher; he was worried about flunking out. When the teacher handed back the papers, he told the class he was holding on to Cosby's because he wanted to read it aloud to the class. It was a first for him; his mind was blown. As the students laughed at his story, Cosby grew more excited. Something was happening. Cosby wrote another paper, this time on procrastination, and once again the teacher read it out loud. He began carrying around a notepad to write down ideas for stories as they came to him. Could he possibly make it as a comedy writer?

Since he still had to pay $350 for tuition each semester, Cosby got a job working as a bartender at a small nightclub called the Underground. The manager, Elwood Johnson, saw how funny he was and how much the customers liked him, so he proposed that Cosby sit on a chair and tell jokes at the end of the bar for an extra $5 a night. This was the true beginning of his comedy career, getting paid for the first time to tell jokes. Looking for ideas, he started listening to comedy albums. He came across a new album, *2000 Years with Carl Reiner & Mel Brooks*, in which they performed improv skits. Cosby loved the album and was inspired to try to put together a two-man act with his friend Joe Johnson Jr. But after performing a few sets with Cosby, Johnson decided a comedy career wasn't for him. Cosby got called to fill in at the Underground for a Black comic named Pop Foster who didn't show up one night. It turned out to be a big break for him.

Cosby did so well that a British couple in attendance offered to hook him up with a friend in New York who owned a club called the Gaslight Café in Greenwich Village. Cosby began to see connections between jazz and comedy: Comedy required hard work, mainly in the preparation, to make it look seamless and free-flowing, just like jazz. He would improvise at times, like with jazz, based on the audience and what he was feeling.

"Jazz was also about listening—how cats had to listen to each other and to the room. When he did stand-up, he wanted to feed off his audience the way a jazz soloist would, sensing when to swing hard and when to lay back, when to cut a riff short and when to take extra helpings. . . . Most of all, jazz was about innovation. Cosby thought about his hero, Miles Davis, and all the times he had changed his sound and his sidemen" (Whitaker 2014, 89).

While in New York that summer, Cosby witnessed a scene in a Chinese restaurant that had a profound impact on him. He observed a table full of people listening to a man who had everyone enthralled with his storytelling. He was acting out different parts as he went on. When he got to the end, the group erupted in laughter. Cosby couldn't get that scene out of his head. He wanted to do the kind of comedy where he would enthrall crowds with his storytelling. Cosby thought to himself, "I want to be the storyteller whose friends all think he is the funniest guy in the world."

While Cosby was finding inspiration, one of his Temple football coaches called a friend at the *New York Times* and told him about a college student moonlighting as a comedian in the Village; the editor was interested and assigned a reporter to profile Cosby. The *Times* had been devoting more coverage to race and the civil rights demonstrations. While the young reporter, Paul Gardner, thought the assignment was about a college jock trying to make it in stand-up comedy, the story that appeared in the paper focused largely on race. The headline said, "Comic Turns Quips into Tuition," which was fine, but the subhead read, "Bill Cosby, Student at Temple, Featured at Gaslight Café; Philadelphia Negro Aims His Barbs at Race Relations." To make it worse, the opening of the piece compared Cosby to an African tribesman "hurling verbal spears at the relations between whites and Negroes."

Cosby was not pleased. This was not the vision he had conjured at the Chinese restaurant of what his act would be. The reporter had reduced him to another angry Negro comic, rather than the thoughtful observer of the human condition that he considered himself. However, he realized that the article wasn't far off base in one respect.

> He *was* trying to have it both ways—to develop his own style and to capitalize on Dick Gregory's popularity at the same time. Cosby couldn't help but identify with Gregory, the St. Louis native who had become famous for his biting barbs at white racism. Not only was Gregory another black

man trying to make it in the white comedy world; he was also a track and field man and a military veteran. Cosby was proud to see how far the older comic had risen—all the way to the couch next to Jack Paar on *The Tonight Show*, a place no other Negro comedian had ever been. He also thought Gregory's material—lines such as "I know the South very well; I spent twenty years there one night"—was very funny. But he knew in his heart that he didn't want to be Philadelphia's Dick Gregory, and reading the *Times* piece left him more determined to go in his own direction. (Whitaker 2014, 97)

Cosby managed to catch other comics that summer in the Village, such as Alan King and Lenny Bruce, whose profanity turned him off, though he liked Bruce's improvisational style. Cosby committed himself to working clean—he thought about how his mother would react if he cursed onstage—and considered profanity a crutch "for comics who wanted to be like Lenny Bruce or Redd Foxx but weren't as talented." Though he didn't like the *Times* article, it did bring out more people to his shows.

This was about the time that Cosby started writing the "Noah" routine that would become one of his most famous. He was inspired to write about Noah when thinking back on the biblical stories his Granddad Samuel used to read to him when he was a boy. Granddad would act out the different parts to bring the story alive. How might Noah have reacted when he first heard from God? Cosby worked on the bit until it was a big crowd-pleaser.

He was having trouble juggling his schoolwork, athletic commitments, and his burgeoning comedy career—so he dropped out of school. His mother was devastated. He was just a year away from being the first family member to graduate from college. His brothers later told him she stayed in bed for a week after she got the news. Cosby's gigs—helped by his new manager, Roy Silver—started to flow in pretty regularly after he dropped out. His career was definitely on the upswing.

One day when Cosby was devouring a "half smoke" sausage from the DC landmark Ben's Chili Bowl, while staying in town with his friend Ron Crockett, he stated that all he needed to be happy in life was "six half smokes and a good woman!" It was as if he conjured Camille Hanks out of thin air with his declaration. Crockett saw her first, a lovely co-ed walking across the University of Maryland in College Park where Crockett was taking classes. He immediately thought of Cosby; Camille looked a lot like Lena Horne, one of his and Cosby's favorite singers. Crockett and Camille had a friend in common; Crockett asked the friend if she would introduce Camille to his friend Bill.

Cosby drove to campus to meet her at a bowling alley where she was taking a physical education class. It didn't take him long to be smitten with this beautiful, brilliant young lady. Camille hailed from a quite distinguished upper-middle-class family in Silver Spring: Her father, Guy Hanks, earned a master's degree at Fisk and was a research chemist at Walter Reed Army Medical Center; her mother, Catherine, was a Howard graduate who ran a nursery. Theirs was a home overflowing with books and art honoring Black history and culture—very reminiscent of the home where the Huxtables would one day live on Cosby's groundbreaking television show.

On their second weekend together, Cosby actually asked the young undergrad to marry him. But it was too soon for her. Cosby was not deterred and would make the four-hour drive to Maryland on the weekends to see her after his set was over. He had bought an MG convertible that had no windshield, so it wasn't a particularly pleasant drive on cold or rainy days. When he took Camille to the movies, he would sometimes fall asleep holding her hand because he was so tired.

"That's when I fell in love with him," Camille said (Whitaker 2014, 110).

Cosby discovered how perceptive and smart she was. She never threw in his face the difference in their families and upbringing. Camille was moved by his ambition to become a gym teacher after he had made enough money onstage. But Camille's parents were not happy about this relationship with a joke teller seven years her senior who spent all his time in seedy nightclubs. Camille's mother, Catherine, tried various tacks to keep her daughter away from him, but none of them worked. For her part, Cosby's mother, Anna, was upset that the Hankses thought they were too good for her son. Camille decided their relationship had too many strikes against it and was not going to work, so she ended it. But Cosby wasn't going to give up that easy.

In order for his career to take the next step, Cosby and his manager, Roy Silver, set their eyes on the comedians' holy grail, *The Tonight Show*. Jack Paar had left and been replaced by a comedian best known for hosting game shows, Johnny Carson. Silver happened to know the talent coordinator for the show, a man named Sheldon "Shelly" Schultz. Silver invited Schultz to catch Cosby's act at The Bitter End. Schultz was impressed and began lobbying for him at the show, though there was at least one writer for the show who had seen him and didn't think he was ready for television. But Schultz kept at it and eventually won over the producers.

Allan Sherman was guest hosting when Cosby went on—and Cosby killed that night. The studio audience roared at everything he did, so much so that he had to slow down a few times and wait for the laughter to subside. When he was done, he got called over to the couch. Dick Gregory had been the first Black comic to ever be invited to the couch on *The Tonight Show*, when Paar hosted. Now Cosby was getting the rare honor. He had been even better than Schultz expected. "He [Schultz] had seen first-time comics get laughs on *The Tonight Show*, but rarely affection. Affection took a while, until comedians had been on several times and the audience felt they knew them. But with Cosby, it happened right away" (Whitaker 2014, 114).

After the *Tonight Show* appearance, Warner Brothers approached Cosby and Silver with an offer to do a comedy album. They set up recording equipment at The Bitter End and built the album around his Noah routine. *Bill Cosby Is a Very Funny Fellow—Right!* had liner notes written by Allan Sherman himself, who was credited on the cover as the producer (Silver was also a producer). Sherman was no stranger to comedy albums, having scored a big hit with his 1963 *My*

Son, the Nut, which featured his spoof on camp songs called "Hello Muddah, Hello Fadduh"—a song that's still played more than sixty years later.

Sherman's liner notes read:

> Bill Cosby's "Noah" (the last three bands on Side One) is a masterpiece, even though nobody has heard it yet. It's warm, and human, and honest, and deeply moving, and it's funny. It's going to be a classic, and that means two things: first, a lot of comics will steal it, even though no one will ever do it as well as Bill; and second, if Bill wanted to, he could make a living for the rest of his life just from the excitement and joy this one great bit will create. But Bill Cosby, if I am any judge of talent, will keep coming up with fresh, new material and will grow everyday in stature and importance on the American comedy scene.
>
> Bill Cosby would be funny if he were green or purple or chartreuse. He's funny because he can feel for people—and he can communicate that feeling. Listen to "Hoof and Mouth" and see if you can avoid falling on the floor at the conversation between the intelligent cow and the stupid one. Listen to "Toss of the Coin," and rediscover (when you stop screaming with laughter) your own sense of fairness. Listen to "Greasy Kid Stuff," which should put an end once and for all to the use of football players in television commercials.
>
> I wish I could look at your face when you first hear this album. I wish I could be with you when you first discover Bill Cosby. I don't know who you are; all I know is that you are one of millions of people who buy records and who made my life so crazy and wonderful during the last year. I want to return the favor. That's why I'm so proud and happy for the chance to introduce you to Bill Cosby.
>
> It isn't everyday that we come in contact with greatness. The day you first listen to this album will be one of those days for you.

BECAUSE OF SHERMAN'S presence in Cosby's early breaks, people assumed that he had been "found" by Sherman. But it was just happenstance that put him on *The Tonight Show* when Sherman was hosting. However, Warner Brothers saw a marketing opportunity by pairing the two and ran with it, hoping to exploit Sherman's popularity with young people by having him introduce Cosby. Cosby's club bookings began rolling in now as well, such as an invitation to appear at the legendary Mister Kelly's in Chicago, where all the big names—Lenny Bruce, Dick Gregory, Cosby-favorite Jonathan Winters—had told jokes.

Cosby started introducing funny, warmhearted stories from his childhood in the Richard Allen Homes to his act, which would become a vital part of his material. He then came up with a three-minute bit that he considered perhaps the best thing he had ever written:

> When I was a child, the grown-ups were trying to murder us. I have proof! We had a perfectly good playground, perfectly good! They tore down some houses, and we called it our playground. It had broken glass and rocks and bricks, but we never lost one kid. Maybe a little gash here or there, but that's all right. . . . And then the grown-ups moved in the monkey bars. We lost one hundred twenty-four kids in one day! Kids were falling off the monkey bars like snowflakes! Broken arms, legs, everything! I made it my philosophy from then on to never play on nothing I didn't see no grown-ups playing on. You never saw grown-ups playing on no monkey bars! They would build them, but they wouldn't play on them! And the last thing they put up was the seesaw. An out-and-out attempt to kill us! They even got another kid in on the plot. There are a lot of kids who never had a chance to have a deep voice because of that seesaw! (Whitaker 2014, 124)

AFTER *THE TONIGHT Show,* Cosby got invited to appear on its chief competitor, *The Jack Paar Show. The Garry Moore Show* came calling soon after, but the week he was booked there, President Kennedy was assassinated. He went on anyway and delivered laughs at a time the country was mourning. That impressed Johnny Carson, who booked him back on *The Tonight Show* in early December. Carson liked Cosby so much that when Carson went on vacation in January 1964, they asked Cosby to guest host. Later that year he released his second comedy album, *I Started Out as a Child*, which sold 150,000 copies in the first year. His career was rapidly taking off.

While he wasn't eager to travel south and join Dick Gregory in protest marches, Cosby was still closely watching the daily battles of the movement. He began sending money to organizers, and he encouraged others to join him—"even if it's only a quarter" (Frierson 2020, 63). He also appeared at fundraisers, offering his talent to the cause. He participated in the NAACP's television special in May 1964 called *Freedom Spectacular*, which also featured Gregory, Lena Horne, Ossie Davis, and Harry Belafonte, among others, with a goal of raising a million dollars.

> In a sense, Cosby's presentation of an essentially colorless comedy routine was revolutionary. No previous African-American comedian had attempted or been allowed to step so boldly into this non-racial territory before non-black audiences. Whether intended or not, Cosby's outward congeniality was crucial to his quick ascendancy. At a time when racial confrontations were escalating in the streets, his relaxed, chatty style and surface image of a clean-cut, sanguine black man was the antithesis of the menacing figures on the street. And mainstream America, though it could abide the slashing satiric wit and more easily perceived anger of a Dick Gregory, seems to have been consoled by the playful brilliance of Cosby's approach. (Watkins 1994, 504)

While he was on the road, Cosby had not forgotten about the lovely Camille Hanks. His career was soaring; maybe now he was an acceptable match for her. In fall 1963, when he called her at her parents' home, she told him in her soft, fetching voice that she still loved him and wanted to be with him—which he said was the "most delicious sound I ever heard." He bought the most expensive ring he could afford—a $250 diamond, with some visible flecks of coal—and left Greenwich Village to head to Maryland. When he got there, he was poised to ask her father for her hand.

"Come down to the basement," her father said. "I want to talk to you" (Whitaker 2014, 129).

Cosby surely didn't expect what he heard next. "Do me a favor," Guy Hanks told him. "Take my girl off my hands because her mother is driving me crazy!"

While Camille's mother wasn't too giddy about the pairing, she hosted the wedding at the Hanks home on January 25, 1964. Camille was just nineteen. She soon found herself thrust into the strange, unpredictable lifestyle of a nightclub entertainer. An early incident illustrates the playful side of Cosby to which Camille quickly had to learn to adapt. It took place during a time when Cosby was obsessed with the genius of John Coltrane, who happened to be doing an extended stint at the Half Note in the Village with his quartet that included drummer Elvin Jones, a friend of Cosby's. When Jones was introduced to Camille, he wrapped her in a hug while dripping with sweat, soaking Camille's dress in his perspiration.

When Cosby waved Jones over to their table on the next night, he got an eyeful from Camille, who gave Bill a pleading look. The look backfired. "Hey, Elvin!" he called out, pointing to Camille. "Guess who's here? Come on over and say hello!"

Cosby's life would change dramatically in 1965. That's when he met Hollywood producer Sheldon Leonard, who was on the hunt for an actor to costar in a television series he was developing about two secret agents pretending to be professional tennis players. As he was describing his idea for the show to Cosby, Leonard paused.

"I intend for one of those agents to be Black!" he said. "And I believe that you have the natural personality to play that role!"

With those two sentences, he not only dramatically changed

Cosby's life, but he set in motion a plan that would transform the face of television.

It was actually Rob Reiner, Carl Reiner's son, who was just sixteen at the time, who had discovered Cosby for Leonard. His parents were out for the evening, so Rob was free to stay up late and watch *The Tonight Show*. One of his dad's former colleagues on *Your Show of Shows*, Selma Diamond, was a guest, in addition to journalist Jimmy Breslin and Bill Cosby. When his parents got home at around one a.m., his father was incensed (Whitaker 2014, 133).

"What are you doing awake?" Carl asked him. "You have school tomorrow."

"I just watched the greatest comedian I've ever seen!" he said. "His name is Bill Cosby. Let me show you the routine he did."

Rob acted out Cosby's "Noah" routine, which he somehow had already memorized. His father loved it. "You're right! That's very funny. Now go to bed!" But Carl thought that perhaps Cosby was the guy Sheldon Leonard was seeking for his new show. Reiner and Leonard were working together at the time as producers of *The Dick Van Dyke Show*. With his partner, comedian Danny Thomas, Leonard had created *The Danny Thomas Show*, *The Real McCoys*, *My Favorite Martian*, and *The Andy Griffith Show*, but he had grown tired of the sitcom format. He wanted to bring a bold new show out into the world. Televisions were growing larger and were now available in color; the shows on television needed to reflect these changes by giving viewers more interesting scenery, outside of studio lots, in the real world. He also wanted to cash in on the public's new interest in espionage after the success of the first James Bond movie, *Dr. No*, which came out in 1962, starring Sean Connery.

As executives at NBC prepared to introduce *I Spy* to the world, Cosby was increasingly being asked his views on race. Racial tensions were boiling over across the country. James Chaney, Andrew Goodman, and Michael Schwerner, three young civil rights workers in Mississippi for the Freedom Summer protests, disappeared on June 21, 1964. Their bodies were found three weeks later, murdered by local Klan members. The national outrage over the murders was a major factor in the passage of the Civil Rights Act of 1964 and the Voting Rights Act of 1965. A Black performer as prominent and successful as Cosby was inevitably going to be forced to speak on the racial fires burning. In a profile in *Jet* by reporter Chester Higgins that was published in August 1964, Cosby's frustrations shone through.

"I am trying to make people laugh," he said in the article. "I think with all the racial tension on the outside, people appreciate coming in to see me. Some people may be disappointed because I don't tell racial tension jokes. But the majority, I believe, enjoy me because I don't. . . . I'm highly aware of the Negro struggle for freedom. Ask me my private views, and I won't hesitate to voice them. But I feel it's time for the Negro to just be a comedian. And I aim to be one who tells funny stories that everyone can identify with."

After Cosby, prominent Black performers and artists would inevitably be confronted with the question, particularly if they seemed inclined to avoid the topic: *Why don't you talk more about race?*

The stakes couldn't have been clearer when the December 23, 1964, issue of *Variety* ran a preview of the fall television season with the headline "Television's Jackie Robinson." The article stated, "For the first time in TV history, a Negro (albeit on a costar basis) will have his name atop the marquee of a continuing prime-time TV series." The comparison made Cosby anxious but determined. For their part, the executives overseeing the show were getting strange phone calls from NBC execs, who were still unsure of the wisdom of casting Cosby, fearing the show would have problems in the South. But they eventually leaned into the idea, taking out a seven-page ad in *Variety* touting the coming drama.

On April 8, five months before the show's premiere, Camille and Bill welcomed their first child, a girl they named Erika. He got some vindication for his comedic decisions as his album *I Started Out as a Child* won a Grammy for best comedy performance. As the show's premiere got closer, NBC execs were nervous about how many stations would refuse to air it. A week beforehand, they got their answer: It would be carried on 180 stations, with just four opting out—in Savannah, Georgia; Birmingham, Alabama; Alexandria, Louisiana;

and Daytona Beach, Florida. The show's first episode was well received by critics and viewers alike.

"Cosby is presented without any emphasis whatsoever on his race," wrote Ben Gross in the *New York Daily News* after the show's 1965 premiere. "His presence is merely taken for granted and thereby more is achieved for better racial relations than by a thousand propaganda exhortations" (Whitaker 2014, 163).

Veteran actor Robert Culp, who started out as the lead, actually wrote scripts for the show that would elevate Cosby's status. In the fifth week, one of his scripts aired, giving Cosby a love interest in the form of the sexy Eartha Kitt. The episode also allowed Cosby to show his developing acting talent after he displayed some awkwardness in the first episode.

Cosby's new television stardom boosted his asking price substantially for his stand-up comedy. He was now getting as much as $20,000 per show, meaning he could gross nearly $100,000 in a weekend. Though he was incredibly busy on *I Spy*, he never stopped doing stand-up. He didn't know how long the gravy train would continue to rumble, and he wanted to exploit every opportunity. His comedy albums were hot now as well, with all four of his Warner Brothers albums sitting on the *Billboard* Hot 100 list, the first time a comedian had accomplished that.

I Spy finished its first season as the second-most-watched drama on television during the spring of 1966. The show got nominated for seven Emmys that year, including nominations for both Cosby and Culp for Outstanding Actor in a Dramatic Series. Ironically, Cosby was nominated for a script written by Culp. Cosby, who was asked to co-host the Emmy telecast, took home the statue—and proceeded to beat Culp for the Emmy each of the three seasons the show was on the air. In the second season, Cosby's character even fell in love, with a female agent played by Cicely Tyson—thus answering the Black critics who wondered when he would have a steady girlfriend.

Cosby was now rich, driving around LA in his Cadillac or his Rolls-Royce, renting an eleven-room house with a swimming pool and sauna for his growing family, which now included a second daughter,

Erinn. Cosby's family members also got to enjoy his successes—when he introduced his stunned mother to Andy Griffith on the lot where *I Spy* was shot, she was so flustered that she reached out and smacked Griffith in the face, with an equally flustered Cosby having to apologize to him.

In the fall of 1968, Cosby was joined on the TV airwaves by two more Black stars—Clarence Williams III in *The Mod Squad* and Diahann Carroll in *Julia*. Surely Cosby's success on *I Spy* had something to do with their casting. In an article in *Ebony*, Cosby voiced words that proved to be incredibly prescient: "Someday I want to do a family situation comedy on television. And it will be a hit because people want to see what goes on in a Negro home today."

Along with his manager, Roy Silver, and film producer Bruce Campbell, Cosby formed a production company, the Campbell, Silver, Cosby Corporation, that garnered a five-movie deal with Warner. They also started a record label called Tetragrammaton. Published reports put the company's net worth at $50 million. Cosby was excited because he was going to be able to hire Black folks and give them valuable experience. "Because the more he thought about it, the more convinced he was that creating jobs for brothers and sisters was the greatest personal contribution that he could make to the Black Power movement" (Whitaker 2014, 205).

Cosby, who remained suspicious of the media because they inevitably would want to ask about his views on race, granted an interview in 1968 with *Playboy*, whose Playboy Interview was becoming a cultural touchstone. In the piece, he voiced a pragmatic racial philosophy whose tone would only grow harsher over the years, suggesting that the best way for Blacks to advance was through education, business, and politics—as opposed to the violence being advocated by the Black Power movement.

"I feel I've really put together a hell of a one-man anti-poverty program," he said. "I took my talent and I put it to work, and today, I've brought up, by the bootstraps, the economic conditions of a mother, a father, two brothers, aunts, uncles, grandfathers, and other family members, and then reached out to help close friends. . . . The next step is to help out other black people. This doesn't simply mean giving them five hundred thousand dollars—although I give plenty. But to me, reaching out to black people means to open up my particular part of the industry."

In 1969, Cosby discovered that his partners had squandered millions of dollars, and he was on the verge of going broke. His agent at William Morris, Norman Brokaw, reported to him that he was down to $50,000 in the bank. Cosby was devastated, outraged, and humiliated that he had allowed it to happen. He fired Silver and severed ties with his production company.

Relying on his popularity, Cosby began to rebuild his coffers, going on the road and then signing a seven-year deal with MCA Records for more comedy albums. He had won four consecutive Grammys for his comedy albums and had even recorded two R&B albums that produced a big hit, "Little Old Man," that reached number four on the *Billboard* Hot 100. After the financial debacle, Cosby put Camille— who had studied accounting at the University of Maryland—in charge of the money, an arrangement that would continue for the rest of his career. Despite the setbacks, April 1969 saw a new addition to the Cosby family—they finally had a son, whom they named Ennis.

In September that year, Cosby developed a new sitcom, *The Bill Cosby Show*, for NBC. With a theme song produced by Quincy Jones and guest appearances by a raft of Black stars, including Mantan Moreland and Moms Mabley, Cosby played a gym teacher, Chet Kincaid, who got ensnared in mishaps every episode. Though the show was nominated for Emmys in each of its two seasons, it got canceled after season two; the strong ratings in the beginning—it finished eleventh in its first season—fell off in the second season, when it dropped out of the top thirty. NBC executives weren't too upset about the show's demise—Cosby had clearly lost interest in the show by season two— because the network's new *The Flip Wilson Show* was an enormous hit, finishing as the number two show on the air for its first two seasons.

With much of his own money, Cosby produced and starred in a Western called *Man and Boy* that turned out to be a big box office disappointment. He also put his money into another venture that turned out to be much more profound: He gave a brilliant young filmmaker, Melvin Van Peebles, the $50,000 he needed to finish filming *Sweet Sweetback's Baadasssss Song*, which in 1971 grossed more than $15 million and became a cult phenomenon. Unfortunately, the film's success spawned a raft of painful imitators, in what became known as the blaxploitation era of Black film, showcasing silly plots and often even sillier performances.

When the producers of *Sesame Street* came up with the concept of a more education-focused program called *The Electric Company*, they recruited Cosby to join a cast that included Academy Award–winner Rita Moreno (*West Side Story*) and an up-and-coming actor named Morgan Freeman. Cosby was only on *The Electric Company* for one season, but that was enough to help it become the most successful program for school-age children in the history of television. The show was even credited with an increase in the nation's reading scores. It also established Cosby's magic with young children. As he left the show, Cosby had reversed his own checkered relationship with the classroom and had earned a master's degree from the University of Massachusetts, after relocating his young family to the East Coast to get away from the madness and crime of Los Angeles.

Cosby was eager to produce his own animated children's television show built around his Fat Albert character. When NBC passed on the idea, CBS's young programmer Fred Silverman jumped on it. The University of Massachusetts allowed Cosby to use the creation of *Fat Albert and the Cosby Kids* as the subject for his doctoral dissertation. The cartoon, which is loosely based on Cosby's childhood experiences growing up in Philadelphia, launched in the fall of 1972 and remained on the air for a remarkable thirteen years and 110 episodes, eventually being named by *TV Guide* as the best cartoon show of the 1970s. Over the years, Cosby would record the voices for Fat Albert, little Bill, and Mushmouth in all kinds of strange places, including backstage in Vegas and at a radio station in Alaska.

When Cosby left Camille behind in Massachusetts—now with four kids—he would take on a different persona out West, gambling in Vegas and spending time with the beautiful women who swirled around him. But his philandering ways caught up to him in the summer of 1975, when a woman named Shawn Berkes, a lovely fair-skinned brunette he met in Vegas, produced a picture of a curly-haired fourteenth-month-old baby girl and told him she was his daughter. Camille, who had warned him that she wouldn't abide by him embarrassing her, didn't leave, but he had to work hard to earn her forgiveness. However, the cheating didn't stop.

While Cosby was on vacation with his friend Sidney Poitier, the Oscar winner asked Cosby if he would costar in a film he was developing called *Uptown Saturday Night*. He also got Harry Belafonte, Flip Wilson, and Richard Pryor to sign on as well, without even seeing a script. It promised to be a huge blockbuster, bringing together three of the funniest men on the planet. With a script by Richard Wesley, a young Black playwright, the shooting commenced with a crew that was a quarter Black by some estimates. It was a reunion for Cosby and Pryor, who had started his career by crafting an act that was a virtual clone of Cosby's, complete with a clean-cut look and wholesome stories of his childhood. When Cosby had gotten reports about Pryor copying him, his team had called Pryor in for a meeting in early 1969.

> When Pryor arrived for the meeting with Cosby's manager, his eyes darted apprehensively around the room. Silver did most of the talking, scolding Pryor for imitating Cosby and pointing out that Cosby had only become a star after he stopped trying to be another Dick Gregory. Pryor made no effort to defend himself, and [Ron] DeBlasio [who worked for Campbell, Silver, Cosby] sensed that the lecture was resonating with a private struggle that was already going on inside the comedian's head. (Whitaker 2014, 261)

It was a powerful moment that would transform Pryor's life and career. Pryor would later say it was the best thing that ever happened to him. Comedians by necessity watch their competitors closely, looking for anything to give them an edge. However, the stakes now felt higher than they did when Timmie Rogers, Slappy White, and Nipsey Russell accused Dick Gregory of stealing their material in 1961. Though Cosby wasn't physically there, this was one of the most consequential meetings in Black comedy history.

Uptown Saturday Night did good work at the box office when it came out in 1974, making more ($7 million in the first year) than all the blaxploitation flicks besides *Shaft*. Cosby and Poitier teamed up two more times—*Let's Do It Again* made twice as much as *Uptown*, while 1977's *A Piece of the Action* fell off quite a bit, partly due to the audience's diminishing appetite for blaxploitation films.

In May 1977, Cosby proudly received his doctorate of education, after submitting a 242-page dissertation exploring the educational benefits of *Fat Albert*, *The Electric Company*, and *Sesame Street*. He walked across the graduation stage and officially had a new title: Dr. William H. Cosby Jr. His mother, Anna, sat in the audience, crying tears of joy and pride.

With his new title, Cosby began to lean in even harder to his ambition to be an educator working with young people. Advertisers also began to recognize the wonder of his interactions with children, using him as one of the country's most effective pitchmen for companies such as Jell-O, Del Monte, Coca-Cola, and Ford Motors. In Cosby's first year hawking Jell-O Pudding Pops in 1979, the popsicles hit $100 million in sales.

After years of reshaping the landscape of American comedy with his unique brand of humor rooted in everyday life, Bill Cosby reached a defining milestone: On Thursday, September 20, 1984, NBC debuted *The Cosby Show*, which in many ways was the culmination of Cosby's two decades of crafting comedy gold by focusing on the zaniness of family life. The show centered on the upper-middle-class Huxtable family—Cliff, a lovable obstetrician; Clair, a sharp-witted attorney; and their five children: Sondra, Denise, Theo, Vanessa, and Rudy.

Though most TV insiders were certain the show would get trounced in its time slot by the ratings juggernaut *Magnum P.I.*, the critics from the *New York Times*, the *Washington Post*, and the *Los Angeles Times* all immediately declared that it was the best new sitcom of the season, and they implored NBC to give the show time to find its audience. But the critics' fears turned out to be unfounded: The show shot past *Magnum P.I.* and was the most-watched TV show of the week with 21.6 million viewers.

Cosby's producing partners Marcy Carsey and Tom Werner pulled him aside during a rehearsal to deliver the news.

"Bill, you're not going to believe this," Carsey said. "The show last week was number one!"

"You mean in our time slot?" Cosby said.

"No, for the week."

"You're kidding," Cosby said. "You mean we beat *60 Minutes*?"

"Yes," she said.

"Call Camille!" he bellowed (Whitaker 2014, 318).

Cosby's interactions with the young cast members, much of it improvised by him, turned out to be comic gold every week. In one episode, called "The Slumber Party," Cosby ad-libbed an entire scene where he is entertaining the friends of young Rudy, played by the adorable Keshia Knight Pulliam, by making them laugh uncontrollably. One of the friends was four-year-old Alicia Cook, who the world would later know as musician Alicia Keys. The part of the youngest Huxtable child was supposed to be played by a boy, but when Pulliam auditioned, she was so natural and cute that everyone quickly pivoted—though they still called her Rudy.

Whitney Houston and Vanessa Williams were considered to play teenage children on the show, but both had other commitments that the world came to know very well.

The show quickly became the third-most-watched show on the airwaves—and the first NBC show to finish in the top ten in years—losing only to *Dynasty* and *Dallas*. By its second season, it would move to the top of the ratings heap, finishing number one for five consecutive seasons—something only also achieved by *All in the Family*. Seemingly overnight, the show became a national institution, remarkably turning the fictional Huxtables into America's favorite family. It was an incredible statement, coming less than two decades after television executives were terrified that a show with a Black star wouldn't attract advertisers. Now, the top show on television was helmed by the nation's top pitchman, an African American who seemed to be sought after by every major brand in America. White fans would tell Cosby that it felt as if the show's writers were eavesdropping on their own families. This was the ultimate sign that the country had undergone dramatic change: white Americans felt as if their lives were reflected in the lives of Black people. It also was a redemption of sorts for Cosby, who had endured considerable criticism in the preceding decades that he wasn't Black enough, that his comedy didn't speak to Black struggles. Cosby's response, that he wanted to create comedy that everyone could identify with—and in so doing, make white people more likely to accept and even embrace Blacks—was now vindicated by the show's success.

The show drew huge ratings, but it also was deeply respected in the industry, winning three Emmys, including best comedy series, in its first year. But Cosby, still bearing the scars from his rivalry with Culp on *I Spy*, refused to be considered for an Emmy during the show's run—leading some observers to claim that his rejection led to the Emmys only rewarding the show with six awards over eight seasons. It was even a big hit in overseas markets such as Europe, where the conventional wisdom said a Black sitcom would never find an audience. *TV Guide* eventually ranked it twenty-eighth on its list of the "50 Greatest Shows of All Time"; in 2014, *TV Guide* named Cosby the "Greatest Television Dad."

The show also achieved another marker, highlighting Black romantic love in a way that had never before been seen on television. "After fighting to 'get the girl' on *I Spy*, Cosby now had the power to control the message he wanted to convey about sexual attraction. He used it to make the Huxtables perhaps the most physically affectionate married couple, black or white, that had ever appeared on television." To Cosby's chagrin, the show pulled back on the physicality of their romance after his costar Phylicia Ayers-Allen married former football star and broadcaster Ahmad Rashad (Whitaker 2014, 323).

As the show continued weaving its ratings gold, Cosby began to see the characters on the show as doppelgangers for his real-life family, also composed of five kids including one boy. That freed him up to dissect his own home life for show material, particularly his relationship with his son, Ennis. In real life, Ennis suffered from dyslexia, so Theo (played by Malcolm-Jamal Warner) on the show had dyslexia too. That resulted in this famous exchange between Cliff and Theo:

"You're a doctor and Mom's a lawyer. And you're both successful and everything, and that's great. But maybe, I was born to be a regular person, and have a regular life. If you weren't a doctor, I wouldn't love you less. Because you're my dad. And so, instead of acting disappointed, because I'm not like you, maybe you can just accept who I am, and love me anyway. Because I'm your son."

The applause from the audience was loud and sustained. Cosby let it sit for a moment. Then he responded:

"Theo, that's the dumbest thing I've ever heard in my life. No wonder you get D's in everything! Now you are afraid to try because you're afraid that your brain is going to explode, and it's going to ooze out of your ears. Now I'm telling you, you are going to try as hard as you can. And you're gonna do it because I said so. I am your father. I brought you in this world, and I'll take you out."

The audience's thunderous applause was even louder this time.

The show was a celebration of Black culture in a way Americans had never seen, with the walls in the Huxtable home adorned with Black art and Cosby honoring historically Black colleges by often donning sweatshirts for particular schools—so much so that bestselling author and Howard alum Ta-Nehisi Coates said he would watch the show to see if Cosby was repping his school that week. Cosby used his platform to honor jazz, one of his first loves even before comedy. He brought on artists such as Dizzy Gillespie and Lena Horne and gave them roles to play. He gave work to many of his friends from his past lives—Leslie Uggams, Rita Moreno, Danny Kaye, Robert Culp. He also had legends such as Nancy Wilson, Sammy Davis Jr., B.B. King, and Stevie Wonder on the show, and he gave exposure to Black artists like Ellis Wilson and Varnette Honeywood—dramatically increasing the value of their art.

One of the show's most famous episodes reflected Cosby's music background. He wanted to have the family celebrate Cliff's parents' anniversary by lip-synching to Ray Charles's 1958 hit "(Night Time Is) The Right Time," which he first heard in the navy. He asked Phylicia Ayers-Allen, a former dancer, to choreograph the family's moves, showcasing her and the four daughters shimmying and shaking like Ray's backup dancers, the Raelettes. Theo mouthed the first verse, then Keshia Knight Pulliam stole the show doing the Ray Charles wail, "Baaabbbyyy!" Cosby came in next, contorting his elastic face in comical ways as he sang the next verse. According to *TV Guide*, the "Happy Anniversary" episode was one of the 100 greatest TV episodes of all time. It was even spoofed by *Saturday Night Live*.

Another endearing plotline in the run of *The Cosby Show* was, as mentioned above, when Theo had an academic breakthrough and discovered his struggles in the classroom weren't because he wasn't smart enough but because he was dyslexic. Theo's storyline reflected the revelation that the real-life Cosbys had experienced with son Ennis, who flourished academically after his own diagnosis. His dad would later beam with pride when Ennis received his diploma from Morehouse College in 1992.

One persistent criticism leveled at the show was that its characters weren't "realistic" depictions of African Americans—which ignored the fact that both Phylicia Rashad and Camille Cosby came from distinguished, well-educated families of professionals very much like the Huxtables. Cosby had grown close to Harvard psychiatrist Dr. Alvin Poussaint, who spent most of his career studying race. Poussaint told Cosby that the critics wanted the show to address chronic problems confronting poor Blacks. In the *New York Times*, historian Henry Louis Gates, one of the most prominent Black scholars in America, wrote a piece that examined the show's representation of Blackness. First, Gates credited *The Cosby Show* with setting the stage for a raft of Black sitcoms that came in its wake, such as *Family Matters* and

The Fresh Prince of Bel-Air. He acknowledged that the 1980s was "the Cosby decade" and credits its profound effect on television:

> Historically, blacks have always worried aloud about the image that white Americans harbor of us, first because we have never had control of those images and, second, because the greater number of those images have been negative. And given television's immediacy, and its capacity to reach so many viewers so quickly, blacks, at least since *Amos 'n' Andy* back in the early '50s, have been especially concerned with our images on the screen.... Later, when American society could not successfully achieve the social reformation it sought in the '60s through the Great Society, television solved the problem simply by inventing symbols of that transformation in the '80s, whether it was Cliff Huxtable—whom we might think of as the grandson of Alexander Scott (played by Mr. Cosby in *I Spy*, 1965–68)—or *Benson* (1979–86), the butler who transforms himself into a lieutenant governor.
>
> Today, blacks are doing much better on TV than they are in real life, an irony underscored by the use of black public figures (Mr. Cosby, Michael Jackson, Michael Jordan, Bobby McFerrin) as spokesmen for major businesses. When Mr. Cosby, deadpan, faces the camera squarely and says, "E. F. Hutton. Because it's my money," the line blurs between Cliff Huxtable's successful career and Mr. Cosby. This helps to explain why Cosby makes some people uncomfortable: As the dominant representation of blacks on TV, it suggests that blacks are solely responsible for their social conditions, with no acknowledgement of the severely constricted life opportunities that most black people face.

In 1988, the Cosbys gave Spelman College an astonishing gift: $20 million. It was nearly half the size of Spelman's $42 million endowment, far more than any individual had ever given an HBCU. The amount was so large that it made the front page of the *New*

York Times. Cosby was able to give that astounding amount because the syndication rights to the show's first three seasons sold for an eye-popping $600 million, making Carsey and Werner tremendously wealthy and netting Cosby an estimated $166 million. Though much of Cosby's wealth came from this, the most lucrative syndication deal in television history at the time, some of it also flowed from his role as America's pitchman, in addition to his many stand-up concerts and now his bestselling books.

THE SHOW PERHAPS created one of the most momentous finales in television history when in April 1992, Clair and Cliff waltzed off the set together, a period on the end of one of the most successful shows ever on television.

In the annals of NBC history, it can't be overstressed how *The Cosby Show* rescued the network from oblivion. And across the television landscape, many of the shows that came in its wake, and the comedians that helmed them, owed their approach to innovations made by Cosby. *Seinfeld* sprouted from the comedic observations of its creator, Jerry Seinfeld, who grew up on Long Island obsessed with Cosby—and who said hearing a Cosby album for the first time might have been the most important event of his childhood. Larry David allowed his actors on *Curb Your Enthusiasm* to improvise, much like Cosby preferred. *Home Improvement* and *Everybody Loves Raymond* were both based on the observation humor of comedians, Tim Allen and Ray Romano, respectively.

The nation was devastated to hear the news on January 16, 1997, that Ennis Cosby was killed during an attempted carjacking on the 405 in Los Angeles. Ennis had been changing a flat tire at 1:30 in the morning when he was approached by an eighteen-year-old who shot him in the head. The news was particularly gut-wrenching to the Cosby family because Ennis had come so far in transforming his life. He was in the process of earning his doctorate in education, after earning his master's from Columbia Teachers College. His parents had promised to finance his dream of opening his own school. The handsome, gregarious Ennis was just twenty-seven. Cosby received a tremendous outpouring of love from a heartbroken public, prompting the family to form the Ennis William Cosby Foundation to focus on learning disabilities.

Cosby's first comment to the public conveyed his immense grief: "He was my hero," he said quietly before walking into the family's Manhattan townhouse.

Three days before Cosby turned sixty-five, on July 9, 2002, he received the Presidential Medal of Freedom, presented to him by George W. Bush. "From television to film, from stand-up comedy to bestselling books," the announcer intoned, "Bill Cosby's good-natured humor has always appealed to our common humanity, helping to bring people together through laughter. The United States proudly honors this truly outstanding American."

But Cosby began to chip away at the bright halo that had long been positioned on his head by an adoring public. His first salvo was what widely became known as the "pound cake" speech. At a black-tie gala in Washington, DC, to celebrate the fiftieth anniversary of the Supreme Court's *Brown v. Board of Education* decision, a frustrated Cosby went after the Black community for what he saw as failures of character, attacking poor Black people, single mothers, absentee fathers, and young Black girls and boys.

"Ladies and gentlemen, the lower economic and lower middle economic people are not holding up their end in this deal. In the neighborhoods that most of us grew up in, parenting is not going on. . . . I'm talking about these people who cry when their son is standing there in an orange suit! Where were you when he was two? Where were you when he was twelve? Where were you when he was eighteen, and how come you don't know he had a pistol? And where is his father, and why don't you know where he is? And why doesn't the father show up to talk to this boy? . . .

"You can't keep asking Jesus to do things for you. . . . God is tired of you," he continued. "Looking at the incarcerated—these are not political criminals! These are people going around stealing Coca-Cola! People getting shot in the head over a piece of pound cake!

Then we all run out and are outraged: 'The cops shouldn't have shot him!' What the hell was he doing with the pound cake in his hand?" (Whitaker 2014, 437)

Cosby kept going, making fun of Black youth for the way they dressed and the names they were given by their parents. He said women were having babies too young and men were sleeping with too many women. The tirade was tone-deaf and it certainly wasn't funny. Many of the things he said were no different than what many Black people have said amongst themselves, but he was saying this out loud, with seemingly not an ounce of empathy or compassion. The reaction to Cosby's speech wasn't uniform in the Black community, as many younger African Americans went after Cosby for being clueless and out of touch, while many older Black people agreed with him—though they weren't pleased about the forum he chose. Ta-Nehisi Coates wrote a vicious piece in the *Village Voice* calling out Cosby for being embarrassed by the Black poor:

> Cosby's audience was reportedly shocked by the classist diatribe. They shouldn't have been. Throughout his career, Bill Cosby has been many beautiful things—brilliant humorist, anti-apartheid activist, champion of historically black colleges, to name a few. But over the past couple of decades, he's played one ugly role that his activist friends like to ignore—patron saint of black elitists. . . .
>
> Race still matters, but largely the problems of black people today are the problems of poor people. In his last days, Martin Luther King turned his attention to class, a focus Cosby's brethren airbrushed away. They could march on Washington every 10 years without having to march on their own drug-riddled corners. They ignore the ghetto or, when emboldened like Cosby, shit on it.

The Black scholar and author Michael Eric Dyson wrote a whole book in response to Cosby, *Is Bill Cosby Right? Or Has the Black Middle Class Lost Its Mind?* that in 2005 made the *New York Times* bestseller list. From the caustic tone of his critique, it's clear that Dyson was choosing the latter of his two options. An enraged Cosby reportedly told friends that Dyson was a "poverty pimp"—someone perceived to exploit marginalized communities for financial or reputational gain (Whitaker 2014, 443). Cosby's own response to his critics came in the form of another book, his 2007 tome *Come On, People: On the Path from Victims to Victors*, which he wrote with Alvin Poussaint. Cosby and Poussaint donated 5,000 copies to schools and prisons across the country.

Ta-Nehisi Coates got an earful from his own father about his attacks on Cosby. W. Paul Coates, a prominent activist and the founder of the Black publishing house Black Classic Press in Baltimore, told his son he should take Cosby's comments more seriously. So, Ta-Nehisi spent considerable time with Cosby to write another piece, entitled "This Is How We Lost to the White Man," comparing Cosby's callout to the actions and speeches of Malcolm X, and aligning Cosby's "organic black conservatism" with the long history of similar thought expressed in Black barbershops, churches, and backyard barbecues.

When Barack Obama was elected president in 2008, many observers credited "the Cosby Effect" with creating an environment where white voters, who had worshipped the Huxtables for years, were now comfortable electing a Black man to the nation's most powerful office.

In October 2014, a young Black comedian named Hannibal Buress did a set in Philly, Cosby's hometown, during which he told a two-minute joke about Cosby that hit the public like a car explosion.

"Bill Cosby has the fucking smuggest old black man public persona that I hate," Buress said. "'Pull your pants up, black people. I was on TV in the '80s. I can talk down to you because I had a successful sitcom.' Yeah, but you raped women, Bill Cosby. So, brings you down a couple notches. 'I don't curse onstage.' But yeah, you're a rapist.

"I want to just at least make it weird for you to watch *Cosby Show* reruns," he continued. "If you don't know about it, trust me. When you leave here, Google 'Bill Cosby rape.' That shit has more results than 'Hannibal Buress.'"

The clip began to gain traction and eventually went viral as more people learned about the vileness of Cosby's sexual past. The attention brought out more and more women who accused Cosby of assaulting them, claiming they were drugged and assaulted or raped. A total of more than sixty women have accused Cosby in incidents that ranged from 1965 to 2008, occurring in ten different states and in Canada.

While the statute of limitations had expired for most of the incidents, Cosby finally was brought to trial in June 2017 on charges of aggravated indecent assault, with proceedings ending in a mistrial. However, he was found guilty of the same three felony charges in April 2018 and sentenced to three to ten years in state prison. His conviction eventually was overturned by the Pennsylvania Supreme Court in June 2021 when it was revealed that the Montgomery County prosecutor had promised Cosby he wouldn't be prosecuted if he agreed to testify in a civil case brought against him by a Temple employee, Andrea Constand. Constand wound up settling her case against Cosby for a reported $3 million. But then a new prosecutor used Cosby's testimony from that civil case to bring criminal charges against him, thus violating the previous agreement. Cosby was allowed to go free. In 2022, a jury ruled that Cosby had sexually assaulted Judy Huth in 1975, when she was sixteen, and Cosby was ordered to pay $500,000 in compensatory damages. In 2023, another nine women filed sexual assault suits against Cosby.

Reruns of *The Cosby Show* were subsequently removed from a number of television channels, such as BET and TV Land, while TV One decided to continue airing episodes. Many colleges and universities revoked the honorary degrees they had granted Cosby and severed other ties to the disgraced comic. In the wake of the revelations, the lawsuits, and the criminal conviction, the public must still grapple with a vexing question: *Do Cosby's misdeeds cancel his massive accomplishments?*

Can we enjoy his gifts to humanity without considering his monstrous actions? That may be a question we each can only answer as individuals.

CHAPTER 12
RICHARD PRYOR

It is sweetly ironic that the greatest comedian of the twentieth century spent nearly the first decade of his career completely at a loss for what kind of comedian he wanted to be. He had grown up in a brothel with a prostitute mother and a pimp father, mostly raised by a grandmother who was one of the most respected—and feared—madams in Peoria, Illinois. But as he began his comedy career in 1960—after getting kicked out of the service—Pryor tried to run as far from his past as he could. Once he witnessed the success of Cosby, he decided to become a genial PG-rated comic telling stories about a wholesome childhood—that was a total work of fiction. In effect, the war that raged in Pryor's head was a microcosm of the battle that Black comedians had engaged in for decades: *How much of private Black life and private Black thoughts should be shared with white people? If we reveal too much, will they reject us? Will they be horrified? Frightened?*

Pryor grappled with these monumental questions. And nobody shared more private Black thoughts than Richard Pryor. He was an incredibly mercurial character, driven by his excesses, his drug use, his sexual appetites, his desire to fight for his people, and his neuroses about being taken advantage of. It all mixed together in an exciting stew of rage and insecurity that bubbled just below the surface—though at times the stew would breach the surface and explode in menacing and riveting ways.

Finally, a performer had mounted the stage whose speech and mannerisms felt like how Black folks talked amongst themselves when complaining about white people. There was very little space between Pryor onstage and the funny uncle who kept every family gathering in stitches.

> Dick Gregory had exposed the wit and acerbic social commentary that often infuses black humor. Bill Cosby had advanced the art of storytelling or 'lying' in his act. And while introducing upbeat comic characters steeped in black street lore, Flip Wilson had revealed not only blacks' pride in their folkways but also the exuberance and joy of much black humor. Pryor incorporated all of these attributes and, thereby, completely unmasked the complex matrix of pride, self-mockery, blunt confrontation of reality, double-edged irony, satiric wit, assertive defiance, poetic obscenity, and verbal acuity that finally define the elusive entity that may be called African-American humor. It was nothing short of revolutionary. (Watkins 1994, 562)

When his third album, *That Nigger's Crazy*, was released in 1974, it was like someone had detonated a nuclear bomb in the precincts of American comedy. Yes, the album quickly went gold and proceeded to win Pryor's first Grammy, but it was the album's tone and content that blew away both the listening public and other comedians. Miraculously, the album topped *Billboard*'s R&B charts even though it carried an X rating. Pryor was mining the familiar comic territory of the differences between Blacks and whites, but it sounded different—more insightful, more profane, more lurid—than anything that had come before. And most profound of all, it just sounded so *Black*. He used his talent of mimicry to render his aunt Maxine sucking on a neckbone: *When she was done with it and threw it on the floor, the family dog looked at her with a puzzled look that said, "What am I supposed to do with that motherfucker?"* Richard turned that piece of profanity, the word *motherfucker*, into high art. A wino coming upon Dracula in the ghetto gives him one look and tells him he better see an orthodontist. These were "characters whose bravado came from embracing their idiosyncrasies" (Saul 2014, 330).

The same could be said of Pryor himself, who eagerly embraced every single idiosyncratic bone in his body. After he won his second straight Grammy for his next album, . . . *Is It Something I Said?*, he declared to the world in a *Los Angeles Times* interview, "Some people say there's no 'best' in comedy. They're wrong. I'm the best."

Between *Lady Sings the Blues* in 1972 and the groundbreaking *Richard Pryor: Live in Concert* in 1979, Pryor appeared in fourteen films. Several were major commercial successes, such as *The Bingo Long Traveling All-Stars & Motor Kings* and *Silver Streak*. Eddie Murphy has called *Richard Pryor: Live in Concert* "the single greatest stand-up performance ever captured on film," while Pauline Kael wrote in the *New Yorker* that it was "probably the greatest of all recorded-performance films. . . . Everything he does seems to be for the first time." There had never been a stand-up performance presented as a major movie release, which is kind of hard to imagine in an age when such stand-up specials are ubiquitous, from the Kings of Comedy (Bernie Mac, Steve Harvey, Cedric the Entertainer, D. L. Hughley) to Dave Chappelle, Chris Rock, and Kevin Hart. Pryor demonstrated that there was no limit to how big an audience a skilled comedian could bring.

Pryor co-wrote the groundbreaking *Blazing Saddles*, along with Mel Brooks and a few others, though he remained bitter till the end of his life that the starring role he was expecting to play went instead to the less threatening Cleavon Little. He suspected Brooks didn't want to share the limelight. He was the first Black actor to be paid a million dollars for a film, 1980's *Stir Crazy* with Gene Wilder. In 1975, he was the first Black actor to host *Saturday Night Live*, in its inaugural season. Both Comedy Central and *Rolling Stone* ranked him number one in their list of the greatest comedians of all time.

Pryor came along and curiously embodied nearly all the personas that Black comedians had embodied over the previous three decades—the smart-ass trickster, the straightlaced storyteller, the unapologetic race man, the profane lancer of American hypocrisy, and the just plain ol' crazy jokester. All in the person of this skinny, neurotic, brilliant child of Peoria.

Located 170 miles southwest of Chicago, Peoria earned its name first for its breweries and distilleries, then for the headquarters of Caterpillar and LeTourneau. It was also a city with a vibrant red-light district when Richard was born on December 1, 1940, to Gertrude and Leroy "Buck" Pryor. They both worked for Buck's mother, Marie, who owned two brothels and was one of the scariest characters in Peoria. Close to six feet tall, Marie was an imposing woman who ruled the North Washington Street thoroughfare where her houses were located. "As a madam, Marie had a motto, 'Don't mess with my money,' by which she meant that you shouldn't mess with the money in her hand, the prostitutes whose bodies she owned, and the johns whose cash she was seeking" (Saul 2014, 330). She entertained men both Black and white, not discriminating if they came with the only color that mattered—green. She carried a straight razor that she would use on the johns who tried to slink away without paying and the girls who didn't hand over her 50 percent take. By one eyewitness account, a lot of men were walking the streets of Peoria "with nasty scars around their face." Marie later upgraded to a pistol she kept strapped to her leg. One of her favorite threats was "I'll put my twelves up in your ass," referring to her shoe size.

When she was growing up, Richard's mother, Gertrude, lived just a few blocks from the red-light district and passed the fancy-looking brothels on her way to high school. By the time she had struck out on her own at twenty, she agreed to join Marie's operation. Buck, a large man who had won a Golden Gloves boxing tournament in Chicago at age eighteen, was the muscle behind his mother's business. They weren't married until 1943 when Richard was three, but seven days after the wedding, Buck was inducted into the army—though he was discharged seven months later, deemed mentally unfit. Gertrude was a fleeting presence for most of Richard's life. That meant he was fated to spend his early days with a brothel as his playground and Marie's stable of prostitutes as his playmates.

This is a scene that occurred outside Marie's brothel and was recounted by one of the neighbors on North Washington Street: "Marie was whaling with her fists on the body of a black woman, most likely one of her prostitutes. Buck the boxer was standing on the sidelines. The woman would struggle to get up; Marie would knock her back down, hard enough to draw blood. As this one-sided melee unfolded, a police car rolled down the street and continued on its way; Marie kept whaling" (Saul 2014, 26).

These were the kinds of episodes Richard witnessed regularly during his difficult early years in Peoria. He also witnessed considerable violence in his own home, as Buck used his boxer hands to regularly beat on Gertrude, prompting her eventually to divorce him. He later told Richard he was glad Gertrude left him because he probably would have killed her. In a custody battle over Richard, the judge—never clued in to what the family really did—awarded Buck custody because of Gertrude's adultery and abandoning her child. She wasn't even granted visitation rights with her son, needing Buck's permission to see him.

At home, Richard experienced the viciousness of his grandmother Marie, a complicated woman who insisted on dragging the boy to Morning Star Missionary Baptist Church every Sunday—after a Saturday night of overseeing her own private Sodom and Gomorrah. She made sure young Richard dressed nicely—but she was quick with the switch when he stepped out of line. He told the story of his grandmother taking him fishing and forcing him to put the worm on the hook to prove he wasn't a "sissy."

"If you couldn't put the worm on the hook, you was a faggot," Richard said. "I always identified with the little worm because it seemed like he was talking—*no, don't put me on the hook!*"

When he finally got it on the hook, she said, "See? I told you he wasn't no sissy."

While he could understand and predict Marie's beatings, Richard had no idea when his father, Buck, would explode. Richard's friends said he was "scared to death" of his father and his cruelty. A police officer in town said they didn't worry too much about Richard getting in real trouble: "At the first sign of it, I'd just march him up to his father and he'd kill him."

In Peoria, young Richard was drawn to the movies. He dreamed of one day being a star like Lash LaRue, the lead in the Westerns

Richard adored, a hero who wore all black and looked and sounded like Humphrey Bogart. He also spent many hours in front of the television set, studying the cartoons. He didn't just watch them, he closely scrutinized every detail so that he could imitate their facial expressions, their gestures. He also discovered how good it felt to him to make people laugh. When he fell off the edge of a railing on purpose and his family broke out in laughter, he did it over and over. When he slipped in a pile of dog poop and everybody laughed, he went back and slipped in the poop all over again.

At age six, he was accosted by a teenage boy named Hoss while he was playing in the alley behind North Washington Street.

"Right away, I knew he was trouble," Richard recalled. "I saw it in his bloodshot eyes. I should've run. But I didn't. Because he was right about me in that sense—I was a little chickenshit."

Hoss pushed him into a dark corner and unzipped his own pants. "Suck it," he told Richard. The six-year-old boy did as he was told. Hoss left him in the alley feeling "dirty, humiliated, and ashamed."

At the Irving School, Richard soon learned that he was not going to be a top student. He struggled in his classes, a pattern that would continue throughout his schooling. (After he got famous and became involved with actress Pam Grier, he admitted publicly that she helped him improve his weak reading skills.) He earned F's and D's in most of his classes and got left back at the end of first grade. By third grade, he was the frequent target of bullies. A frail child, he did have one weapon in his arsenal to get back at them: his mouth. He heard plenty of spicy language at the brothel, and he wasn't shy about repeating what he heard.

In addition to his horrible grades, Richard gave his teachers a hard time by acting up in class at every opportunity—throwing spitballs, breaking out in Tarzan imitations, pretending to be Tarzan's chimp buddy. When he made the school basketball team, he entertained his classmates by trying out some of the moves he had seen performed by the Harlem Globetrotters—and was kicked off the team by the end of his first week.

As a fourth grader, Richard had noticed that the white girls at the school were much nicer to him than the white boys. One girl caught his eye and as a gift he gave her a scratchboard—the kind where you could draw on the board and then lift a plastic sheet to erase it. Giddy, she told him it was her new favorite toy. But the bonhomie didn't last long. Her father showed up to the school the next day, demanding to be told which "little nigger" gave her the toy. His teacher gave him up in an instant.

"Nigger, don't you ever give my daughter anything!" the father shouted at him.

Richard didn't understand why this man he didn't know would call him that word. *Why did he hate me?* he wondered.

"If I was four and a half feet tall then, the girl's daddy cut six inches off," Richard said. "Zap. Six inches of self-esteem gone. That was my indoctrination to the Black experience in America."

Richard's father got remarried in 1950, when Richard was nine, to a woman named Viola Anna Hurst, known by everyone as Ann. A light-skinned Creole who likely could pass for white, Ann was a mother figure of sorts to Richard, advocating for him when the Irving School didn't want to take him back after a suspension. Ann made a living on the mattress working for Marie; Richard called her "Mom" anyway. Ann took him out of the Irving School and enrolled him in a Catholic school for fifth grade. But when someone notified school officials how the family made its money, the school told Richard he couldn't come back.

Richard caught a break at his new school, called Blaine-Sumner, when he wound up in the sixth-grade classroom of Margaret Yingst. She saw the talents in the new kid and told him if he got to school on time, she'd let him entertain the class for ten minutes on Friday afternoon. It is a story remarkably similar to those of a legion of comedians who lucked upon a teacher who decided to join them rather than try to beat them, giving up classroom time for them to tell jokes. Cosby, Pryor, Martin Lawrence, Jamie Foxx, all tell stories of being so disruptive in class that a teacher gave them the floor during a specified time—usually Friday afternoon—to entertain.

In seventh grade, Richard stuck out as the only Black student among hundreds of white students at Trewyn School, which had recently opened. One afternoon he went to his teacher, sporting a bloody lip and torn clothes. "What happened?" the teacher asked, staring at the crying boy.

"Those kids out there called me a nigger," he said.

She responded loud enough for the rest of the class to hear. "Well, Richard, that's what you are. Why are you so upset?"

These scarring incidents stayed with Richard long after his schooling days were over. "His later crossover comedy returned to the psychic scenes of his sixth- and seventh-grade classrooms, where there were no other black faces in the room and he had to play to an audience that could not intuit where he was coming from" (Saul 2014, 66).

When Richard was fourteen, he found life at the George Washington Carver Community Center, a plain-looking brick building about a mile from the red-light district where teenagers liked to hang. There he stepped into the tutelage of a young Black woman named Juliette Whittaker, who ran the theater program at the community center. They were working on Whittaker's bohemian version of the classic play *Rumpelstiltskin*. As soon as he watched them rehearse, Richard was desperate to become involved.

"I can do that!" he told her.

When she apologized that the play had already been cast, he said, "I don't care. I'll do anything. I'll do anything." She gave him a bit part as a servant who walks onstage and sneezes. But that didn't last long: He stepped in when the kid playing the king didn't show up to rehearsals—and, Pryor already being Pryor, he had his own interpretation of how the king should act. He modeled his king after his playboy uncle, Dickie, who could unspool quite the smooth lines to the ladies.

"Hey baby, you keep on spinning that straw into gold for me and I'll get you a car," said Richard as king. "Something fine. Something for your mama. I'll make you my woman."

That's what you get when you raise a child in a brothel. Whittaker and the other kids thought he was hilarious. Richard watched his teacher handle every aspect of play production—writing, directing, choreography, set design, costume design. While the other teachers saw Richard heading straight for a brick wall, a dead end, Whittaker saw something else. Over the next year he spent considerable time in his teacher's small office, helping her write and plan future shows. It was his first writing collaboration—something he would repeat often during his storied career with writers such as Mel Brooks and Lily Tomlin. Whittaker brought Richard outside of his neighborhood to introduce him to the world, places such as the local museum or play productions.

Richard transferred for ninth grade to Central High School, where he acted up one time too many in science class and his teacher grabbed him by the scruff of the neck and dragged him from the classroom. But Richard wasn't going along—he took a swing at his teacher. He was expelled from Central. He proceeded to work odd jobs when his father insisted he bring in something to put "in the pot"—shoeshine boy, janitor in a strip club. During *Live in Concert*, Richard acted out the story of what happened when he tried to stand up to Buck and tell him he wasn't going to take any more ass whoopings.

"What? You a man now, motherfucker?" Buck responded.

> He hit me in the chest—hard. He hit me so hard my chest caved in and wrapped around his fist, and I held on to it with my chest. I would not let go so he could hit my ass again. And everywhere he moved his arm, I was hanging on.

When he was fifteen, Richard got a girl pregnant. In a panic, he ran to his father and stepmother, Ann, in tears. He knew he wasn't ready for this yet. Buck, who had fathered four children out of wedlock, asked Richard whether he was sure the child was his. The baby was born in April 1957, but Richard stayed away from the mother and child.

In April 1959, he reported for the US Army. He thought it would allow him to escape from a dead-end life in Peoria and see the world. "Peoria felt like a closed circuit: a third of its restaurants still refused to serve Black customers, and around this time Richard was turned away from the Pantry, a downtown fixture, when he tried to get a hamburger with friends after a late-night movie" (Saul 2014, 82). He was five-foot-ten, with flat feet, and weighing in at an alarmingly skinny 126 pounds. The army decided he was best suited during his two-year tour of duty to be a general laborer—meaning he wasn't really suited for anything.

Pryor found plenty of racism in Europe, especially at the Kaiserslautern base he was assigned, a place that to many Black soldiers felt like Mississippi—after all, the village had embraced the Nazis a little more than a decade earlier. The white GIs warned the German bar owners in the town of Rhineland-Palatinate that they would boycott their bars if they served Black soldiers. So, they confined the Black GIs to one street of bars, known as Little Harlem. A German woman caught with a Black GI might be charged with prostitution and sent to jail. Richard kept messing up, missing reveille, missing formation. Eventually he was kicked out of the army after pulling a switchblade on a superior.

In his memoir, Richard described the incident that led to his expulsion. It happened after the unit had been watching the 1959 film *Imitation of Life*, about a light-skinned Black woman passing for white and her Black mother subsequently dying of heartbreak. One of the white GIs "laughed at the wrong spot," according to Richard. One of the Black GIs, a friend of Richard's, started hitting the white GI who laughed. Richard watched the fight along with the rest of the soldiers, but when it appeared that his friend would lose, Richard joined the tussle—and stabbed the white GI in the back six or seven times, though it didn't appear to slow him down. Richard was sent to the stockade, where he spent the next month before his discharge. A superior said of Richard in his report that he had "a history of violence."

> His retention in the service would be detrimental to unit moral[e] and the personal saf[e]ty of the men forced into contact with him. . . . He does not get along with other men and he continually feels he is being "picked on."

The report doesn't mention race, which was likely the most important factor affecting Richard's behavior in the service. But Richard did leave the army with a clearer idea of his future. Asked to list his occupation during his exit physical, Richard wrote *actor*.

After he got back to Peoria, living with his father again, Richard bounced around town, trying to get into something. He found a welcoming spirit down at the nightclub run by an old neighbor, Harold Parker, a tough guy who used to be married to Peoria's top madam, China Bee, and whose nightclub had become the fanciest in town. Richard lied and told Harold he could sing and play piano. But when he sat down at the piano, flop sweat pouring down his face, he hit the four chords he knew on the piano and sang something best described as nonsense.

"You've got more nerve than anybody I've ever seen," Harold told him. He offered Richard a job as bartender but also allowed him to fill the fifteen-minute intermission between music sets by telling jokes. It was his first professional gig as a comedian. He used it to good effect, assuming different characters onstage that were straight from the surrounding streets of Peoria, like a local preacher and the local wino.

When Richard was twenty, he fell for a curvy seventeen-year-old redhead from Missouri named Patricia Watts. She got pregnant a few months later and accepted Richard's proposal to get married. They were married on June 11, 1961, in Marie's living room; they moved into Marie's house right after the wedding. A local crackdown on Peoria's vibrant vice industry resulted in Marie having to close her brothel. She was now selling liquor from her home, and she converted space into a restaurant serving fried chicken and fish. Patricia had a miscarriage, then quickly got pregnant again. But she decided she'd had enough of Richard's philandering; she moved back into her parents' home just eighty days after the wedding. Richard moved back in with Buck. Patricia had the baby, which they named Richard Jr., but Richard Sr. was not much of a presence in the baby's life.

In the fall of 1962, Richard hit the road, trying his hand on the well-worn Chitlin' Circuit. It's a crucial fact in his evolution that he was effectively the last major Black comedian to go through the gauntlet of the old-school Black clubs and dives. Comedians such as Eddie Murphy and Whoopi Goldberg, who came in Pryor's direct wake, never had to labor on the backbreaking circuit. Murphy became an enormous star virtually overnight, while Goldberg—birth name Caryn Elaine Johnson—had a one-woman show on Broadway called *The Spook Show* and a Grammy for the show's recording before she turned thirty, and an Academy Award before thirty-five for *Ghost*. (Goldberg first made her name playing Moms Mabley in a one-woman show named, simply, *Moms*.)

Pryor had many mishaps on the road—getting robbed in East St. Louis; getting arrested in Pittsburgh for beating up the woman he was dating and spending more than a month in jail. While in Toronto, he opened up *Newsweek* to see a profile of Bill Cosby, whose career was taking off after he stopped talking about race in his act.

"Goddamn it, this nigger's doing what I'm fixing to do," he said to himself. "I want to be the only nigger. Ain't no room for two niggers" (Saul 2014, 114).

And thus began Pryor's two-decade-long dance with Cosby, admiring him, imitating him, arguing with him, befriending him, resenting him. On the road, Pryor's act sounded a lot like Cosby's. He bought a train ticket to New York so he could witness the Cosby phenomenon up close. His first stop was Harlem.

"In two blocks, I saw more Black people than I'd ever seen in my life," he remembered. "Just two blocks, and it was beautiful and it was exciting. And I looked and I felt it and I loved it, and I wanted to be part of it. Everyone talks about 'Don't walk in Harlem.' I felt safer than I ever felt in my life."

But the booking agent at the Apollo told Richard he needed to try Greenwich Village, which he had never heard of. It was a great time to be arriving on the shores of the Village, this hip, bohemian headquarters. Comedian Buck Henry would say of the Village in the early 1960s, "It was a time when every doorway late at night had someone standing in it who would later be famous" (Saul 2014, 117).

Richard found his people among the hippie dope smokers and cocaine sniffers, while he tried his material at clubs such as the Cafe

Wha? and The Bitter End. But he didn't feel totally comfortable living among the Village denizens, who he thought were snobbish, so he rented a small apartment in Brooklyn. He was still trying to run from his past in his act, still trying to channel Cosby. He was blown away when he caught Cosby live at the Cafe Wha?

"The man was amazing. Truly amazing," he said. "Do you hear me? I was amazed."

He studied Cosby's records to dissect what made them work. He tried to do some Cosby-esque storytelling in his act, which consisted mostly of impressions of characters such as Sammy Davis Jr. and Alfred Hitchcock. Other comedians confronted him about stealing from Cosby, but he said he was following the money. It was no secret—a review in the *New York Herald Tribune* said that Pryor has "got guts. He uses Bill Cosby's style, mannerisms, inflections, and much of Cosby's material without batting an eyelash. Be yourself, Richard, so we can pan (or applaud) you on your own."

The owner of Cafe Wha?, Manny Roth, told him he can't be Cosby. "You'll never be Cosby in a million years. But you know what? You're going to be bigger and better than Cos."

Cosby was a calm, genial figure onstage, but calm and genial just weren't in Richard's nature. He was twitchy, anxious, beleaguered. He didn't allow the audience to relax. His success would come when he figured out how to lean into that discomfort. But in order to do that, he had to stop running away from his past. He discovered that he had an affinity for improvisation; he would commit to the sketch and make it go on far longer than his peers. He even got fully naked onstage because he thought the sketch needed it—though many folks got upset with him. With his friend Henry Jaglom, an extremely wealthy Jewish bohemian, he tried writing his own scripts for movies he envisioned starring in. They came up with a concept for an interracial buddy comedy starring a pair of detectives—but were gutted when Cosby and Culp debuted *I Spy*.

For Richard in the mid-1960s, improv became more than an art form to be practiced onstage. It was a way of life, a survival tactic, a means of turning his frustration and rage into the stuff of a joke. When he and his comic buddies gathered at each other's apartments, they would play improv games until daybreak. (Saul 2014, 126)

Richard got elevated above all the other comics playing the open mic at Cafe Wha? when Manny Roth gave him his own slot in the evening for $15 a set. Even more, Manny decided to be Richard's manager—by Roth's own admission he also became a father figure of sorts to Richard. He was determined to make his new client rich and famous, but first he had to prepare Richard for his big break. He brought Richard to the YMCA to swim and work out with weights, trying to flesh out Richard's bony frame. They worked on Richard's material, his delivery, his stage demeanor. Roth discouraged Richard from using a slower style that would look too much like Cosby. They dressed Richard in nicer suits and shoes. But in his sets at the time, he was still pretending to be something other than what he was. This is how he described himself during his first television appearance, on a variety show hosted by singer Rudy Vallée called *On Broadway Tonight*:

> I'm going to tell you a few things about myself because a lot of you probably don't know me. I'm not a New Yorker. My home's in Peoria, Illinois. I'm from an average-type family— eleven kids. No mother and father, just kids. . . . I had a wild neighborhood because my mother's Puerto Rican, and my father's Negro, and we live in a really big Jewish tenement building in an Italian neighborhood. Every time I go outside, the kids say, "Get him! He's all of them!" (Pryor 1995)

Yes, it was funny, but the only truthful words he uttered were that he was from Peoria. Everything else was fiction. But Richard did mine his childhood for a routine that would bring him great success. It was about him appearing in a production of the play *Rumpelstiltskin* when he was a child. He did change the facts quite a bit—he was in Juliette Whittaker's production when he was fourteen, but he moved the age all the way down to kindergarten and he changed Whittaker to a white "Mr. Conrad." The routine went over big with Merv Griffin when Richard appeared on his show; the same with Ed Sullivan when Richard debuted there. He was on *Merv Griffin* more than twenty times in less than a year, and he agreed to appear on *Ed Sullivan* every two months. He signed with a big-name talent agency that boasted the Beatles and the Supremes as clients. His career was starting to take off.

He snagged a gig at the Apollo in August 1965; he was so excited that he talked Bill Cosby into riding with him uptown to see his name on the marquee. In the cab, Cosby tried to give Richard advice about playing the Apollo, counseling him that he shouldn't curse or play the fool.

"But I'm being paid to be a fool," Richard responded.

"You know what I mean," Cosby said.

They got to 125th Street and looked up at a marquee that broadcast "Billy Eckstine and Opening Acts."

"Where's your name, Rich?" Cosby asked him. "I see Billy Eckstine's. But not yours."

"Right there. Underneath," Richard said.

"I don't see it."

"What do you mean?" Richard said. "Right there. 'Opening Acts.'"

But Richard's made-for-TV jokes didn't impress the Apollo crowd during his weeklong gig; he didn't get asked to come back. After Richard taped an appearance on *Merv Griffin* with Redd Foxx months later, the two comedians headed uptown so Redd could show him around. Richard heard Black folks calling out to Redd wherever they went. When they had been downtown at Merv's show, Richard had been the celebrity, while nobody knew Redd.

He thought to himself: *Wait a minute. I'm in the wrong place, I'm in the wrong town. I want to be here. I want people to talk to me like they talk to Redd.*

He knew he needed to focus on connecting with his people.

After he got offered a gig as a recurring special guest on the *Kraft Summer Music Hall*, he moved to Los Angeles. He was excited about trying to become an actor. He brought his girlfriend, Maxine, a young Jewish girl who looked like Audrey Hepburn, and they moved into a place in Beverly Hills. In Hollywood, Richard got in with the right folks, the hungry young actors and singers looking for their big break. One of his new friends was the crooner Bobby Darin, who had exploded a few years earlier with his cover of "Mack the Knife." Darin hired Richard as his opening act for his stay at the Flamingo in Vegas, for which Richard would get $2,400 a week.

He got rave reviews in Vegas, lots of backslapping, but Richard wasn't satisfied. Part of it was how he still was being perceived. Funnyman Don Rickles came backstage one night and told him, "It's uncanny. You sound just like Bill Cosby." Richard still hadn't escaped Cosby's long shadow.

He started getting small acting parts, first in the Sid Caesar film *The Busy Body*, then on the TV show *The Wild Wild West*. He wasn't choosy; he just wanted to work. The parts might not have been impressive, but when he returned to Peoria for the first time in four years, he was regaled as a conquering hero. After all, how many Black folk had left Peoria and wound up on television? His father told the local paper that "the thrill of our son making it good tugged at our hearts and brought a tear or two."

As anger and disillusionment raged across Black communities in 1966 and 1967—largely fueled by frustrations over systemic racial discrimination in housing, employment, education, and policing—Richard was holed away in Beverly Hills, far from the uprisings and fires. He was trying to figure out how all this dissension, this frustration, this deep-rooted Blackness, would find its way into his act. He got inspired by the Harry Belafonte–produced, Sidney Poitier–narrated special *A Time for Laughter: A Look at Negro Humor in America*, which brought together a stable of top Black comedians to announce that Black humor was ready for its close-up. Pryor appeared in a skit as a young funeral director delivering a eulogy for a man he didn't know. He joined a cast that included Redd Foxx, Pigmeat Markham, George Kirby, Moms Mabley, Godfrey Cambridge, and Dick Gregory. Pryor knew he wasn't their first choice.

"They wanted Bill Cosby," he said. "He was contractually committed so they took me. There was a time in my career when it wouldn't have mattered. For about a year I *was* Bill Cosby" (Saul 2014, 168).

Watching the old guard work their magic shook up Richard, who felt he hadn't yet figured out his act. "Working in a show like the Belafonte special has convinced me I've got a long way to go to really make it," he told one TV critic. He opened up a few months later in *Ebony*, telling some truths about his family for the first time—though hilariously, the reporter didn't believe him. He told her he lived in a brothel until he was fifteen, but she was "shocked by his lie." Pryor began incorporating stories about his crazy upbringing into his stage routines. He also demonstrated his penchant for self-sabotage on more than one occasion. Feeling disrespected, high on cocaine, Richard punched the night clerk at his apartment building in the face, breaking his glasses and lacerating his cornea, causing permanent vision loss in his left eye. In Vegas at the Aladdin, he walked off the stage just seven minutes into his act and drove all the way back to Los Angeles without telling anyone why. He later told the *Los Angeles Times*, "I was doing material that was not funny to me. I saw how I was going to end up. I was false. I was turning into plastic." In *Rolling Stone*, he said he felt like he was becoming a robot, programmed to tell the same jokes over and over. He recounted the story in his memoir of walking out and seeing Dean Martin staring at him from the front tables, waiting for the first laugh.

> Who was Dean looking at? I didn't know who Richard Pryor was. And in that flash of introspection when I was unable to find an answer, I crashed. . . . I imagined what I looked like and got disgusted.

Richard was profoundly influenced by the Black Power movement and the counterculture hippie movement, both warring inside him and giving him energy to push his act into new places. He sobbed uncontrollably the night of King's assassination as he drove around the streets of Chicago with the booker from Mister Kelly, the famous

Chicago nightclub. He canceled an appearance on *Ed Sullivan* and returned to LA, where he performed at a King memorial in front of ten thousand people at the Hollywood Bowl. Richard's message that day wasn't quite as peaceful and hopeful as the other speakers', who included Cosby and Barbra Streisand: "All these people here are giving money, but if your son gets killed by a cop, money don't mean shit."

As Richard's anger and grief fueled his performances, he began to channel the rawness of his emotions into his comedy, blending his personal pain with his growing sense of activism. This shift became evident as he mined his childhood for a routine that was one of his most brilliant of the period, talking about an after-hours joint in Peoria he called "Hank's Place" that was the home of the characters he grew up with—hustlers, prostitutes, gamblers, pimps.

It was a remarkable eleven-minute routine because it was the first time he leaned so heavily on the real Peoria.

As he sought to bring more edginess to his act, he became close with fellow comedian and writer Paul Mooney, who would be an important collaborator for the rest of Pryor's career. Together they began stalking the Black clubs, looking for inspiration, feeding off the lively crowds. Richard found freedom at the Redd Foxx Club and another trendy LA spot called Maverick's Flat—whose colorful décor inspired the Temptations song "Psychedelic Shack." Onstage at these venues, Richard was free to say anything he wanted without fear of censorship or judgment. "It was an extraordinary feeling, this sensation of creative freedom. For him, the worm was turning: those parts of himself that had been buried, by shame or censorship, were now his creative fuel" (Saul 2014, 216).

By this time, Richard was leaning heavily on the word *nigger* in his act. By saying it aloud in mixed audiences, he was taking the final step: This was the epitome of private Blackness out loud, using a word that *some* Black folks used unselfconsciously among themselves for generations. Bill Cosby, not one to relish the public use of the N-word, had high praise for Richard during this period: "Richard would walk in [the Redd Foxx Club], and he'd blow Foxx away. He'd blow me away, with no problem. That was mainly because Richard was bringing in a new kind of language at the time—not really bringing it in, but using it and using it well" (Saul 2014, 217).

Starting in the late 1970s, Richard stayed busy with a couple of Aaron Spelling–produced TV movies of the week for ABC. The first was called *The Young Lawyers*, about a couple of jazz musicians victimized by racism; the second was *Carter's Army*, about an all-Black World War II platoon. He also had parts in *The Mod Squad* and *The Partridge Family*. He released an album called *'Craps' (After Hours)*, recorded at the Redd Foxx Club, that contained many themes—sex, racism, marriage—that would become standard fare for him. He even talked about the fluidity of his sexuality for the first time, stating that he had had sex with a gay man.

Richard was literally shaken by the Sylmar Earthquake that rocked Los Angeles in February 1971 and decided he needed to leave LA. He hit Berkeley, ground zero of the counterculture movement, that same month with the goal of simplifying his life. During the seven months he spent there, he became close with a group of Black intellectuals—writers such as Ishmael Reed and Claude Brown—who expanded his worldview and provided new energy to his comedy. This period marked a turning point for Richard, as he paused his relentless pursuit of success and, for the first time in years, allowed himself the space to reflect, recharge, and recalibrate both personally and creatively.

The act he was trying out in Berkeley got rave reviews from critics such as Phil Elwood in the *San Francisco Examiner*, who wrote that Richard was "a major figure among contemporary hip theatrical figures of American society. . . . In the vernacular, he is one of the 'baddest niggers' around.'"

Ishmael Reed gave Richard a biography of Bert Williams, the minstrel superstar who managed to bring an air of respectability to blackface. Richard felt a connection to Williams, how he used the makeup to conceal himself. He also was moved by the work of his new friend Claude Brown, whose bestselling book *Manchild in the Promised Land* had set critics' heads spinning.

Brown also recounted how much cocaine Richard was doing in

Berkeley with the story of a visit from Richard's drug dealer. The dealer asked Richard, "How much you want?"

"How much you got?" Richard answered. "Just leave it there. I'll see you tomorrow."

But the drugs did inspire Richard to come up with one of his best routines, called "Wino and Junkie," about the life of an addict. When he returned to Los Angeles, he stepped into a moment of transformation in Hollywood—an experimental phase of storytelling that embraced bold voices and new perspectives. Among those pushing boundaries was Motown founder Berry Gordy, who was expanding into film. Richard landed a small role in Gordy's latest project, *Lady Sings the Blues*, a vehicle for Diana Ross. With a mix of sharp instincts and fearless improvisation, Richard ad-libbed his way into a much larger role—ultimately securing third billing behind Ross and Billy Dee Williams. His part originally consisted of one scene and one line—he was the piano player who nudges the nightclub owner to try out the young Billie Holiday as a singer after she messes up as a dancer. "Hey, Jerry, give the girl a chance." That was supposed to be it for Pryor. But he cocked his fedora to the side and poured oodles of personality into the camera, channeling a charismatic jazz pianist he knew in Peoria named Jimmy Binkley. They decided to keep him in the next scene, when Billie sings her song, and he improvised such a lively patter that the movie's writers expanded his scenes until Piano Man is in a third of the film.

The irony of the role was that while he was acting in a film chronicling an artist's destruction through addiction, Pryor was deep in the throes of addiction himself. That sometimes meant he was a threat to those around him. When the Motown limo pulled up to his cottage one morning, Richard's current girlfriend, Patricia Heitman, tried to rouse him. He'd been up most of the night at a late-night card game.

"Bitch, if you touch me one more motherfucking time, I'm going to beat the shit out of you," he warned her.

"The car is here," she said. "Richard, please."

He proceeded to punch her in the face. She ran off, leaving him to the efforts of the limo driver. When Richard got back later that evening after a day of shooting, he found his girlfriend sporting a bandage on her nose and a black eye.

"Who fuckin' did this to you?" Richard yelled. "I'll kill the motherfucker!"

After Mel Brooks convinced him to help spruce up the script to what would become *Blazing Saddles*, Richard showed up late to his first day with the other writers in New York. As he settled into his seat and listened to Brooks, Richard took out a vial and snorted some coke. He pushed it in Brooks's direction. "Brother Mel?"

Brooks joked, "Never before lunch," but the writers were all shocked. One of them didn't even know what cocaine was. Richard turned the movie into a darker, more sinister, but ultimately hilarious take on race in the Old West.

That boldness carried over into his next project. Richard did voice-overs for the groundbreaking music documentary *Wattstax*, in effect bringing his stage act to the screen as he waxed poetic on the ridiculousness of bigotry in America. Many Americans, even Black Americans, had never seen Richard so racially incendiary. After watching the film, a critic for the *Los Angeles Times* called Pryor the "Here and Now Black Man of the Moment."

Richard was in usual Richard form when he returned to the US after traveling to the Cannes Film Festival in 1973 for the screening of *Wattstax*. In his appraisal of the trip, he complained that the French didn't understand his sense of humor. Why? Because they didn't know how to translate *motherfucker*.

In the summer of 1974, Richard's album *That Nigger's Crazy* hit number one on *Billboard*'s R&B charts. After witnessing the collapse of President Nixon in the Watergate scandal, Richard said of the accusation that he was too profane, "Nixon took justice and broke its jaw. Now *that* is profane." The album went on to win the 1975 Grammy Award for Best Comedy Album. The next year, his album *. . . Is It Something I Said?* also won the Grammy, as did his next release, 1976's *Bicentennial Nigger*.

Amid the wave of critical and commercial success, Richard found himself stepping into a new kind of spotlight—one that brought his past to center stage. Richard was asked by Mike Douglas to guest host his show for a week, and during his week he had his grandmother Marie on as a guest. She commanded the stage and kept the audience rocking in laughter as she regaled them with stories of how bad Richard was as a child. "There ain't no sense in nobody going on," said Sammy Davis Jr., who was to go on after her. "The show belongs to her." Asked about her appearance, Richard would later call it "the greatest moment of my life."

Before *Saturday Night Live* even went on the air, its young creators Dick Ebersol and Lorne Michaels engaged in a pitched battle with NBC executives about having Pryor as one of the new show's first guest hosts. The executives thought Richard was far too dangerous for a live show. Michaels responded, "I can't do a contemporary comedy show without Richard Pryor." Michaels actually quit in protest, though NBC execs lured him back. Pryor went on to host the show's seventh episode on December 13, 1975, creating comic gold in unforgettable moments with Chevy Chase and John Belushi in particular. The network insisted on adding a five-second delay when Richard appeared—something Michaels agreed to, though he never told Richard because he feared Richard would walk away.

Had the internet and social media existed in the 1970s, they would have gone into overdrive over the romance between Richard and actress Pam Grier—two of the decade's biggest Black stars. But the relationship was a rocky one, partly because of Richard's competitiveness. She beat him once in tennis and he wouldn't talk to her for the rest of the day. He got upset when she tried to correct his game.

"I'm supposed to take instructions and have you beat my ass too?" he said to her. "No way."

He thought she was too focused on her career to focus on him. "I was put off by how much I thought Pam believed that stardom belonged to her," he said later, clearly with misgivings that the relationship didn't work out. "In my head there was only one Numero Uno, and it wasn't her."

For her part, she was scared off by his drug addiction, telling him, "I don't feel safe living here yet because I don't know who you are" when he proposed they move in together. Yet, she brought structure to his life, improving his diet and pushing him to work out. When she left him, all that clean living swirled down the drain.

In 1977, one of the strangest experiments to hit the television airwaves debuted with *The Richard Pryor Show*. It only lasted for four episodes, but it was unlike anything that had ever been seen on network television. The show's first cold open gave some preview of what was to come: It featured John Belushi as the captain of a slave ship, whipping dozens of shirtless Black men. Eventually Belushi singles out Pryor for even worse punishment: to work for NBC. In another skit, Richard played the first Black president in a scene that presaged the way Fox News would harass Barack Obama three decades later. This is what happens when you give Richard Pryor money and creative control. The critics were stunned, thrilled, bewildered. John O'Connor in the *New York Times* said that Pryor was one of America's most innovative and talented performers. "And he is also extremely imaginative and unpredictable. In the style of Lily Tomlin, he can be exaggeratedly goofy or movingly poignant. Often, he is somewhere in between, defying easy categorization. In any event, his material is unmistakably adult, and NBC has obviously made a tactical error in subjecting him to the acknowledged and unwritten restraints of the early-evening schedule."

Other guests included Sandra Bernhard, Tim Reid, Marsha Warfield, and Robin Williams, a year before he would detonate as the star of the TV show *Mork & Mindy*.

There was so much cocaine on the set of his show that at the end of the day Richard might be found passed out on the floor.

Richard abused drugs so hard when he made *The Wiz* that he said he was surprised when he woke up every morning. "I answered my wake-up calls by saying, 'Oh shit, I made it again.'" His aptitude for self-destruction was unrivaled. While having sex with a prostitute back in Peoria, Richard felt his heart racing and pounding in his chest and he struggled to breathe. He thought he was having a heart attack and rushed to his grandmother's house, yelling, "Help me, Mama!" He was only thirty-six.

"They were probably closer to death than I was," he said of his family. "They saw their money supply gasping for air, moaning, and writhing in pain. They probably wondered if this wasn't some sick joke. Me coming home to die in front of them."

In *Richard Pryor: Live in Concert*, he tells the story of his heart attack, giving his heart the voice of a domineering taskmaster: "Don't breathe," he says, using his right fist to hit the left side of his body with an uppercut.

"Huh?" Richard says, looking around for the voice.

"You heard me, motherfucker. I said don't breathe." The voice hits him with another blow to his chest.

"Okay, I won't breathe, I won't breathe."

"Then shut the fuck *up!*" the voice says.

"Okay, okay, don't kill me, don't kill me."

"Get on one knee and prove it!"

"I'm on one knee, I'm on one knee, don't kill me," Richard pleads.

"You're thinking about dying now, aren't ya?"

"Yeah, I'm thinking about dying, I'm thinking about dying," Richard says.

"You didn't think about it when you was eating all that pork!" The voice hits Richard again, dropping him to the floor. When Richard tries to put in a call to God, an angel puts him on hold.

"Was you trying to talk to God behind my back?" the heart asks him.

"Nooo," Richard says.

"You're a lyin' mother*fucker!*" the heart says, dropping him to the ground again.

After his grandmother Marie died, Richard went deep into a troubling funk, locking himself in his bedroom with a bottle of liquor, cocaine, a pipe, and a Bic lighter—the tools for freebasing. On the night of June 9, 1980, amid voices he said he heard, voices from people he knew, came an idea: to set himself on fire. So that's what he did. He poured the liquor over his head, dousing himself, and sparked the lighter. But as he felt himself burning, he realized he wasn't ready to die. The folks who were with him tried to use a sheet to smother the flames, but he thought they were trying to kill him. He ran out of the house, down the driveway, into the street, with his shirt burning and melting into his skin. When he was approached by a police officer, he started running. After a half mile, he was physically forced into an ambulance and brought to the hospital. The fire incident would become fodder for one of Richard's funniest stand-up routines, which he told in the brilliant concert film *Richard Pryor: Live on the Sunset Strip*.

But it seemed as if the fire burned away much of Richard's brilliant edginess. Observers described the new Richard as gentle and mellow, words rarely used in the same sentence as "Richard Pryor." "People call me up and say, 'You're not like you used to be,'" he said in 1983. "I say to them, 'That's right, but do you know what I was really like then? Do you know what kind of insanity I was into, with the drugs and liquor? I'm not going to start doing that again. I'm going to be nice to myself. I don't have the same desire to succeed anymore. I don't have that push, push, push I used to have. I think I had it until I burned up."

Subsequent films such as *The Toy*, *Brewster's Millions*, and the semi-autobiographical *Jo Jo Dancer, Your Life Is Calling* didn't have the same Pryor energy, reflected by disappointing box office receipts. In August 1986, Richard got diagnosed with multiple sclerosis—MS stood for "more shit," he said. Eventually he was relegated to a motorized scooter when he could no longer walk. He did a farewell tour as a comedian in 1983, at age forty-two. In 1995, he published a memoir. A decade later, on December 10, 2005, the greatest comedian to ever live suffered a heart attack and died at a Los Angeles hospital. He had turned sixty-five just nine days before.

"He unleashed a galaxy of street characters who traditionally had been embarrassments to most middle-class blacks and mere stereotypes to most whites," Mel Watkins wrote in the *New York Times*. "And he presented them so truthfully and hilariously that he was able to transcend racial boundaries and capture a huge audience of admirers in virtually every ethnic, economic, and cultural group in America."

His career had dropped off considerably, but everyone knew: The king was dead.

CHAPTER 13
EDDIE MURPHY

When once asked to name his biggest comedic influences, Eddie Murphy didn't hesitate: Bill Cosby and Richard Pryor. It was the continuation of a pattern that began long ago with early Black comedians like Bert Williams—looking to predecessors for inspiration and guidance. Or, to state it honestly, for material—though many of them might deny that last bit. The ancestral line has continued for nearly a century, connecting through the decades like strands of DNA molecules, carrying instructions for their offspring. In this way, Murphy is connected to Bert Williams, who is connected to Moms Mabley, who is connected to Redd Foxx, who is connected to Dave Chappelle. Joined by their fidelity to their craft and to their people, birthing the next generation of joke tellers, providing Black folk with the vital energy to laugh, to escape the strife thrown at them simply because of their hue.

Murphy was like a shooting star—dazzling, electrifying, and impossible to ignore at his peak. He ascended to heights few comedians have ever reached, captivating audiences with his sharp wit, boundless energy, and magnetic presence. His success was so monumental that it seemed almost unstoppable, a testament both to his talent and his ability to connect with audiences across generations. Like Pryor, he was a game changer in comedy and film, setting new standards and redefining what was possible for a Black entertainer in Hollywood. But over time, the formula that once felt fresh began to lose its spark, and some of Murphy's later projects struggled to recapture the same magic. Few misfires were as infamous as the 2002 film *The*

Adventures of Pluto Nash—a movie so widely panned that even his own son didn't hold back.

"I remember the first time we watched *Pluto Nash*, I had my son Myles with me," Murphy told the *New York Times*. "He was probably about 8. Myles is sitting there with me, and the movie's all soft. Then at the end, it goes silent, and my little baby son goes, 'Corny.' *That* was challenging. [Laughs.] Even the baby knows it's corny."

Not every venture was a triumph, but even the missteps—whether *The PJs* or *Pluto Nash*—remain mere footnotes in a career defined by groundbreaking success.

When nineteen-year-old Eddie Murphy joined the cast of *Saturday Night Live* in 1980, the show was on life support. The original cast had exploded onto the nation's consciousness in October 1975 and made *SNL* must-see TV before the term had been invented. John Belushi, Chevy Chase, Bill Murray, Jane Curtin, Dan Ackroyd, and Gilda Radner all became big stars, making movies and grabbing headlines. But upon the expiration of their four-year contracts, they all wanted out, seeking to leave behind the grueling show and see what Hollywood was offering. NBC was desperate to keep the franchise afloat. Lorne Michaels had left the show as well. Michaels's replacement wasn't impressed by Murphy's audition, but the grapevine reported that the show needed a Black cast member to break up the sea of whiteness that was *SNL*. Murphy auditioned three times before the show gave him the nod.

"He competed against every Black face you ever saw on TV and film," his mother, Lillian, said.

They didn't give him much work in his first season, with a staff of Ivy League writers who had no idea what to do with the brash teenager. But when showrunner Jean Doumanian was replaced by Dick Ebersol the next season, Murphy got his chance—and was so creative and hysterically funny that he became an instant superstar. From Gumby to Mister Robinson's Neighborhood to pimp Velvet Jones, he created characters people are still talking about more than four decades later. After *SNL*, Murphy went on to rack up a dazzling list of career accomplishments: an Emmy Award, a Grammy Award, a Golden Globe Award, as well as nominations for an Academy Award and a BAFTA award. In 2015, he was honored with the Mark Twain Prize for American Humor; he received the Cecil B. DeMille Award in 2023.

Murphy's first solo leading role, *Beverly Hills Cop*, was the highest-grossing comedy of all time and the highest-grossing R-rated film of all time. After Murphy's box office champions *48 Hrs.* and *Trading Places*, the success of *Beverly Hills Cop* established him as the most bankable star in the country. Every Hollywood executive wanted to be in the Eddie Murphy business.

But then a curious thing happened: Murphy lost his sheen. People stopped flocking to his movies. His adult-targeted films began to disappoint at the box office, so Murphy turned to children's movies, finding much more success clowning for the babies.

Why did Murphy stop being funny? Like Pryor, he lost the dangerous edge that made him unpredictable and hilarious. Like Pryor, you never knew what Murphy was going to say. Or how he was going to say it. You just knew it was going to be funny. Perhaps it was the enormous wealth, but something caused him to lose his connection to the larger Black community, to the comic thread that always kept Black folks in stitches. He lost his bite.

While his public image portrayed him as the sweet middle-class kid from Long Island, Murphy's early years actually were tough. Maybe not Pryor tough, but certainly not the *Leave It to Beaver* upbringing that the public believed. Murphy was born in Bushwick, Brooklyn, and lived in the projects for the early years of his life. His mother, Lillian, worked as a telephone operator, while his father, Charles Lee Murphy, was a police officer for the New York City Transit Authority. His brother Charles Jr., known as Charlie, was two years older than him. His parents divorced when he was three; Eddie didn't have much contact with his father—though people used to tell him he walked like his father and held his head like his father. When Eddie was eight, his mother got very sick, requiring hospitalization that stretched on for a year. Charlie and Eddie were placed in foster care, suddenly under the auspices of an abusive woman Eddie called the "Black Nazi."

"One day she gave us pigs' tails for dinner, and then, when I told my grandmother that we were being fed snakes, the woman grabbed Charles and whipped him," Murphy recalled. "Those were *baaad* days. Staying with her was probably the reason I became a comedian."

The Murphy clan was rescued from their hood struggles by a man named Vernon Lynch, who married Lillian and moved the family out of Brooklyn when Eddie was eleven. Vernon drove a truck and worked as a foreman at the Breyer's Ice Cream plant. A former welterweight boxer who retired with a 17–4 record, Lynch used boxing as a disciplinary tool, forcing the boys to square off against him in the makeshift "ring" in the basement when they messed up.

"If he wanted to, I think he'd be a dynamite middleweight boxer. He don't like to be hit, but he's quick to learn," Lynch said after Eddie's career took off. "His reflexes are good, terrific."

One time when Lynch, who sometimes had visitations with the liquor bottle, came home drunk after work, he woke up the boys and challenged them to a fight. He actually placed his paycheck down and said the winner could take it all.

"We beat the shit out of the motherfucker," a grinning Eddie said from the stage during his act.

In 1969, tragedy barged into Murphy's life over Labor Day weekend: His biological father, Charles, was stabbed to death by a jealous girlfriend. Though he wasn't close to his dad, the death left a mark.

"It was really traumatic," Murphy said. "Richard Pryor's father died fucking. That's a good way to go."

The *National Enquirer* exploited the tragedy later by blasting it on the tabloid's front page: "Eddie Murphy Haunted by Dad's Brutal Murder—He's Afraid He'll Die the Same Horrible Death." An enraged Murphy sued the tabloid in federal court for $30 million, claiming the story was "totally false and defamatory."

Two years after his biological father's murder, his stepfather, Vernon, moved the family to Roosevelt, Long Island, a lower-middle-class, heavily Black suburb on the south shore. "We always wanted to go forward," Vernon said. "Eddie never knew anything about no ghetto" (Sanello 1997, 9).

As a kid, Murphy was obsessed with cartoons, particularly Bugs Bunny and Tom and Jerry. As he got a bit older, his obsession switched to Elvis Presley. He would study Elvis's moves and recreate them in the basement—complete with a gold lamé coat given to him by an uncle. He later said Elvis was the only entertainer he'd want to trade places with.

"We never encouraged him to be a comedian," his mother said. "He really did it all on his own. But humor has got to be a trait in the Murphy blood. Eddie's father was a weekend comic and emcee. What's strange is that Eddie never knew him."

Murphy also closely studied Bill Cosby. He did study people who were physically closer, such as his elementary school principal. When he stood outside the boys' bathroom and bellowed loudly in imitation of the principal, alarmed students would hear the voice and scatter, running to class. His impression of his grandmother, which Vernon said was dead-on, would show up decades later in 1996's *The Nutty Professor*, which grossed $200 million and announced his arrival into the children's film genre. After *The Nutty Professor*, he would go on to make eight children's films, including *Mulan*, *Dr. Doolittle*, *Shrek*, and *Daddy Day Care*—demonstrating that his obsession with cartoons and children's television as a child paid off handsomely.

He was clearly a bright kid, but Murphy struggled in school, primarily because he didn't care enough. His GPA in high school was somewhere in the 2.0 range, which caused his mother much distress.

"I used to come home with report cards when I was fifteen with zeroes on them, and fifties and sixties," he recalled. "My mother would say, 'What's wrong with you?' and I'd say, 'I'm going to be famous, Ma.'"

He went to school every day wearing a suit, a tie with a collar pin, and a briefcase under his arm. His uncle gifted him a cashmere coat, which he draped over a shoulder. It was a pretty strange getup for a high schooler, but it worked for Murphy. Rather than seeing him as goofy or corny, his classmates saw cool.

"I was voted most popular," Murphy said. "I was like a little celebrity. I was hot shit."

Murphy was told his grades were so bad that he needed to repeat eleventh grade. It hit him that his graduation was in danger, so he attended summer school—still sporting the cashmere coat in midsummer—to graduate with his classmates.

At age fifteen, he was asked to serve as emcee for a talent show at the Roosevelt Youth Center. It was his first public performance, not counting acting up in school. Between acts, he played an Al Green song, swiveling his hips like Elvis. The crowd loved it. When he saw the awe on the faces of the crowd, "I knew that I was in show biz for the rest of my life."

At sixteen, he was a big deal on Long Island, headlining at multiple comedy clubs. His stepfather would drive him to gigs until he was old enough to drive himself. That single fact made his show business start radically different than that of his idols Cosby and Pryor—and virtually every other Black comedian who came along before him. It's a long, winding road from Redd Foxx hopping freight trains to try to get to New York, to Eddie Murphy being driven to clubs by his parents. In many ways, what could better signify an arrival into the middle-American mainstream than a teenager being driven to nightclubs by his parents to tell jokes? He pronounced to his parents that he was going to be a millionaire by the time he was twenty-two. Turns out that prediction wasn't aggressive enough; he got there a year early.

His mother was shocked when she went to one of his shows and heard how much her little boy cursed onstage. "That's not the real Eddie," she said. "He knows what people want to hear. It's his act."

His stepfather agreed, stating that "he doesn't talk to me or anybody else in the family that way."

As he got more serious about turning comedy into a career, he had to get more serious when choosing his idols. Elvis wouldn't suffice anymore. He turned his attentions to Cosby and Pryor.

"Pryor on an artistic level," he explained. "Cosby on a moral level. Cosby was this cool guy and Pryor was brilliant. I wanted to combine the two. Be funny *and* have a clean life."

Clearly, Murphy's description of Cosby's morality didn't age well. But when it came to comedy, his true north was Richard Pryor—especially in his unapologetic use of profanity. Even as a teenager, Murphy was cursing onstage, drawn to the way Pryor wielded language as an art form.

"He paints pictures with words," Murphy once said. "He can tell you a story, and you can see the whole thing. He was a genius."

That deep admiration was palpable during their first encounter. Murphy recalled the moment to the *New York Times*: "I was on a plane coming from Georgia, and Richard Pryor was on the plane. That's when I first met him. I gave him my cassette of my first album, and I sat two, three rows on the other side, just watching the back of his head. And he was laughing. I could have died right there."

When he was seventeen, Murphy formed a comedic trio with two white guys, Rob Bartlett and Bob Nelson. Their name? The Identical Triplets. The joke was supposed to be on them, since they obviously weren't triplets. They got some gigs in the area, made some people laugh, but the group didn't have legs. When they were bombing at a teacher's convention, Murphy snatched the mic and made a pronouncement to wake up the ladies, who were no longer paying them any mind. "Listen up. We're going to be on the *Tonight Show* in two years." He wasn't wrong—though he probably shouldn't have said "we."

His big break came at seventeen. His friend and partner Bob Nelson knew the owners of Manhattan's Comic Strip comedy club, Bob Wachs and Richie Tienken, and asked them to give Murphy an audition. But his arrogance almost killed his big chance. He showed up at the Comic Strip and immediately announced to Wachs, a Harvard-trained attorney, "I'm Eddie Murphy. I'm ready to go on."

Wachs was offended. "Wait a minute," he told Eddie. "We have systems around here, procedures. You don't just walk in and say, 'I'm here and I'm going on.' Get the hell out."

Murphy was also shown the door at a competing club, The Improv, whose co-owner Silver Friedman found his arrogance "appalling." He went back to the Comic Strip two weeks later, taken down a few notches, and agreed to the late-night shift—not a treasured time slot because the audience would be tired and drunk. Wachs wasn't in love with Murphy's material, which was not going to be particularly elevated from a seventeen-year-old, yet he found his style and energy immensely appealing—so much so that he and Tienken decided to be Murphy's managers. This was a big deal; hundreds of comics came through the club, but they picked Murphy to manage. They proceeded to get their young charge plenty of work in the New York region and beyond.

Murphy saw another rising young comic at The Improv—Keenen Ivory Wayans—and went backstage to meet him. "Hi, I'm Eddie Murphy," he said. "I thought I was the only funny Black guy in New York. Now I see there are two."

The two young men quickly hit it off. Wayans said it was like a bonding between two gunslingers.

"Everybody talked about his presence. He had an amazing amount of confidence onstage," Wayans said. "His stage presence was years beyond his material. At fourteen, fifteen, your material is limited in terms of what you've experienced, so it's juvenile. But Eddie had a command of stage and audience that people ten years his senior could only wish for."

After a show in Florida, legendary comedian Rodney Dangerfield told him his act was too dirty. "You're funny, but where you gonna go with that shit?" Dangerfield said.

Murphy heard him, but he was more than a little taken aback. "I ain't taking his motherfuckin' advice. Dangerfield is a funny guy, but how old was he when he got famous—in his fifties?"

After he was added to the *SNL* cast, Murphy amazed observers with his ability to say extremely offensive things without anybody getting offended. According to Dick Ebersol, people were drawn to the "smile dancing in his brown eyes."

"Wit sometimes enables us to act rudely with impunity," Ebersol said.

Murphy became such a dominant force on *SNL* in his second year that on the bulletin board where they pinned index cards describing upcoming sketches, some of the cards read, simply, *Eddie*. That meant the twenty-year-old could do whatever he wanted. After starting his first season making $750 per episode, Murphy had jumped to $8,700 per show by the middle of the second season.

"He has carried *SNL* virtually by himself since the show lost the entire original cast," *New York* magazine wrote at the time (Sanello 1997, 36).

Hollywood soon came calling. In Murphy's first movie, *48 Hrs.*, he played a role originally intended for Richard Pryor. When he broke up a redneck bar in one of the film's most memorable scenes, it was clear that Murphy had a certain charm that endeared him to white folks. While the white dudes in the bar stare at him like they're going to bite off his head, he whips out his (borrowed) badge and declares, "I'm your worst fucking nightmare, man. I'm a nigger with a badge. That mean I got permission to kick your fucking ass whenever I feel like it."

One can imagine Pryor pulling off such a scene, though there wouldn't be as much wink-wink when those words came out of Richard's mouth. For Cosby, delivering those lines would have been unthinkable.

"Eddie can tiptoe along the narrow line between anger and laughter in a way that shows everybody how silly we are to imprison ourselves with racial stereotypes," *Newsweek* wrote. "He thinks he can walk that same line in his career."

As this book has explored, the evolution of Black humor in America is, at its core, a study in comfort—how freely can Black comedians reveal their true selves onstage? Can they speak their minds without restraint? These questions extend far beyond comedy; they echo the everyday realities of Black life in America. How much of their authentic selves can Black people comfortably express in predominantly white spaces? And at what cost? Murphy reflected the shifting times by refusing to hold his tongue, challenging white audiences to be uncomfortable—and daring them to be offended.

As he became a movie star, Murphy understood his own humor better than anyone. He began rejecting most of his *SNL* skits, saying they weren't funny. For a show that had to go on the air every week regardless, this was a problem. Ebersol feared that Murphy's head was getting too big, but in fact he was just exercising his newfound clout. He was not going to walk out there and embarrass himself in corny skits. He threatened to boycott the show if he didn't start getting recognized in the credits as a writer—so they gave him writer credit.

Murphy also began experiencing drastic mood swings—what eventually would become known as bipolar disorder.

"Sometimes I'll wake up and want to cry," Murphy said during this period. "And not really have any reason: just a bunch of small stuff, wondering about my career. Or sometimes I'll get depressed about certain places I can't go anymore, like the park."

Murphy replaced Pryor again for his second big film, *Trading Places*. Pryor had dropped out of the project to make the ill-fated *The Toy*, with Jackie Gleason. Gene Wilder was also attached to *Trading Places*, but Murphy didn't want to work with him because he thought Wilder was too closely associated with Pryor, with whom Wilder had made the successful *Stir Crazy*. The studio proceeded to replace Wilder with Ackroyd.

In assessing the difference between him and Pryor, Murphy felt Pryor was often laughed *at* on-screen, the humor coming from his victimization.

"But I'm not funny like that," Murphy said. "When I'm being cocky, straightforward, that's when I'm the funniest. I'm funniest when I'm a wiseass."

In his analysis, Murphy might have inadvertently identified what happened when his adult movies failed to find an audience. He kept being served to the public as the cocky wiseass, but his cocky wiseass stopped being funny. If he's not funny, he's just . . . a wiseass. However, his adult humor was very much on display in two movies that made an indelible impact on the Black community, *Delirious* (1983) and *Raw* (1987). Many decades later, people still quote lines and scenes from the stand-up shows. People who tuned in to *Delirious* expecting PG Eddie from *SNL* were not prepared for what they saw: He said the word *fuck* 230 times and *shit* 171 times.

After 1984's *Beverly Hills Cop* blew up, a survey conducted by MGM, TriStar, and HBO revealed that Murphy was the most popular performer in the country, ahead of Bill Cosby and Richard Pryor.

Murphy himself was keenly aware of the trail he was blazing. In an NBC interview, he reflected on the genre-shaping success of his early films: "It's pretentious to actually say it," he admitted, "but my films kind of pioneered—*48 Hrs.* is the first action comedy, and *Beverly Hills Cop* was the second one. And then after *Beverly Hills Cop*, everybody, all the cops were like, 'Hasta la vista, baby.'"

It wasn't just bravado. By pairing razor-sharp comedic timing with the pacing and stakes of a big-budget thriller, Murphy created a blueprint that Hollywood would copy endlessly. His wisecracking, street-smart characters—never the sidekick, always the star—proved that a Black lead could dominate the box office in a genre long reserved for white actors. What studios once considered a gamble became a formula: buddy-cop banter, high-octane chases, and a charismatic lead whose humor was as essential as his heroics. Murphy had not only cracked the code; he had rewritten it.

Film critic Kenneth Turan wrote an essay explaining why Pryor makes the public squirm while Murphy makes them relax and laugh. "Eddie Murphy, though he absorbed Pryor's attitudes, does not have his background; he grew up not in a whorehouse but in a middle-class suburb. He doesn't have to strive to become one of us, he *is* one of us, and consequently his humor never disturbs, never creates discomfort."

Turan said Murphy was "nasty but safe, a thrill we can live with."

In 1984, Cosby placed a call to Murphy that would become the phone call heard around the world—that is, after Murphy described it in *Raw*. He said that Cosby started out by telling Murphy that he needed to stop being so profane onstage. Murphy is doing a dead-on Cosby impersonation as he describes the conversation. After a bit of back-and-forth, which takes longer than it should because Cosby refuses to repeat the offending curse words, Murphy tells him, "I'm offended that you called. Fuck you."

"That's what I'm talking about," Murphy as Cosby says. "You cannot say . . . fuck. In front of people."

Murphy says he got mad because Cosby was acting as if his entire act consisted of profanity. "Like I walked out onstage, cursed, and left," Murphy says. "I manage to stick in some jokes between the curses."

Murphy says he was so mad that he called up Richard Pryor.

"Yo, Richard, Bill Cosby just told me I was too dirty," Murphy says.

Murphy as Pryor responds, "The next time that motherfucker call, tell him to suck *my* dick. . . . Whatever the fuck make the people laugh, say that shit."

It was a momentous moment—Cosby essentially calling for Murphy to be respectful and well-mannered in front of the white folks, and Murphy telling him that was no longer necessary because Black people were now saying things without caring what white people think. We all knew the rules had changed when peak-irreverent comedies such as *In Living Color* and *Martin* hijacked the airwaves in the 1990s—shows made for the Black gaze.

"What makes a lot of comics bitter is that they have to pay dues a long time," Murphy said early in his career. "I got my break when I was nineteen. I've got nothing to be bitter about."

Many commentators might add that when the disappointing box office receipts came in for movies such as *Another 48 Hrs.* and *Vampire in Brooklyn*, Murphy began to understand what bitterness felt like. He also had some career missteps in the 1980s, such as turning down Michael Jackson's offer to be part of "We Are the World." He feared he'd be stuck in the back row next to La Toya Jackson after the release of his critically panned song "Boogie in Your Butt." He also turned down the Bill Murray part in the enormously successful *Ghostbusters*, which he later said he regretted.

After the enormous splash of his movies in the 1980s, Murphy's film career resembled a rollercoaster once the 1990s began. He found success with 1992's *Boomerang*, whose costars include Martin Lawrence and Halle Berry, but then followed it up with the disappointing *Beverly Hills Cop III*. After the success of 2006's *Dreamgirls*, which earned him his first Oscar nomination, he followed it up with the tedious *Norbit*, which was attacked as sexist and insensitive for Murphy's portrayal of Norbit's morbidly obese wife Rasputia.

His has been a career of dramatic firsts, mind-boggling successes, but also significant disappointments. Murphy turned stand-up comedy into the terrain of the rock star with his flash and sass. The sold-out arena tours and multimillion-dollar streaming deals of Hart, Rock, and Chappelle are all the progeny of Murphy. He transformed the realm of the possible for the profession of stand-up comedian.

CHAPTER 14
A DIFFERENT WORLD

The 1990s stand out as a golden era of Black creative expression—spanning music, film, literature, television, and especially comedy. After decades of catering to mainstream expectations, Black comedians in the '90s found freedom to craft humor centered on the experiences and culture of Black people. African-American culture became the heart of their work, and their comedy boldly reflected that focus. While others could join in and laugh, the success of a show was no longer dependent on a broader audience. It became clear that Black comedy could thrive on its own terms, carving out its own space in the cultural landscape.

In some ways this development was bittersweet: Advertisers and executives discovered, according to Nielsen surveys, that Black households consistently spent more hours watching TV per week than white or Hispanic households. That sparked a realization: Black audiences craved Black-led shows, and advertisers saw an opportunity to tap into a powerful consumer base. This shift in television not only reshaped programming but also transformed the career trajectory for ambitious comedians, opening doors that had rarely existed before. It was now television, much more than stand-up, that was going to offer comedians the two things they craved—exposure and money. Fame and fortune. Starting in the 1990s, a talented comic hoped more than anything to land a spot on a television show. That was the golden ticket to fame and fortune. From Martin Lawrence to Jamie Foxx, Bernie Mac to Cedric the Entertainer, Steve Harvey to Damon Wayans, the next generation to come along after Cosby and Pryor was much more interested in television than the stand-up comedy circuit—and they saw their celebrity soar after they got TV shows.

Shows that came along in the wake of *The Cosby Show* revealed a much more sophisticated, nuanced portrayal of Black people and Black life. That was certainly true with *A Different World*, the *Cosby* spin-off that debuted in 1987 but didn't really hit its stride until the 1990s.

"The portrayal of Blacks in the '80s and '90s, you begin to see an expansion of our identity," said Gil Robertson, then-president of the African American Film Critics Association, in an interview with *The Atlanta Journal-Constitution* in 2020. "Whereas back in the '70s or back in, certainly, earlier periods, African American identity was pretty one-note. In the '80s and the '90s you started seeing people in TV with different personalities outside of being either a person's sidekick or being the token Black person. You started to see a truer representation of Black people."

Sixteen-year-old Lisa Bonet was an early breakout star of *The Cosby Show*, with her cutting-edge bohemian fashion and her teenage snarkiness. Growing up in Los Angeles, Bonet witnessed her parents' rocky marriage. Her father, Allen Bonet, was a Black opera singer, while her mother was a Jewish schoolteacher named Arlene Litman. Lisa always thought she was ugly and was awkward and shy at her school, Reseda High School in the San Fernando Valley. But *The Cosby Show* transformed all that in an instant.

"Overnight, young viewers became obsessed with Lisa Bonet. When junior writers on the staff went out with her in public, fans gawked at the actress, shouted greetings, and hounded her for style tips. Boys thought she was gorgeous in a particularly exotic way, with her light skin and doe eyes and dreadlocks. Girls loved her bohemian sense of fashion, which every week produced funky clothes that Bonet made herself, often with little input from the wardrobe department" (Whitaker 2014, 346).

This perception of her as "exotic" largely came from the mainstream audience, who hadn't seen many biracial characters like her on television. For the average Black viewer, the Black bohemian type was well-known. However, for many outside that community, the setting of *A Different World*, with its fictional HBCU campus at Hillman College, introduced a whole new world. Cosby saw an opportunity to spotlight the importance of HBCUs by giving Bonet her own show—while also providing a way to navigate the growing tensions surrounding her role on *The Cosby Show*.

The first season of *A Different World* struggled to find its identity. The show wavered in tone and direction, and the casting of twenty-three-year-old white actress Marisa Tomei—fresh off the soap opera *As the World Turns*—only added to the confusion. When Phylicia Rashad flew out to LA for a guest appearance on *A Different World*, she came back to New York and told Cosby his spin-off was in trouble.

"It's not up to your standards," she said. "It doesn't represent you" (Whitaker 2014, 346).

Phylicia Rashad suggested bringing in her sister, actor and choreographer Debbie Allen, to direct the second season and infuse the show with greater authenticity—particularly given Allen's own experience attending an HBCU, Howard University. With Marisa Tomei's departure, Allen shifted the focus to the blossoming romance between Jasmine Guy's spoiled Southern belle, Whitley Gilbert, and Kadeem Hardison's lovable nerd, Dwayne Wayne. She also steered the series toward more complex, socially relevant storylines that deeply reflected Black culture.

Allen's job became easier after the departure of Lisa Bonet, whose presence had grown increasingly complicated. Bonet had recently starred in *Angel Heart* alongside Mickey Rourke, a film so sexually explicit that British director Alan Parker reportedly had to cut scenes to avoid an X rating. Around the same time, she eloped with rock star Lenny Kravitz and announced her pregnancy—a development that did not sit well with Bill Cosby, who disapproved of the rebellious image she was cultivating. At Bonet's request, she was written off *A Different World* and made occasional returns to *The Cosby Show* after giving birth to her daughter, Zoë. Her absence created an opportunity to introduce another precociously charming child to the series: Raven-Symoné, who played her on-screen stepdaughter, Olivia.

Two years after Bonet's return, Cosby ultimately wrote her off the show for good. He was "so annoyed and disappointed by her moodiness and lack of professionalism that he fired her."

Yvette Lee Bowser, who began her career as a writer's apprentice on *A Different World* before rising to producer and later creating *Living Single*, had a front-row seat to the show's transformation between its first and second seasons.

"It shifted dramatically. And yet there was a core there that was consistent," she said. "There was a lot of honesty, there was a lot of creativity. There was a lot of great ideas buzzing around. But there was also a lot of chaos. There was absolutely chaos at the very beginning in particular. It was really interesting to be in a position where I didn't have any real responsibility. I just had opportunity to observe, to contribute. And I really have to credit that situation for helping shape how I approached the work—not only the work creatively, but just managerially. I learned a lot about what not to do."

Yvette Lee Bowser's path to television was anything but conventional for a Black college student. Her breakthrough came from an unexpected realization—she had a family connection in the industry. During her senior year at Stanford, she and her best friend Kim were watching *The Cosby Show*, as they did every Thursday night. That evening, Bowser found herself in what she called a "pity party." She was on track for law school after graduation, but a sudden vision struck her—she was meant to write for television instead. As the credits rolled, a familiar name caught her eye, setting her career on an entirely new trajectory.

"For the first time ever, I recognized the name of someone that I knew in the credits," she said.

It was a man who was close to her family when she was growing up; she called him Uncle Stu. He was the music composer for *The Cosby Show*, Stuart Gardner. But she hadn't spoken to him in years. She figured she would have to remind him who she was. She tracked down the number for NBC's main switchboard and, after some persistence, secured a contact for *The Cosby Show*'s production offices—a far more challenging task in the pre-Google era. After navigating a few hurdles, she finally reached Stu Gardner on the phone.

"I told him that I just had this vision that I was supposed to be writing for television, but I didn't know anyone who had written for television or what it really entailed. And he said, 'Well, I totally remember who you are. You were a bright and shining star as a child. I happen to be headed to the Bay Area to meet up with my friend Dr. Cosby, who is shooting a movie in the Bay Area.'"

Cosby was in the midst of filming the ill-fated *Leonard Part 6*, which critics have widely decried as one of the worst films ever made. Bowser referred to the fact that Cosby was shooting in the Bay Area as "serendipity."

"A week after I made that first phone call, I was sitting in front of Dr. Cosby telling him I had this creative energy that had to be tapped," Bowser recalled. "And he told me, 'There's nothing for you out here. Go to law school.' I said, 'No, you don't understand. My family's financial situation is such that if I go to law school, I'll never come back and take a chance on this. I have to take this risk now or never.' So he read some of my writing samples and he chuckled. Then he said, 'Okay, I'll set you up as a writer's apprentice on my new show, the spin-off of *The Cosby Show*.' I was very, very excited. And months went by, and I kept waiting for this phone call to come."

When the call finally arrived, Bowser joined the staff of *A Different World* in August 1987, just as the show was set to debut the following month. Working with producers Thad Mumford and Susan Fales, Bowser said they aimed to bring dignity and substance to a groundbreaking show centered on Black college life—territory that had never been explored on television before. The team worked tirelessly during the first season, often pulling twenty-hour days, with little time for anything but their work.

"There was a lack of vision," she recalled. "No one who had created the original show came to work on *A Different World*. And no one was empowered to define its vision. Then they hired Ann Beatts, the creator of *Square Pegs*, to run the show. She was constantly trying to create something else, and Susan and I knew there was a lack of authenticity. We fought many worthwhile battles during that first season."

Given that the show revolved around a fictional HBCU, it was crucial for the writers to understand that world. However, none of the creators had attended an HBCU, and most were long-removed from their college years. As one of the few staff members fresh out of college, Bowser was uniquely able to relate to the characters' experiences. She recalled her role being so undefined that she was writing script notes and lunch orders simultaneously. Early episode themes, suggested by the more seasoned writers, often felt juvenile, more suited to high school. Bowser, Thad, and Susan embarked on a whirlwind tour of HBCUs to immerse themselves in the culture and truly capture the spirit of these institutions.

"That tour ended at Dr. Cosby's house, where we met Debbie [Allen]," Bowser explained. "We were told she was coming on board as a producing partner. From that point, it was 'go-time.' Everything was very symbiotic. We all shared the same vision. We knew we had something special—something that could shift both entertainment and culture. You always hope for entertainment, but when it does more, it's a bonus."

Bowser later had an encounter with veteran actress Loretta Devine, who had been part of the show's first season. After their brief conversation, Bowser thanked Devine for a moment she'd never forgotten from the set.

"We had a script that just wasn't coming together," Bowser recalled. "The writers and actors had a meeting, and Loretta just looked at the showrunner and said, 'Your script don't make no sense.' I told myself, 'I will never be on the receiving end of a note like that [again].'"

Darryl Bell, who joined the cast midway through the first season as Dwayne Wayne's best friend, Ron Johnson, emphasized Allen's insistence on authenticity, down to the smallest details.

"She walked around The Pit [the students' gathering spot and diner] and said, 'Honey, this is a Black school. Where's the hot sauce?'"

And so hot sauce ended up on all the tables," Bell said. "Those little, but crucial, touches made all the difference."

Bell stressed that the show's main goal was always comedy. Despite the tendency of shows with Black casts—created by white producers—to lack authenticity, *A Different World* marked a new era of storytelling.

"Often, a true word is said in a joke," Bell said. "Because our show was so funny and the characters were so well-developed, it made it easier to discuss difficult topics. Humor opened the door, and we had such a diverse point of view. Our characters ranged from 18 to 75, with every demographic and sensibility represented. Viewers could say, 'I identify with Mr. Gaines,' or 'I identify with Lena.' And that's what made *A Different World* resonate and remain relevant today."

Bell recounted the moment when he realized just how successful the show had become. He knew the show had a strong shot at success, given its prime placement between *The Cosby Show* and the iconic *Cheers*. NBC took to calling it "must-see TV."

"I just remember after our first week, that Friday morning, at some point in time there was one of the script supervisors onstage, and she was on the phone. She hung up the phone and she was like, 'We got a 49 share!' And I was like, Wow! You know that 49 percent of all televisions were watching you last night, and I knew how big that was. If you look at some of the biggest stars in the history of television, they've never been on the number one or number two show. So, I knew this is rare air that we're in right now. I knew it was different. I knew it was significant."

Allen made the cast members negotiate a clause in their contracts that they would be allowed to direct episodes—even if they didn't have a desire to direct. Glynn Turman directed four episodes, Kadeem Hardison directed four and wrote two, while Jasmine Guy directed one episode and wrote three.

"'The more you do, the less they can tell you you can't do,'" Guy recalled Allen telling her. "She said, 'We'll never have this opportunity again, so do everything you can while we're in this position.' She was an advocate for us."

Guy reflected on how Allen helped deepen their characters by giving them homework: writing about their characters' futures.

"Debbie made our characters feel real," Guy said. "She knew the difference between going to a Black college and a predominantly white university: You are loved, nurtured, and part of a community. You're not going to fail. She brought that essence to our work."

Despite *A Different World* ranking number two in ratings during its first season, and consistently in the top five for the next three, the cast often felt overlooked by the industry. Hardison pointed out that no cast member was ever nominated for an Emmy, nor were they ever invited to the ceremony.

"We never got that recognition," Guy said, recalling that Roseanne Barr got to sing the national anthem at a Padres game, notoriously poorly, while *A Different World* cast members never had that opportunity. "And we had five singers in our cast!"

Despite this, Guy took it in stride. "I always felt the exclusion. But you can't put too much stock in praise or criticism. You have to know who you are and where you belong."

The cast has many behind-the-scenes stories from their time on the show, especially given the grueling production schedule of up to twenty-six episodes per season. One memorable moment was when the show planned to name a building on campus after Supreme Court Justice Thurgood Marshall, only to realize they had no clearance. In a frantic scramble, a producer called the US Supreme Court, where "Miss Mary" on the other end informed them that Justice Marshall had no issue with the use of his name.

"When they asked if we got clearance, she said, 'From the Supreme Court,'" Bell recalled. "That was a moment."

After *The Cosby Show* ended, *A Different World* struggled to maintain its earlier momentum. NBC's conflicts with Allen grew, particularly after the controversial sixth-season storyline involving Whitley and Dwayne's honeymoon in Los Angeles during the 1992 riots. NBC's resistance to these tough, timely topics signaled the beginning of the end.

"They didn't care about serious issues like date rape, apartheid, or

HIV," Guy said. "They just wanted us to be funny. But I could see it coming. They treated us like monkeys, and we weren't monkeys. We were more than that."

In the same period, a show was emerging that would revolutionize television and forever alter the relationship between creators and networks.

CHAPTER 15
IN LIVING COLOR

Four months into the new decade, on April 15, 1990, more than 22 million viewers sat glued to their television screens, eyes wide with astonishment. They weren't just watching a new show—they were witnessing a cultural shift. *In Living Color* didn't simply premiere; it crashed onto the airwaves, disrupting the status quo with fearless, unfiltered comedy. And at the helm of this revolution was Keenen Ivory Wayans, the visionary mastermind behind it all.

What would Hollywood look like without *In Living Color*? Would we have witnessed the rise of Damon Wayans, Jim Carrey, Tommy Davidson, Jamie Foxx, Kim Wayans, Shawn Wayans, Marlon Wayans, David Alan Grier—even Jennifer Lopez—without the vision of Keenen Ivory Wayans? If you didn't experience the phenomenon firsthand, it's hard to grasp just how radical and subversive the show was. Nothing like it had ever aired before—a show that tackled race with fearless irreverence, confronting topics television had long treated as untouchable. At its core, *In Living Color* was an unprecedented cultural shift, unapologetically reshaping comedy and representation on TV.

This was two years before LL Cool J's FUBU line hit the streets, but *In Living Color* was already moving with a "For Us, By Us" spirit. Something was in the air—a new generation of Black artists was using their craft to push back against racism and the decay around them. Crack had ravaged inner cities, and the homicide rate for Black men under twenty-five doubled between 1984 and 1994.

Public Enemy's *Fear of a Black Planet* dropped just five days before *In Living Color*'s debut, racing into the *Billboard* Top 10 and selling over a million copies in two months. Spike Lee's *Do the Right Thing*, powered by Public Enemy's incendiary anthem "Fight the Power," proved there was a hunger for art that challenged the establishment. And then there was Arsenio Hall—Keenen's longtime rival—who had already tapped the zeitgeist. His trailblazing late-night show, launched in 1989, wasn't just a hit; it was a cultural shift, electrifying young audiences, especially Black viewers.

"There was something special going on at that time," said Chuck D, leader of Public Enemy.

For months, Keenen and the cast had been grinding, fine-tuning sketches without knowing which would make the cut. Fox, meanwhile, was on edge—eager for a hit but wary of just how much ground this groundbreaking show might actually break. Their fears proved unfounded. The premiere drew a staggering 23 million viewers—an astronomical number for a fledgling network that wasn't even airing programming seven days a week.

Fox slotted *In Living Color* right after its two biggest comedies, *The Simpsons* and *Married . . . with Children*, but by then, the show was already a hot topic. The network had dragged its feet so long on airing the pilot that bootleg copies started circulating within the industry—and beyond. In New York City, street vendors were selling tapes of the unaired episode months before its official debut.

One of those copies found its way to *Details* magazine writer Martha Frankel, thanks to producer Tamara Rawitt, who discreetly passed it to her over dinner. Frankel wrote a glowing piece, raving about the show and questioning why Fox was holding it back. The next day, Fox executives scrambled and finally greenlit eight episodes.

The public was primed, but the network remained jittery. Fox execs sought reassurance from prominent Black figures, including the NAACP and activist C. Delores Tucker—who would soon gain notoriety for her crusade against rap music—by privately screening the pilot for them. Some wanted to be paid as consultants, a move that infuriated Keenen. He had no interest in seeking approval from self-appointed gatekeepers—especially ones looking for a payout. To him, it was a double standard; white executives weren't forcing filmmakers like Woody Allen to get a stamp of approval from the Anti-Defamation League. He refused to play along.

"At one point, Fox brought this old Black man that they wanted to hire as a consultant to the show," Keenen said. "They told me how he'd marched with Dr. King and had a lump on the side of his head from when he got beat up. I said, 'I respect all he has done, but if he ain't got no jokes, I don't need him. He's no blacker than me. I don't need him to validate me.'"

A closer look at the sketches in the pilot demonstrates just how far Keenen was willing to go to upend norms and rattle people—and just how subversive his vision was. Keenen was eager to take down whoever he felt would get a laugh—including menacing heavyweight champion Mike Tyson. That alone was new ground for Black comedy on television, which hadn't been ready thirteen years earlier for the strange, rebellious vision of Richard Pryor on *The Richard Pryor Show*.

"What was cool about those guys is that they'd mock the heroes of their community, which is a real threading of the needle," Les Firestein, co-head writer of the show, said of Keenen and his younger brother Damon. "Having the ability to make fun of yourselves as a culture is a show of great strength. One of the things that was seminal about *In Living Color* was that Black people enjoyed laughing at Black people. That was the seismic change. You had an entire culture getting to the point where they said we're strong enough that we can laugh at the more ridiculous parts of our own culture."

One of the first things the audience sees in the *In Living Color* pilot is Keenen stepping onto the stage, introducing his cast—but, in true form, he doesn't play it straight.

"I'll tell you what I'm most proud of," he says, locking eyes with the camera. "Unlike other shows, I've got nothing but qualified Black people backstage making decisions."

With perfect timing, he swings open the door to the writers' room—only for a swarm of panicked white writers to scurry out. Keenen, deadpan, assures the audience they're just the cleaning staff. He then gestures toward a bewildered Black woman holding a mop. "And this," he says with a grin, "is our head writer."

The bit lands perfectly—sharp, subversive, and hilarious. Then, without missing a beat, Keenen moves on and introduces the cast.

"We went nationwide to find the most talented people in the country," Keenen announces with a straight face—before rattling off a lineup that sounds more like a family roll call than a casting list. "Damon Wayans, Kim Wayans, Crystal Wayans, TJ Wayans, Toney Wayans, Tommy Wayans . . ."

The joke lands instantly. The message is clear—and hilariously ironic. Many cast members would later (half) joke that the surest way to get on the show and thrive was to have "Wayans" on your birth certificate.

KEENEN BRAGS ABOUT how integrated the show is—and then opens a door that is labeled WHITE CAST MEMBERS ONLY, with white cast members Jim Carrey and Kelly Coffield shining shoes and ironing clothes while grinning and singing "Camp Town Ladies."

"Oh, those people," Keenen says. "Always singing, always happy."

For the viewer, the message is obvious: This show is eager to take on the peculiarities of race and affirmative action in a boldly clever way but also isn't scared of making fun of itself by pointing to the nepotism elephant in the room—the overemployment of the Wayans family.

The first sketch, "Love Connection," features Jim Carrey as the ever-smarmy Chuck Woolery, while Keenen steps in as Mike Tyson, paired with Kim Coles as his new wife, Robin Givens. Keenen leans into the broad caricature—giving Tyson the signature lisp and playing him as a clueless, sexist ogre. From the jump, the show made its stance clear: No one was off-limits.

That particular Tyson impression may have aged out, but in 1990, Mike was still young, ferocious, and not yet a go-to punch line. He had just been knocked out by Buster Douglas in Japan two months before the episode aired—though the sketch had been written before that stunning defeat. It didn't take long for Keenen to learn that Tyson wasn't amused. One night at a club, Mike spotted him and stormed over.

"That was the scariest moment of my life," Keenen recalled. "All I feel is this paw land on my shoulder. I turn around and it's the heavyweight champion of the world. He stepped to me. He goes, 'What? I kill your mother or something?'"

He said he didn't like the impression.

"Yo, you gotta freeze that," Tyson said.

Keenen, who had had years of martial arts training, knew there was no point in trying to defend himself—or worse, step to Tyson.

"In my mind, I was like, *I'm going to have to take this.* Ain't nothing I can do right now. He shut me down." A few months later Keenen saw Tyson again, and he wasn't quite so upset. "He was actually really cool," Keenen said. "He was like, 'Yo, I was just going through some things. You do your thing.' He gave me the green light to go ahead and get back to it."

Kim Coles had a very different kind of Tyson encounter. She was on tour as Luther Vandross's opening act when she ran into the boxing champ.

"He pretended like he was mad," Coles recalled, in an interview with *Entertainment Tonight*. "Like, 'I don't appreciate you making jokes about me on the show!' But he had a good sense of humor about it."

Then, Tyson extended an invitation.

"He invited me to his hotel room, and I promptly got on the tour bus," she said. "He was like, 'I'm having a party back at my room.' I was like, 'I gotta be on the tour bus. Sorry. Bye!'"

(A year after *In Living Color*'s debut, Tyson was accused of raping beauty pageant contestant Desiree Washington. He was later convicted and served three years in prison.)

The show never shied away from making fun of Black culture, as seen in the recurring sketch "Great Moments in Black History." One of the most memorable bits claimed that a Black man had "invented" self-serve gas stations. The punch line? Cast member Tony Riley playing an apathetic gas station attendant who yells at a customer, "Get it your damn self!"

The studio crowd for *In Living Color*'s pilot exceeded even Keenen's wildest expectations.

"Black audiences don't just laugh at stuff, we stomp our feet, we high-five," said Paul Miller, the show's primary director. "People were literally running up and down the aisles during the taping, high-fiving each other. One of the executives turned to me and said, 'Did you pay these guys to do that?'"

Kevin Bright, a supervising producer in the first season who later co-created *Friends*, had never seen anything like it. "At *Friends*, I'd never seen a first taping of anything where the audience was that crazy. They were on fire."

For Larry Wilmore, a writer on the show's first three seasons who went on to co-create *The Bernie Mac Show* and produce *The Office* and *Black-ish*, working on *In Living Color* often felt "surreal."

"In those days, if you worked on *In Living Color*, people went crazy," Wilmore recalled. "They would say, 'So what do you do?' I go, 'Oh, I write for television.' 'Oh, really?' They didn't seem that impressed. 'Well, what shows do you write for?' 'I write for *In Living Color*.' And they go, '*In Living Color*! Oh, my God!' The energy they had for that show, it was so interesting. And I think because we were pushing boundaries at that time that hadn't really been pushed before, especially in race and culture. And people were so excited to see that on their television."

Keenen Wayans's knack for sharp, subversive humor had deep roots. For the first six years of his life, the Wayans family lived in a Harlem tenement on 145th Street and Amsterdam Avenue. His mother, Elvira, grew up immersed in the Harlem Renaissance's art, music, and literature, and Keenen called her a "radical," fully committed to Black Power and the "Black Is Beautiful" movement. His father, Howell, a Jehovah's Witness, worked tirelessly at multiple jobs, yet keeping food on the table was a constant struggle—especially as the family expanded.

By 1972, the Wayans family had ten children. They had moved in 1964 to the Fulton Houses, a newly built public housing project in Chelsea, an area that—long before its transformation into an enclave of art galleries and luxury high-rises—was a rough-and-tumble, working-class neighborhood filled with run-down tenements, bodegas, and mom-and-pop shops. The Wayanses had one of the larger units, a four-bedroom, but with a dozen people crammed inside, space was tight. Shawn and Marlon, the two youngest, slept head-to-toe in the same bed until they were old enough to drive.

Food was scarce. "My mother would look at us and say, 'Look, babies, there ain't no food in the house. We're having sleep for dinner. Now brush your teeth and get ready for bed. Keenen, you make sure everyone gets a little extra toothpaste tonight,'" Damon wrote in his book *Bootleg*.

Keenen, born in 1958, was the second oldest, after Dwayne. Then came Diedra, Damon, Kim, Elvira, Nadia, Devonne, Shawn, and Marlon. Howell took on jobs as a supermarket manager, a sales rep for Guinness/Harp, and a worker at Drake's Cakes before going into business for himself—hustling surplus goods that hadn't been claimed at the post office. Sometimes he brought the kids along to help knock on doors. Elvira, who once performed at the Apollo as part of a singing group, worked as a social worker for a time, but her primary job was running the household.

Marlon, the youngest, had a front-row seat to his parents' unique dynamic.

"My dad would annoy the shit out of my mother and she'd curse him out," Marlon said. "When my mom cursed my dad out, she was like Richard Pryor with titties. I thought his name was Motherfucker until I was nineteen. . . . We got to watch the best buddy comedy ever. Fuck Tom and Jerry. Fuck Daffy Duck and Bugs Bunny. We got to watch Elvira and Howell."

With so many quick-witted personalities crammed into one apartment, laughter wasn't just entertainment—it was survival. The siblings constantly tested each other's comedic chops, often at their mother's expense. Keenen once recalled how Shawn and Marlon found a bell that sounded exactly like the family's telephone. They hid under Elvira's bed, ringing it repeatedly, until she was convinced it was a woman calling for Howell. She stormed through the apartment, unleashing a string of expletives that could've rivaled a Richard Pryor set. That was their goal all along. In the Wayans household, if you were too sensitive, you wouldn't last long.

"If you were getting a whipping from my father, there would be five of us in the room laughing about how you were getting hit," Marlon said.

Howell, meanwhile, carried the weight of feeding ten children.

"I used to watch my dad wake up, put his hand on his head, read his Bible for a little while, look up to the sky, take a deep breath, and go, 'How the fuck am I going to feed these ten motherfuckers today?'" Marlon said. "He'd somehow magically go out and bring dinner home."

The Wayans kids even turned comedy into a competitive sport. They played a game called Make Me Laugh or Die, which, in hindsight, was early improv training.

"Everybody would sit down and then one of us would have to get up and make everybody laugh," Damon recalled. "You couldn't just make one laugh—you had to make everyone laugh at the same time, in unison. If you didn't, we all thought about what your 'die' is. We'd pick something like 'You've got to go drink Daddy's last beer in front of him.' 'Go fart in Mama's face.'"

To avoid these punishments, the siblings got really good at suppressing laughter, making it harder for the performer to win. Years later, when Keenen was running *In Living Color*, cast members would remark on how difficult it was to get a laugh out of him—so when it happened, it was earned. That standard undoubtedly came from growing up Wayans.

Keenen's introduction to Richard Pryor came by accident. One day at PS 11, the elementary school five blocks from the Fulton Houses, he got into an argument with a classmate who declared that they would fight after school. At 3 p.m. sharp, instead of waiting for the showdown, Keenen bolted like a fugitive and made it home so fast his favorite cartoons hadn't even started yet. When he flipped on the TV, instead of animation, he saw a young, skinny Black man standing in front of a crowd, telling jokes.

It was a clean-cut version of Richard Pryor—named "Richie" Pryor—years before he found his raw, irreverent voice, spinning family-friendly tales about his childhood. One joke was about a school bully, woven into stories of growing up poor.

"I was laughing, so amazed that this guy could take this horrible moment and make it funny," Keenen recalled. "I was like, 'Who is this man? I want to be like this man.'"

Though they were close, Keenen and Damon were opposites. Keenen was straightlaced, rarely one to stir trouble. Damon was a rebel—his mother's favorite, partly because he was born with a clubfoot and had to undergo multiple corrective surgeries, wearing special orthopedic shoes as a child. His older brother Dwayne resented the attention and took it out on him.

"He used to beat me up," Damon said. "When my mother made him babysit, he'd hang me on the door hook. If I tried to get down, he'd hit me."

Damon's limp made him an easy target in the neighborhood, but it also sharpened his comedic instincts. He developed a razor-sharp tongue as self-defense, learning that words could hit harder than fists.

He was a small kid—while Keenen was over six feet at sixteen, Damon was still under five feet past his fourteenth birthday—but he got into plenty of fights. He ran with rough kids, smoked weed, and committed petty crimes. By tenth grade, he'd dropped out of high school.

"I just wanted to survive," he said.

Survival in the Wayans household meant being fast, funny, and fearless. The world would soon see just how well-prepared they were.

The kids were always getting into fights, but if you were picking a fight with one Wayans, you had to fight them all. Especially when it came to their archrivals, a family named the Andersons. The Wayanses and Andersons were the ghetto Chelsea version of the Hatfields and McCoys.

"Damon got into a fight with the youngest, and he went and got his brother," Keenen remembered. "Soon, I was fighting the middle kids. Then Dwayne was fighting the older brother. It went on for four years after school."

By the time the 1980s rolled around, the fighting had slowed down a bit, but little Marlon still found himself in the mix. "I would always find the biggest dude, then 'pop,' one punch, and turn around and go, 'Shaaaawn!' My sister would kick him, my nephew would bite him. It was like fighting an octopus. Everybody would jump in."

Their mother had a keen sense about her kids and understood how much Keenen loved comedy. When Richard Pryor was on TV, she'd wake him up. "That little skinny boy is on TV," she'd whisper, even though she didn't know Pryor's name. Their father was more strict, forbidding them from listening to Pryor and Redd Foxx albums, even spanking them if they got caught. "He'd beat us, but we'd take the beating," Damon said. "That's how funny Pryor was."

Keenen wasn't much of a student, but an uncle convinced him to apply for a United Negro College Fund scholarship. That's how, in 1976, Keenen ended up at Tuskegee Institute in Alabama, far away from Chelsea. For him, it was a revelation.

"Being in a city that was predominantly Black, I knew for the first time in my life what white people feel every day—that is, what it's like to be in the majority," Keenen said. "You have no blinders on because you look around and the mayor is Black, the police chief is Black, and the janitor is Black. You can take your pick: You can be anyone."

At Tuskegee, an upperclassman from New York heard Keenen tell hilarious stories about growing up in the city and offered some life-changing advice: "Hey, when you go home, you should check out The Improv." The next time he was in Manhattan, Keenen found the club in the phone book and couldn't believe it was only a twenty-minute walk from the Fulton Houses. "The irony was it took me going two thousand miles away to find out about a club that was one mile from my house."

By the late 1970s, The Improv had become a huge deal, America's premier comedy club, and had hosted legends like Lily Tomlin, Rodney Dangerfield, George Carlin, and certainly Richard Pryor. Comics didn't get paid, but they performed to try out new material, sometimes with agents, managers, and TV bookers in the audience. It was a way to get discovered.

In the summer of 1978, Keenen stood in line for his shot at a five-minute set. He met the only other Black guy there, Robert Townsend, and the two became inseparable. Keenen bombed his first set, but it didn't matter.

"I bombed terribly. It was an out-of-body experience," he said. "I was standing onstage, but at the same time I was able to see myself. [There] was only about five people in the audience and [there] was . . . scattered laughter. Still, I was looking at myself like, You're doing it. It was like I'd stepped into my dream—all those years and the feeling was as good as I thought it was going to be. I didn't care about laughter at that moment because I knew I could do this."

Keenen studied other comics closely, analyzing how they crafted jokes. Townsend recalls one of Keenen's early jokes: "He goes, 'I'm from a family of ten kids. My father had stretch marks,'" Townsend said. "Even as a young comedian, Keenen was kind of a master craftsman. He knew instinctively how to set up a punch, deliver the joke, rewrite the structure, make it funnier."

Those were skills that would serve him well with *In Living Color* twelve years later.

But when Keenen came home from Tuskegee in his second year to tell his parents he was dropping out to pursue comedy instead of engineering, they didn't understand. Marlon, still in elementary school, was there to witness the moment.

"My mother cursed Keenen out," Marlon said. "My mother said, 'Boy, a stand-up comedian? I known you your whole life and you ain't never said nothing funny. This shit is the funniest thing you ever said! You're going to be a stand-up comedian? Let me tell you something, boy. You better go out there and get your engineer's degree and a job with some benefits!'"

Keenen knew there was very little chance they would understand. "I might as well have said I was going to smoke crack," he said. "But I knew deep in myself what I wanted to be. I knew I was going to do it."

Keenen thrived in the world of stand-up comics who gathered at clubs to dissect jokes and share their craft—comedians like Larry David, Jerry Seinfeld, Jay Leno, Bill Maher, Robin Williams, and Rodney

Dangerfield. For most, the goal was clear: Get on *The Tonight Show* with Carson, sit on the couch, and get their big break.

Keenen spent most of his time with Robert Townsend, talking comedy at Townsend's apartment. Townsend, a poor kid from Chicago, had also dropped out of college, and he and Keenen had much in common.

"We just clicked," Townsend said. "I'd visit him in his neighborhood in Chelsea and he'd have his friends try to rob me. He wanted to see what [I] was gonna do. He thought that shit was funny. His sense of humor can be twisted."

Townsend soon invested in video equipment and turned his apartment into a mini studio. He and Keenen didn't know what to film, but they were determined to make something, even if it was just the gatherings of Black comedians they called the Kitchen Table. Keenen suggested they include Damon.

"Damon was working at Smiley's Deli at the time," Townsend recalled. "I remember Keenen saying, 'We gotta get my baby brother involved. He's really funny and can do characters.'"

The other comedians were impressed by Keenen's leadership and ability to bring everyone together. But what really stunned them was Damon's natural talent. "He was so damn funny it made me insecure," Townsend said. "That's your baby brother?! He's working at a deli?!"

Damon had already developed a host of characters, like a gay film critic and a neighborhood hustler. "All those characters he'd eventually do on *In Living Color*, I saw in my apartment," Townsend said.

Keenen dreamed of a time when the Kitchen Table could focus entirely on skits and improv. That thought never left him. In 1980, he moved to California to try his hand at Hollywood, though he was so broke, he had to walk everywhere, even ten or fifteen miles. Walking in LA is so suspicious that he even got pulled over by the cops one night.

He auditioned for the Comedy Store, a West Coast version of The Improv. There, he met Arsenio Hall, another young Black comic, who had come to LA from Cleveland. Neither Keenen nor Arsenio got picked to perform at the main club, but Mitzi Shore put them on at her second club in Westwood, a kind of junior varsity.

In 1981, Keenen landed a development deal with NBC and was cast as Irene Cara's boyfriend in a pilot called *Irene*. Keenen had had a crush on Cara ever since seeing her in *Sparkle* when he was sixteen, even telling a friend he would marry her one day. Unfortunately, the relationship wasn't meant to be, nor was the pilot, which didn't get picked up, though Keenen did get a few on-screen kisses.

"I was a young, naïve boy and she was a woman," Keenen said.

Keenen convinced Townsend to join him in LA, but they soon discovered the disheartening reality: The industry expected young Black men to only play thugs or pimps.

"YOU'VE GOT THIS dream, then you get to Hollywood and find yourself in line to play some crack dealer," Townsend said. "You're like, 'Wow. This is what they think of us.'"

Both he and Keenen were often told they sounded too articulate, too well-educated. "I'm from a family of ten in the projects, and I find out I'm not 'Black enough,'" Keenen said.

These experiences fueled their drive to write *Hollywood Shuffle*, the razor-sharp satire that exposed racism in the industry. But before that, Keenen was just another struggling actor trying to break through. If you blinked, you might've missed his face on *Cheers*. He got arrested by Erik Estrada on *CHiPs* and played a stand-up comic in Bob Fosse's *Star 80*. He even starred in a short-lived series, *For Love and Honor*, playing an illiterate boxer. But his biggest break came when he landed a spot on *The Tonight Show*.

By then, he was five years into his stand-up career—seasoned, confident. He told a joke about his older brother, Dwayne, who, as Keenen put it, "finds racism in everything."

"He's like, 'The white man don't want to see you make it! They don't want to see you get ahead. They got a conspiracy out there!' Does he think there's some secret organization sitting around going, 'Now, there are too many Black people making it in this country. They're making too much progress. Now, let's see . . . We got Malcolm X, we got Martin Luther King . . . Dwayne! He's up for promotion at McDonald's! Stop him!'"

The crowd erupted. Then came the ultimate trophy—Carson called him over to the couch. They were headed to commercial, so there was no time for an interview, but as the show cut away, Carson's voice could be heard: "That's funny stuff."

"Next time you come back, we'll have time to talk," Carson promised after the break.

Keenen grew close with Eddie Murphy and even closer with Townsend. Along with Arsenio Hall and Paul Mooney, they formed what Mooney later called the Black Pack, a nod to Sinatra's Rat Pack. Eddie was the king, far more successful than the rest. Keenen and Arsenio vied for his attention. Meanwhile, Damon moved to LA to try his luck in comedy, his style sharper and angrier than his brother's.

Eddie was so impressed with Damon that he cast him in *Beverly Hills Cop*, playing the flamboyant hotel clerk who slips Axel Foley some bananas.

"That got a huge laugh," Damon said. "I was working in the mailroom, making $12 an hour, and I had to quit my job because everyone wanted me to be the banana guy."

Back in New York, while Keenen was hanging out with Murphy, his family still lived in the projects. When he was home, he slept in the same bedroom he once shared with Damon. Shawn and Marlon were just kids, but already funny and irreverent.

One night, Murphy pulled up to the Fulton Houses in his limo to take Keenen out. His arrival caused a stir—Hollywood royalty didn't exactly frequent the projects.

"You ever see *The Birds*?" Shawn joked, referencing Hitchcock's horror classic. "Where they're trying to escape at the end? It was that—with project people. You had to step over them."

Murphy planned to scoop Keenen and leave, but he ended up staying for hours. Keenen had even bought a new couch for the occasion, embarrassed by the old one.

"He didn't want Eddie sitting on the roach-infested couch that my mother still had plastic covers on," Shawn recalled.

Shawn and Marlon weren't starstruck—they saw a guy in cow-skin pants.

"He walked in, he had some cow-skin pants on—ain't too many Negroes in the projects got cow-skin pants," Marlon said. "So while he was there, me, Shawn, and Craig [their sister Diedra's son] were snapping on Eddie, cracking jokes about his pants. Every time he sat down, we'd go, 'Moooo!' We tagged him for hours."

After Murphy left *SNL* in 1984, Damon joined the cast. But he was underused, his ideas dismissed. He wasn't going to be the next Murphy. He sulked around 30 Rock in sunglasses. If anyone asked why, he'd reply, "It's too white in here. It hurts my eyes."

The breaking point came when they cast him as a spear-holding slave—with no lines.

"I told Lorne [Michaels], 'My mother's gonna watch this. I'm not standing there with no spear. Unless I could stab everybody in this scene, I'm not doing it.'"

Lorne begged him to be a team player. So did his manager, Brad Grey. But Damon refused. Then came a *Miami Vice*-style cop sketch with Randy Quaid. Frustrated, Damon played the cop as the same flamboyant character from *Beverly Hills Cop*.

Lorne was furious. He cursed Damon out and fired him. Told him he'd just torched his career.

Damon didn't care. He wanted out.

Meanwhile, Townsend was equally frustrated. He had a strong role in *A Soldier's Story* alongside Denzel Washington, but after that, it was back to playing addicts and criminals.

So, he and Keenen got to work.

"We didn't know how to write a movie," Keenen said. "We just went with the things we did know. We'd lay out pieces of clothing that represented different characters. We'd set up a video camera and improvise. Whenever we'd switch characters, we'd put on a hat or a scarf or whatever. Then we'd watch it back. Stuff we thought worked, we'd write down. What didn't work, we discarded."

They used Townsend's savings to shoot scenes guerrilla-style, dodging cops, filming without permits. They spoofed movie tropes—like "Death of a Break Dancer," where Keenen played the prime suspect, Jheri Curl. They did a Siskel and Ebert parody called "Sneakin' in the Movies." But the most biting satire was "Black Acting School," a skit that summed up their Hollywood experience:

A classically trained Black British actor and other well-educated Black performers advertise a school where aspiring actors learn to play pimps, muggers, and street thugs—complete with a white instructor teaching them the proper way to say, "Jive turkey motherfucker."

The film featured Keenen, Townsend, Damon, Kim Wayans, and their friends from LA's Black comedy scene.

Then they saw *She's Gotta Have It*.

Watching Spike Lee's indie breakthrough, they recognized a kindred spirit—someone doing in New York what they were trying to do in LA.

They knew they were onto something.

In 1987, Arsenio took over hosting *The Late Show* on Fox, and the rest of the Black Pack was right there backstage, cheering him on. Having Eddie as a guest was a huge boost for the show's ratings.

"We became a bit of a clique," Townsend said. "We were all young artists. When you're young and have healthy egos, you want to take over the world. You look at Hollywood and you're like, 'We could do this.'"

Eddie's manager, Richie Tienken, couldn't help but notice the rivalry brewing between Keenen and Arsenio for Eddie's attention.

"Keenen and Arsenio didn't get along," Tienken said. "It was like watching two broads try to pick up a guy." (That dynamic would find its way into *In Living Color*, where Keenen impersonated Arsenio—cranking up the volume on Hall's signature moves, from the exaggerated fist pumps to the over-the-top reactions to guests. With an oversize suit and an even bigger attitude, Keenen's parody was as ruthless as it was hilarious, turning Arsenio's late-night swagger into pure comedic gold.)

Townsend's career skyrocketed with the release of *Hollywood Shuffle*. Made on a shoestring budget—financed entirely with Townsend's savings and credit cards—the film cost between $60,000 and $100,000 to produce. It went on to gross $5.2 million and earned critical acclaim. In the Black community, Townsend was now seen as the next major comedic voice.

But Keenen felt overshadowed. He believed his contributions to *Hollywood Shuffle* went unrecognized and was especially frustrated that he didn't get co-writing credit for the opening of Eddie Murphy's *Raw*, which featured a skit he had written—young Eddie performing stand-up for his family, only to deliver a wildly inappropriate joke that sends them into chaos.

Keenen wanted a project that was unquestionably his own. That was when he turned his attention to *I'm Gonna Git You Sucka*.

The idea had actually come from Murphy. "We were all hanging out and he said, 'Wouldn't it be funny to make a parody of blaxploitation movies?'" Keenen recalled. "He actually said, 'I'm gonna get you sucka.' We all started riffing and throwing out ideas. Then it sat."

On the advice of Tamara Rawitt, the sharp-witted executive running Eddie's production company, Keenen got Eddie's blessing to use the idea. He wrote the script and brought it to Rawitt, who pushed him through at least twenty rewrites before they finally sold it to United Artists for a modest $2.7 million budget. Because the investment was so small, UA agreed to let Keenen direct.

Keenen starred in the film but also recruited blaxploitation legends—Bernie Casey, Jim Brown, Isaac Hayes, and Antonio Fargas—to reprise variations of their iconic roles. The cast also included a slew of Wayanses, David Alan Grier, Anne-Marie Johnson, John Witherspoon, and Robin Harris. Chris Rock had a brief but unforgettable role as a cheapskate trying to haggle Isaac Hayes down to selling just one rib at the rib joint. Rock has said he gets more comments from the public on that part than almost anything else he has done in his career.

"I don't want to get punched in the face, but Keenen basically stole a joke of mine," Rock admitted. "It was in the script. I think Eddie was like, 'Hey, isn't that Chris Rock's thing?' Next thing I know, I got flown from New York to LA for a movie that only had a two-million-dollar budget."

Despite minimal marketing from UA and opening in just five cities, *Sucka* still debuted as the third-highest-grossing new release that weekend, trailing only *Rain Man* and *Dirty Rotten Scoundrels*. As word spread, UA doubled its theater count, and the film eventually earned $20 million—an incredible return on a $2.7 million budget. More importantly, it proved that Keenen could carry a project on his own.

At the same time, Fox was desperate to break through as the fourth major TV network and had hired twenty-eight-year-old Garth Ancier from NBC to run programming. They were eager for Keenen to create a show for them, offering him a blank check. Initially, he hesitated—his focus was on making movies. But the more he thought about it, the more the idea intrigued him.

"He thought of the characters he and Damon had been making each other laugh with since they were kids. He thought back to those improvs they'd filmed with the Kitchen Table. He thought about *Saturday Night Live*—his brief audition, Damon's disastrous stint, Eddie's triumph—and how the show felt made by, for, and about white people. He thought about all the Black comics and actors he knew, people he'd met at the Comedy Act, on *Hollywood Shuffle*, *Partners in Crime*, or *Sucka*. Hollywood had no idea what to do with any of them. But he did."

Assembling the cast for *In Living Color* proved to be a challenge—even with his siblings in the mix. Keenen saw *SNL* as a writer-driven show, but he wanted *ILC* to be performer driven, where the writing would serve the cast. His plan was to build the show around Damon and add the best talent he could find.

"Damon was at a point comedically where he was the most brilliant guy on the planet," Keenen said. "The way he thought, the way his point of view was completely different than mine or anybody else's. He was really on the edge."

Kim had moved to LA after graduating from Wesleyan and was

working as an assistant at the powerhouse talent agency CAA. She'd landed guest spots on *A Different World* and *China Beach*, but Keenen still made her audition.

"It was very exciting but also nerve-racking," she said. "The last thing I wanted to do was embarrass my brother."

Keenen hired Shawn as a production assistant, while Marlon was supposed to start at Howard University in the fall—though he kept hanging around the show.

"The Wayanses are kind of a comedy troupe in and of themselves," said Rob Edwards, a Black writer on the show who created "Great Moments in Black History." "They'd go out to dinner—they eat as a family all the time—and try to crack each other up."

The next day, they'd bring those stories to the writers' room.

"The writers would take as much of this down as humanly possible," Edwards said. "They have incredible characters, timing, and a great sense of what's funny."

Kim Wayans, according to Edwards, had considerable influence over Keenen's decisions, while Marlon—still a teenager—was already being recognized as just as funny as Damon and Keenen.

Jim Carrey came in on Damon's recommendation. The two had met at the Comedy Store, where Carrey—then a struggling Canadian comic—was trying to evolve beyond his early work as a pure impersonator. Despite a decade in Hollywood, steady work had eluded him. His NBC sitcom *The Duck Factory* had flopped after just thirteen episodes in 1984. He'd starred alongside Damon in *Earth Girls Are Easy* and had auditioned for *SNL* multiple times. But he was still waiting for his breakthrough—someone who truly understood how to harness his talent.

"I remember loving Damon's stand-up because he took such huge chances and wasn't afraid to say anything on his mind," Carrey recalled. "He had one really sick bit where he talked about his sister being beaten senseless by her husband. He said, 'Why are you with this guy?' And then, imitating her swollen lips and half-shut eye, he'd answer, 'I dooownn't knooow. Dere's joust somefin' about 'im.' It was so wrong. I remember thinking, *This is one of the angriest comedians*

I've ever seen. One day he came up to me after seeing me experimenting onstage and said, 'Man, you're one of the angriest comedians I've ever seen in my life!' We became friends."

One of about 150 hopefuls, Carrey went all out at his audition, firing off a rapid succession of characters—including a Nipsey Russell impression—that left the room buzzing.

"They were just falling on the ground," he said.

Keenen knew immediately: "At that point, Jim became an obvious choice."

David Spade also auditioned, making it through the first few rounds before being cut.

"I'm not a great improv-er, but they needed a white guy," Spade said. "I didn't know I was against Jim Carrey. If I [had] known, I would've skipped it. I wasn't very good. I don't do characters. He was so perfect. I was like, 'Why did you waste all of our time?'"

Martin Lawrence tried out as well, fresh off his minor role as a neighborhood kid with a lisp in *Do the Right Thing*. He was joined by Bonnie Hunt and Thomas Haden Church. Meanwhile, performers like David Alan Grier, Kelly Coffield, and T'Keyah Crystal Keymáh were hesitant about auditioning, since they saw themselves as actors rather than comedians.

Keenen encouraged Grier—who had been in his and Townsend's orbit for years—to go for it. Initially, Grier declined the offer. But Kim Wayans convinced him to reconsider.

Chris Rock had been hopeful about landing a spot, but the offer never came, something he later attributed to being based in New York while the show was happening in LA.

"Chris was a genius writer and great at being Chris, but the show needed people who could do a myriad of characters and accents. That's not what he did," said Tamara Rawitt. "If we had our own 'News Update' desk [like *SNL*], he could've owned that space."

Damon, however, was proving to be a thorny hire. Keenen was adamant about him being on the show, but Damon was holding out for more money. Fox, frustrated with the negotiations, knew they had to keep Keenen happy—otherwise, they would have likely cut Damon.

Their compromise was making Damon a "guest star" for the pilot, with the option to revisit his status if the show got picked up.

Damon wasn't satisfied.

"When I walked into *In Living Color,* they treated me like Keenen's little brother," he said. "I had a one-year deal. They didn't even respect me enough to make me a regular. I was a recurring character."

He said he was paid just $1,500 per episode.

"I don't think Fox knew what I could do."

From the very beginning, one of Keenen's firmest ideas was incorporating a hip-hop dance troupe that would perform throughout the show. Almost no one understood why.

One night, he spotted a young dancer, AJ Johnson, moving on the floor at a club and approached her. AJ, who had appeared in Spike Lee's *School Daze* while still at Spelman, had been her sorority's step captain. Over lunch, Keenen explained his vision, but she still wasn't sold.

"I don't get why you want dancers coming out in the middle of a comedy show," she told him.

"I'm telling you, it's going to be one of the hottest parts of the show. It's gonna be crazy!"

"I still don't get it," she said. "You're going to have some dancers out there for a couple of seconds. Big deal."

Keenen was undeterred. "When I saw you dance in the club that night, that's when the vision hit," he said. "Everybody in America's gonna wanna do these dances. Everybody in America's gonna wanna dress like these girls. Trust me!"

But before things could move forward, AJ was offered a role in *House Party* and decided to take it over the show. It was a difficult decision—especially since she and Keenen had begun a relationship. Still, she made a recommendation for her replacement: Rosie Perez, the dancer who had electrified the opening credits of *Do the Right Thing.*

Keenen's casting director, Robi Reed, had worked with Perez before and arranged a meeting. Keenen liked her and assured her a producer would be in touch to finalize a contract. But the call never came. When Perez followed up, she was told someone else had been hired.

"I couldn't believe it," Perez said. "I didn't have Keenen's number. I didn't know Keenen like that, so I said, 'Will you leave a message with Keenen?' He didn't call me back."

Instead, Perez took a job choreographing LL Cool J's tour. Keenen later chalked up the miscommunication to a mix-up, but by then, the show had moved on and hired veteran choreographer Carla Earle. The pilot featured an all-Black group of dancers, but when the show was picked up, Fox wanted a more diverse look—something akin to a Benetton ad.

Then, LL's tour rolled through Los Angeles, and Keenen went backstage to talk to Perez. He wanted her for the show and was willing to pay double whatever LL was giving her. When she hesitated, he offered even more. Perez told LL about the offer, and he gave his blessing: "Go get that TV money."

At first, Perez struggled to connect with the dancers. Most were classically trained and looked down on her. She wasn't impressed by them either.

"What they thought was hip-hop wasn't hip-hop," she said.

Determined to bring authenticity, she also took over the show's music selection, ensuring the dancers performed to the hottest hip-hop tracks. She even flew back to New York to hit the clubs and stay ahead of the trends.

"When Rosie came on, she helped to shape the look and the whole style," Keenen said. "She was connected to underground hip-hop, so all the dance moves were stuff people hadn't seen yet. They were coming straight out of the clubs. A lot of the credit for the Fly Girls goes to her."

During a club visit, Perez saw Leaders of the New School perform and was mesmerized—especially by one wild, charismatic rapper named Busta Rhymes. That night, she had a new idea: Instead of just playing artists' music, why not bring them on the show to perform live? Keenen was skeptical—guests cost money. But Perez pushed until he relented (though he would later claim live music had always been part of his plan).

The first musical guest was Queen Latifah, who killed it. After that, artists lined up to appear. By the second season, the show featured Monie Love, KRS-One, 3rd Bass, Leaders of the New School, and Public Enemy.

Keenen's authority over the show was undisputed. He had strong ideas, and whether people saw him as confident and visionary or arrogant and dismissive, he commanded respect. He wasn't a screamer or a tantrum thrower, but his presence was intimidating. He took input, but not dissent.

"It was a dictatorship," Keenen admitted.

And that dictatorship worked. Right before the premiere of season two, *In Living Color* won an Emmy for Outstanding Variety, Music, or Comedy Series—beating *The Arsenio Hall Show*, *Saturday Night Live*, and *Late Night with David Letterman*. Keenen especially enjoyed besting *SNL*, which had unceremoniously dumped Damon. But Hollywood had no interest in rewarding the show beyond that—*In Living Color* never won another Emmy.

Keenen had big plans for the Fly Girls. He wanted them to become their own brand—land a TV spin-off, maybe even sign a recording contract. But first, he needed more dancers. The search was massive, drawing thousands of women. To speed things up, Keenen personally walked the line and cut anyone he deemed "busted." Some women were so enraged that one even took a swing at him.

On the second day, Perez spotted a "curvy, heavyset, big-ass beautiful girl" from the Bronx: Jennifer Lopez. She wasn't the best dancer, but she had undeniable star quality. However, when Keenen let the Fly Girls themselves choose the new member in a national TV stunt, they picked Carla Garrido—some suspected because they saw her as less of a threat than Lopez.

Keenen wasn't happy. He told Perez he still wanted Lopez. Fox offered her a holding deal, and she joined the cast in season three. But from day one, she clashed with the other dancers—especially Perez.

Resentment brewed among the other Fly Girls, who felt their friends had been cut to make space for her. Adding fuel to the fire, Lopez's ambition was obvious, and it rubbed some the wrong way.

"There was a feeling that Jennifer Lopez seemed most interested in what was best for Jennifer Lopez's own career as opposed to what was best for the group or the show," Perez said.

Perez later admitted she was young and didn't handle the situation well, but she also blamed Keenen for stoking the tension.

"He would always call me on the red phone reserved for producers during live and pre-tapings, telling me to take her out of a certain number if he thought she looked fat that week or too clunky," Perez said.

Perez passed the notes along but never told Lopez where they came from. Finally, Lopez exploded.

"You pick on me, me and only me, every fucking day!" she yelled at Perez. "Every fucking day! I work my ass off, deliver, and you keep pushing me aside, treating me like I'm shit! I know I'm good! I'm better than any of these girls and you know it!"

Eric Gold, a show executive who would later manage Lopez, recalled the moment vividly.

"She's bossing Jennifer around, and Jennifer's like, 'Fuck you!' Let's go in the parking lot right now!'" Gold said. "This turns into like a Brooklyn-Bronx thing. Rosie's like, 'Fuck you! I'll kill you!' And they're going in the parking lot to fight. Somehow Keenen intervened and it worked itself out."

As for Keenen's grand plan for the Fly Girls, it collapsed in the worst way.

They were close to signing with Virgin Records when disaster struck. At the time, one of Virgin's top artists was Paula Abdul, whose career had been rocked by rumors she wasn't actually singing on her own records. *In Living Color* aired a brutal parody of Abdul, so vicious that Perez refused to choreograph it out of respect for her.

During a break in their Virgin meeting, some of the Fly Girls went to the bathroom and started badmouthing Abdul—without realizing she was in a stall listening. Furious, Abdul stormed into the executive's office and issued an ultimatum:

"They go or I go."

Virgin dropped the Fly Girls immediately. The spin-off TV show also collapsed.

One of *In Living Color*'s most enduring creations was Homey the Clown, played by Damon Wayans. As writer David Peisner observed, Homey embodied the raw, unfiltered id of Keenen and Damon—angry, irreverent, and hilarious. While many assumed Paul Mooney had created the character, Homey was actually inspired by him.

"Homey is Paul Mooney," Keenen explained. "Instead of an angry comedian, he's an angry clown. He's a guy whose job is to be funny but he's the antithesis of that."

Damon infused Homey with elements from his own stand-up act, particularly his "Angry Comic" bit. In the character's debut sketch, Homey performs at a children's birthday party, where a little girl asks him to "do a silly clown dance." He refuses to "degrade" himself. "I don't think so. Homey don't play that," he says, before smacking the child with a weighted sock. When asked to perform a magic trick, he simply takes a dollar from a kid, folds it up, and pockets it.

Seemingly overnight, "Homey don't play that" became a catchphrase across the country.

"As the character developed over the course of the coming seasons," Peisner wrote, "Homey often felt like an alternate mouthpiece for Keenen and Damon to express their frustrations with the show, with Fox, with their own careers, and with the wider world. Homey the Clown was, in some sense, *In Living Color*'s aggrieved, outspoken id."

By this point, Keenen was appearing less frequently in sketches, but his presence was undeniable.

"Keenen is one of the true geniuses of sketch comedy," said David Alan Grier. "Meaning, you do a scene, it's all flat, and Keenen says, 'If you pick up your pencil, look to the right and say the same joke, it's gonna work.' You trust him, you do it, and it kills. Most people don't know comedy. They can't fix it. You stumble on a great joke, you don't know why it's great. But Keenen had that ability. I've been acting over 30 years, there's maybe two or three people like that."

By the time Jamie Foxx joined in season three, the show had hit its stride. But breaking in wasn't easy.

"When I saw Damon walk in and Jim walk in, it was like fucking

Jurassic Park," Foxx recalled. "I was the eighth-funniest person in the room at any given time. I had to be quiet sometimes to learn my way."

The other cast members quickly recognized his talent.

"Jamie fucking scared me," Tommy Davidson admitted. He played opposite Foxx's breakout character, Wanda, and saw firsthand how effortlessly Foxx commanded a scene. "Jamie was so talented, it was like, Whoa."

One of the show's most lasting contributions to pop culture wasn't a sketch or a character—it was a revolution in television. The Super Bowl halftime show had traditionally been a dull affair, featuring marching bands and forgettable acts. Fox executives had an audacious idea: *In Living Color* should hijack halftime, luring viewers away from CBS.

Keenen was immediately on board.

"I thought, *This is genius*," he said. "The Super Bowl was the biggest thing in television. No one would dare take on the Super Bowl. We have to do that."

At the time, CBS's halftime programming featured Olympic skaters Dorothy Hamill and Brian Boitano performing alongside a thirty-foot inflatable snowman in a segment called "Winter Magic"—a transparent attempt to hype their upcoming Winter Olympics coverage. It was an easy target.

Frito-Lay backed *In Living Color*'s counterprogramming with a $2 million sponsorship. With sketches like "The Homeboy Shopping Network," Jim Carrey's "Fire Marshal Bill," and Damon and Grier's flamboyant "Men on Football," the bold move paid off. *In Living Color* drew 29 million viewers, and the Super Bowl's ratings plunged by ten points in the second half.

"It was this little show that took on this giant and crushed," Keenen said.

In a single night, *In Living Color* transformed the Super Bowl halftime show forever. The next year, Michael Jackson took the stage, ushering in the era of blockbuster musical performances that continues today.

"We swooped in like pirates and took over that halftime half hour," Carrey said proudly. "We're the reason why you see all that amazing entertainment at Super Bowl halftime now."

After *In Living Color*, Shawn and Marlon went on to star in the WB sitcom *The Wayans Bros.*, in addition to such hit films as *Don't Be a Menace*, *Scary Movie*, and *White Chicks*.

David Alan Grier didn't hesitate when asked whether *In Living Color* could exist in today's world. "Oh man, we can't do it this time," he said. "The world has changed. You can't be doing that crazy stuff we did. I mean, we barely got away last time because when *In Living Color* was originally on, you could call the station to complain. You could write a letter, snail mail, or you could do the latest technology at the time, which was fax, there was no social media, right? No, we could not do the show as it was now."

He wasn't just talking about shifting audience sensibilities—he was talking about an entirely different media landscape. Back then, controversy took time to build, and complaints had to be mailed, faxed, or called in. Now, backlash is instantaneous. In his view, the same boundary-pushing comedy that made *In Living Color* revolutionary would never make it past today's hyperaware, quick-to-react cultural climate.

CHAPTER 16
FAMILY MATTERS

While *In Living Color* broke ground with its raw energy and comedic audacity, a new wave of Black family sitcoms was taking root across network schedules. These shows didn't shout; they invited you in. And leading that charge was a series that started with a simple story about a working-class Chicago family.

Family Matters debuted in the fall of 1989, as part of ABC's iconic TGIF (Thank Goodness It's Friday) programming block—a lineup that would come to define Friday nights for a generation of American families. TGIF wasn't just a scheduling strategy; it was a cultural event. With a mix of heartwarming humor, family-centered storytelling, and just enough chaos to keep kids laughing and parents watching, the block became appointment television in an era long before streaming.

At the heart of *Family Matters* was a breakout character no one saw coming. But before he became one of the most recognizable faces in American television, Jaleel White was just an innocent kid getting his start on the set of *The Jeffersons*. "At that age, I'm just wide-eyed and can't believe I'm at a table reading with George Jefferson and Florence and Mr. Willis," he recalled in a 2011 *Vanity Fair* interview. "It was amazing and it was surreal. I didn't know what the heck I was doing. I was just being a cute kid. That was such a fun week and I remember Sherman Hemsley being so nice to me." That early role as a child-prodigy pianist was his first taste of the television world—a world that would eventually center around him.

White nearly took a very different path. As a child, he auditioned for the role of Rudy Huxtable on *The Cosby Show*—a part originally written for a boy. His agent was so confident he'd land it, she told his parents to start apartment-hunting in New York. "We were all packed up and ready to go," he recalls.

But in a fateful twist, the network decided to rewrite the role for a girl—a decision that would change both White's trajectory and Keshia Knight Pulliam's.

"I remember this little girl walking in, and even at eight years old I was like, 'Who's she?'" he says. "They told me, 'She's auditioning for Rudy too.'"

It was White's first taste of the industry's sharp edges. "I walked into this room with thirty people staring at me like, 'Okay, make me laugh,'" he says. "The producers were in such a rush to start filming that they cast the roles on the spot, calling out names one by one—Malcolm-Jamal Warner, Tempestt Bledsoe—right in front of everyone.... The rest of us just went home crying."

The sting faded over time. "Obviously, I'm grateful things worked out the way they did."

They certainly did. In 1989, White was cast in a sitcom called *Family Matters*, a *Perfect Strangers* spin-off that centered on the working-class Winslow family in Chicago. Jo Marie Payton's character, Harriette, had appeared on *Perfect Strangers* as an elevator operator, and now she and her TV husband, Carl Winslow (Reginald VelJohnson)—a penny-pinching police officer with a death grip on his wallet—were getting their own series. Their kids—Eddie and Laura—filled the typical roles of teen sitcomdom. Bills were paid, mishaps were resolved, and values were affirmed. *Family Matters*, while charming, was struggling in the ratings.

Then, in episode 13, everything changed.

Jaleel White was brought on for what was supposed to be a one-off role: Steve Urkel, the Winslows' nerdy, love-struck neighbor with a high-pitched voice, thick glasses, suspenders, and a penchant for cheese. "I thought, great, I can have fun for the week," he said. But his performance struck a nerve—and struck gold. Urkel was instantly unforgettable. Viewers couldn't get enough of the nasally-voiced inventor with a heart of gold. By the time his catchphrase "Did I do that?" became a national joke, the direction of the show had irrevocably changed.

Family Matters was no longer an ensemble family sitcom. It was the Urkel show.

White's sudden rise to the center brought challenges behind the scenes. "Things were definitely strained in the early going," he admits. "There was a division between myself and the rest of the cast, but over nine years and 215 episodes, obviously relationships get better. I still talk to certain cast members to this day."

As much as White may have felt like an outsider within the cast, he was becoming a household name to the American public. Urkel joined the ranks of cultural icons, a character who, like Jimmie Walker's "Dy-no-mite"-spouting J.J. Evans, became synonymous with the show he was never meant to lead. "I catapulted Urkel into the pantheon of American pop culture," White notes, not without a hint of irony.

As *Family Matters* grew into one of the longest-running Black sitcoms of the 1990s, it painted a picture of familial stability and sitcom comfort. Week after week, viewers tuned in to see the Winslows navigate everyday life—mishaps, lessons, and laughter—with consistency and love. But behind the scenes, the Winslow family was quietly undergoing a change that would never be addressed on-screen. One member of the household simply stopped appearing, and the show moved on as if she had never been there at all.

If you blinked, you might've missed her. And if you didn't blink, you probably wondered what happened. Judy Winslow, the youngest daughter of Carl and Harriette Winslow, vanished without a trace midway through the fourth season of *Family Matters*. No goodbye. No storyline explanation. No spin-off. She simply went upstairs one episode and never came back down. In the sitcom canon, this phenomenon became so common it earned a name: "Chuck Cunningham Syndrome"—after the older brother on *Happy Days* who similarly evaporated from his show.

But the case of Judy Winslow, played by Jaimee Foxworth, is particularly emblematic of the way Hollywood's choices have real-life consequences, especially for young Black actors and especially within the framework of shows that were ostensibly about Black families—but often became more about ratings than representation.

It wasn't just viewers who were left in the dark; so too was Jaleel White: "Shoot, I didn't get an explanation. Her momma asked for too much and they sent her upstairs. That was it. Back then, family television had a way of getting away with certain things that, obviously, you couldn't get away with now."

For Foxworth, the impact was real and lasting. Being cut from the show without closure or compensation left emotional scars. In later interviews, she described struggling with depression and substance abuse. In the early 2000s, she made headlines when it was revealed she had briefly entered the adult film industry under a pseudonym—a choice made, she later said, out of financial desperation.

Foxworth eventually got sober, became a mother, and began to speak publicly about her experience—both the trauma and the recovery. She appeared on *Oprah* and *Life After*, telling her story with candor and strength, offering a window into what happens when a child actor is discarded by an industry that builds up characters but not always the people behind them.

While Foxworth wrestled with being written out of the story, Jaleel White carried a different kind of weight—the pressure of being its unlikely centerpiece. As the show's breakout star, his character became a cultural lightning rod, drawing scrutiny and debate, especially from within the Black academic and cultural spheres.

Years later, as a film and television student at UCLA, White found himself confronting a more personal version of that critique—on the receiving end of intellectual disdain for the very character that had made him famous. A teaching assistant in a lecture hall dismissed Urkel as a modern-day Sambo, suggesting that his character was crafted to make white audiences more comfortable watching a Black family. "I was deeply uncomfortable, and I was steaming," he recalled in his 2024 memoir *Growing Up Urkel*. "But I didn't say a word."

To be labeled a caricature in front of 200 classmates while sitting silently in the back row was a surreal reversal: The actor whose performance had helped keep a hit show on the air was now being dismissed as emblematic of cultural regression—by critics with little understanding of how television actually gets made. "No one created my character with those overreaching intentions," White writes.

He didn't argue. He didn't need to. *Family Matters* was doing its job: entertaining families. It wasn't trying to be *A Different World*. White argues that the criticism often lacked nuance, failing to see the clear genre distinctions between a show like *Family Matters* and edgier, adult fare like *Martin* or *Living Single*. "That's like comparing *Seinfeld* to *Full House*. You wouldn't do it. They are two very different shows with different goals, created by and for different demographics."

White's defense of *Family Matters* isn't just about Urkel—it's about legacy. "We all stand on the shoulders of those who've come before us," he writes. "Would there be any of the Black shows on the fledgling WB network in the mid-aughts if *Family Matters* hadn't been on the air for nine years? I would argue not."

Yet as the 1990s drew to a close, culture evolved faster than *Family Matters* could keep up. The rise of hip-hop culture, Black sitcoms with sharper wit and topical edge, and the emergence of online communities all meant that Urkel's quirky innocence began to feel out of step. "Maybe that's an indictment of the show," White concedes. "Or maybe that's just the reality of a 30-minute family sitcom."

What *Family Matters* never tried to do was speak for all Black people—nor should it have.

"*Seinfeld* doesn't speak for all Jewish people. *Friends* doesn't speak for all white people. But no one ever thinks they should or did. They are not examined with that same lens."

But for Black shows—especially popular ones—there has long been an unspoken expectation that they must be both entertaining and representationally responsible.

Urkel complicated that.

For a generation of Black kids, he was both an inspiration and a source of teasing. It was just about impossible for a bookish, bespectacled Black kid in the '90s to show up to school and avoid being called Urkel. He was the archetype no one asked for—but everyone remembered.

In the end, *Family Matters* mattered. It lasted nine seasons, spanning a time of enormous cultural change, and helped open the door for the next wave of Black-led television. Its legacy is complicated but not undeserved.

CHAPTER 17
THE FRESH PRINCE OF BEL-AIR

Growing up on the unforgiving streets of Philadelphia as an imaginative, awkward, somewhat goofy kid with ears that his teasing peers said made him look like a "trophy," Will Smith used humor at an early age to try to disarm the bullies often threatening to beat him up. Though he didn't grow up to be a classic stand-up comedian, Will's story mirrors that of many other comics who got their start using wit to evade the blows of neighborhood bullies.

"It is impossible to be angry, hateful, or violent when you're doubled over laughing," Will said in his memoir, *Will*, written with Mark Manson. He seesawed between the white kids at the Catholic school where his parents insisted on sending him and the Black kids in the middle-class Philly neighborhood called Wynnefield where he grew up.

"I learned to move between these two worlds," he wrote. "If I was making the kids on the corner laugh, I wasn't getting my ass kicked. If I was making the white kids at school laugh, I wasn't a nigger."

Willard Carroll Smith II was born on September 25, 1968, the oldest child of Willard Carroll Smith and Carolyn Elaine Bright—called "Daddio" and "Mom-Mom" by Will and his siblings, twins Harry and Ellen, who were three years Will's junior. Tall and good-looking, Daddio was a former military man who owned a refrigeration and ice-making business that at its height had a fleet of ice trucks and employed seemingly half the neighborhood in the backbreaking labor of making ice and delivering bags all across the city and even beyond Philly. Daddio was a talented man—he was funny, a gifted singer and guitar player with a magnetic, commanding presence. Will's mom said he reminded her of Marvin Gaye.

Mom-Mom was in many ways the opposite of Daddio—petite, reserved, sophisticated, well-educated. She attended the prestigious Carnegie Mellon University in Pittsburgh, where she was born and raised. She used her education to run her husband's ice business, handling the payroll, contracts, taxes, permits while he concentrated on the work. He expanded from ice-making to installing and maintaining refrigerators and freezers in major supermarkets in Philly and the surrounding suburbs.

Daddio was also a strict taskmaster who demanded hard work and discipline from his children, particularly his sons, Will and his brother, Harry. When Will was eleven and his brother eight, their father made them build a new wall, brick by brick, in front of his refrigeration shop—mixing the mortar, carrying the two-gallon buckets of water, and stacking them into a wall. The task, which the two boys considered impossible at the start, took them nearly a year, working weekends, holidays, vacations, through the summer.

"My father never took a day off, so neither could we," he said in *Will*. "There were so many times I remember looking at that hole, totally discouraged. I couldn't see how this was ever going to end."

But one day when Will and Henry were getting increasingly discouraged by the enormity of the task and were complaining between themselves, their father marched over and snatched a brick out of Will's hand.

"Stop thinking about the damn wall!" he said. "There *is* no wall. There are only *bricks*. Your job is to lay *this brick* perfectly. Then move on to the next brick. Then lay that brick perfectly. Then the next one. Don't be worrying about no wall. Your only concern is *one brick*."

Will took that fatherly advice to heart throughout his career, focusing on the bricks, not the entirety of the wall. "I started to see that the difference between a task that feels impossible and a task that feels doable is merely a matter of perspective. Are you paying attention to the wall? Or are you paying attention to the brick?"

Though Will said his father was his hero, Daddio was also a violent, foul-tempered man who often beat Will's mom and the kids. But Mom-Mom was a tough, proud, stubborn woman who wasn't going to take a beating passively. Will recalled a time when Daddio slapped her and she egged him on.

"Oh, you're such a man!" she yelled. "You think that hitting a woman makes you a man, huh?"

When he hit her again, she fell to the ground. She stood up, glared at him, and said something that stayed with Will the rest of his life. "Hit me all you want," she said calmly, "but you can never hurt me."

"I have never forgotten that," he wrote. "The idea that he could hit her body but somehow she was in control of what 'hurt' her? I wanted to be strong like that."

In his memoir, Smith goes on at length about how he felt afraid for much of his childhood, of his father, of the kids in the neighborhood, of everything. While his sister was strong-willed like their mother, and his younger brother was able to stand up to "the monster," Will was terrified of him. "In a family of fighters, I was the weak one," he wrote. "I was the coward."

Because his instinct was to make their father laugh to placate him, when this failed and Daddio got violent, Will internalized it as his fault. This feeling intensified that night the children watched him hit their mother so hard she fell to the ground.

"And it's in this compulsive desire to constantly please others, to keep them laughing and smiling at all times, to redirect all the attention in the room away from the ugly and uncomfortable, toward the joyful and the beautiful—it's there that a true entertainer is born," he wrote.

"But that night, in that bedroom, with me standing there in the doorway, watching my father's fists collide with the woman I loved most in this world, watching as she collapsed on the ground, helpless, I just stood there. Frozen."

In that moment, he forged a new way of considering himself, one that would stay with him for the rest of his life.

"No matter what I have done, and no matter how successful I have become, no matter how much money I've made or how many #1 hits I've had or how many box office records I've broken, there is that subtle and silent feeling always pulsating in the back of my mind: that I am a coward; that I have failed; that I am sorry, Mom-Mom, so sorry."

In the scorching heat of his shame, Smith made a silent pledge to himself: "One day, I would be in charge. And this would never, *ever* happen again."

It doesn't take a PhD in psychology to envision how a man with this mindset might respond when a comedian insults his wife from the stage in front of a global audience. *Will* came out in 2021. A year later, Smith marched onstage and smacked Chris Rock in the face for making a joke about Jada Pinkett Smith's close-cropped hair. Some might surmise that he wasn't smacking Rock; he was really smacking Daddio—some forty-four years later.

Smith used humor to astounding effect during his teenage years after he discovered hip-hop and began to forge an identity as the rapper Fresh Prince, roaming the streets of Philly with his friend and beatbox companion Ready Rock C, searching for rappers to battle. Humor became his secret weapon in these battles, stitched onto his tireless work ethic—which he said he got from Daddio—of incessantly practicing and writing rhymes. He even rapped in front of a mirror to learn to control his facial expressions and dramatize his words even more. He said he was "invincible" in these rap battles. While some rappers might have more clever wordplay or smoother flows, nobody was funnier.

> What nobody seemed to ever understand was that you *can't beat funny.* You can spit all the tough gangster shit you want—you can rip rhymes about all the money and women in the world—but if your pants are just a little bit too far above your shoes, and somebody says,

> *Look at you, homey, pretendin' you all fly*
> *looks like your shoes went to a party and your pants got high*

and forty people laugh? You're done. It's over.

When Smith was a senior at Overbrook High School, he met Jeffrey Allen Townes—otherwise known as DJ Jazzy Jeff—at a house party Jeff was working. Jeff, who was three years older than Smith, had already established a reputation as one of the best DJs in Philly. When Jeff's emcee didn't show up to the party, Smith offered to partner with him—and, as the cliché goes, the rest is history. The pair became inseparable, spending nearly all of their time in Jeff's basement, working on tracks. Jeff had already graduated from high school, so he could prepare tracks for Will's vocals while Will was in school. James Lassiter, Jeff's best friend since childhood, otherwise known as JL, spent some time in the basement with them when he wasn't in class at Temple law school working toward his law degree. JL became the duo's very serious, very competent manager—originally because he was the only one with a fax machine when they needed to send back a signed contract for a $1,500 gig, which was big money for them.

After Jazzy Jeff won the Battle for World Supremacy, an early Olympics of DJing and emceeing held yearly in New York City, he and Will returned to Philly as even bigger names on the local rap scene. Smith makes a strong case in his memoir that Jeff is the best DJ of all time.

"He pioneered techniques and styles in those Philly basement parties as a teenager that are still used by thousands of DJs all over the world today," he wrote. "He could manipulate records in ways that no one had seen or heard before."

Dana Goodman, a local Philly entrepreneur, asked them to be the first acts on his new independent record label. Dana's brother Lawrence Goodman had founded Pop Art Records in New York, one of the first New York–based hip-hop labels, and the competitive Dana wanted to surpass his brother's success. They recorded a single that contained two tracks, one of which was "Girls Ain't Nothing but

Trouble." Dana was hustling, selling the vinyl out the trunk of his car, but sales were painfully slow. Russell Simmons, possibly the most important person in hip-hop at the time, the force behind Run-DMC, the Beastie Boys, Whodini, and LL Cool J, was a huge fan of DJ Jazzy Jeff and the Fresh Prince. He felt that hip-hop needed a clean, parent-friendly act like the duo to counter the attacks on rap for its misogynistic and violent lyrics. Russell and Lyor Cohen at Rush Management became the managers of Jazzy Jeff and the Fresh Prince. The duo later got out of their contract with Dana when lawyers realized Will had signed it when he was only seventeen and he did so without a parent or guardian present—rendering the contract invalid.

Smith decided he wasn't going to attend college, which he knew would break his mother's heart. He had gotten over 1200 on his SATs, a respectable score that would grant him entry to some good colleges. His mother had it all planned out—she even created a spreadsheet containing top engineering schools, since math and science were Smith's best subjects in school. When he broke the news to Mom-Mom, she was enraged and demanded he go to college. There was a tense standoff between them that went on for a week before Daddio interceded. Will's father was sympathetic to his son because he felt he could have made it as a performer but had been told his dreams weren't practical. He sat down Will and Mom-Mom and pronounced that they would give Will a year to try to make it as a rapper. At the end of the year, if he hadn't found success, he would go to college.

When Mom-Mom called the admissions dean at the University of Wisconsin, a prestigious public university in Madison where Will had been accepted, seeking to defer his admission for a year, she told the dean it was unfortunate that her son wanted to take a gap year to do "something called 'rapping.'"

"I think that's incredible, Mrs. Smith," the dean said.

"What?" a shocked Mom-Mom responded.

"For a young man his age? He would *never* get that kind of experience here. He should *absolutely* do it."

It wasn't the reaction she was expecting.

"And certainly we'll hold a spot for him. If his album doesn't work out, he can attend next year. That's no problem."

Smith never made it to Madison.

"Girls Ain't Nothing but Trouble" was all over Philadelphia radio in the spring of 1986. The duo recorded their first album, *Rock the House*, and went on tour, opening for Public Enemy and 2 Live Crew, two of the country's biggest rap acts. *Rock the House* went gold, selling more than 500,000 copies, and reached #83 on the *Billboard* 200 chart. Those numbers weren't mind-blowing, but the duo were on their way. Their next album, *He's the DJ, I'm the Rapper*, fueled by the single "Parents Just Don't Understand"—and its equally entertaining music video highlighting Will's comic persona—went triple platinum, selling more than three million copies, and reached #4 on the *Billboard* 200. Even better, it won a Grammy, beating out Salt-N-Pepa ("Push It"), LL Cool J ("Going Back to Cali"), J.J. Fad ("Supersonic"), and Kool Moe Dee ("Wild Wild West"). They were the first rappers to ever receive a Grammy—since it was the first year the Grammys included a rap category. At age twenty, Smith was a Grammy-winning, freshly minted millionaire. He bought his beloved grandmother, Gigi, a fancy apartment overlooking the Main Line in Philly, and Smith moved into her old house with his girlfriend, Melanie, his first love. However, their relationship was doomed because he spent so much time on the road. It wasn't Will succumbing to groupies—he proclaimed himself a one-woman man and was even getting upset with his crew for entertaining groupies at every stop—but it was Melanie's eyes that wandered when Will was gone.

When he brought Daddio to his house to show him the three fancy cars he had purchased, his father responded, "Boy, why you need *three* cars? You only got *one* ass."

But Smith lost it all for not paying his taxes. The IRS took everything. He even spent a weekend in jail when his bodyguard and best friend Charlie Mack beat up a guy who was apparently sent by Dana Goodman to intimidate them. Broke and profoundly depressed, Will moved out to LA to get away from the craziness in Philly. He moved in with a new woman, a beautiful Southern Cali girl named Tanya

Moore. After he spent weeks wallowing in his grief at her place, Tanya told him his hiatus was over; it was time to get "back to life." She suggested he hang out at *The Arsenio Hall Show*, LA's hippest spot, and see if he might make something happen. He had become friendly with Arsenio during his rise with Jazzy Jeff.

"Go to Arsenio and do *what*?" he yelled at Tanya.

"Arsenio likes you! Just go to the *show* and hang out. *Meet* people."

"You sound crazy as shit," he told her. "So, you want me to go to *The Arsenio Hall Show* and stand around like a dickhead so I could might meet somebody?"

"Yes, exactly—so you *could might meet* somebody!"

"I'm not doing this wit' you. That's dumb, and I'm not in the mood for this shit."

He and Charlie Mack went to the show almost every day for months. Charlie would venture out until he saw somebody famous, then he would drag them—whether they liked it or not—over to meet Will. One night, he met an A&R executive (an "artists and repertoire," dealmaking exec) with Warner Bros. Records named Benny Medina, a major player in hip-hop who oversaw acts such as Queen Latifah, De La Soul, and Big Daddy Kane. After talking for a while about the music business, Medina asked him, "Do you know how to act?"

Smith had never acted before, but he wasn't about to tell Medina he couldn't do it. He lied and said, "Yes."

"I figured you could," Medina said. "I can see it in your music videos. I might have something to talk to you about. Let's keep in touch."

Medina was already working on creating a show based on his own life as an Afro Latino teenager taken in by a wealthy white family in Beverly Hills. A few weeks later, Will got a call from legendary producer Quincy Jones, who told Will he had an idea for a television show he wanted to pitch Will. Will was in Detroit doing a show, but he hustled out to LA to attend Quincy's birthday party. He walked into Quincy's glorious castle of a house to see a dizzying array of A-list stars, from Steven Spielberg to Stevie Wonder and Lionel Richie.

That night, after introducing Will to Brandon Tartikoff, the head of NBC, Quincy announced to the entire crowd that Will was going to "audition." Terrified, Will's knees buckled, and he told Quincy he couldn't do it. But you can't say no to Quincy.

"Quincy Jones understands magic," Smith said in *Will*. "He sees the universe as an infinite playground of magical possibilities. He recognizes miraculous potential in every moment and every thing and everyone around him. His superpower is that he has learned to present himself to the universe as a lightning rod, placing himself perfectly to capture and conduct the ever-present, ever-recurring magical flashes of brilliance surrounding us all."

Smith followed Quincy into his private library to have a conversation with him. He told Quincy that he needed more time to prepare; Quincy wasn't having it.

"But right now, everybody that needs to say yes to this show is sitting out there in that living room waiting for you," Quincy said. "And you are about to make a decision that will affect the rest of your life."

Will did the script reading and got a big ovation from everyone assembled, who all later certainly would tell the story of witnessing Will Smith transform his life before their eyes. When Tartikoff, egged on by Quincy, said that he liked the performance, Quincy practically demanded that Tartikoff's chief counsel, who also had been "strategically" invited to the birthday party, go out to their limo and draw up a deal memo. That's how *The Fresh Prince of Bel-Air* was created.

The party took place on March 14, 1990; they were shooting the pilot in mid-May; the pilot aired on September 10, 1990. In six months, Will Smith went from a flailing rapper to a television star. In Hollywood, that kind of speed, from deal to airing, was unheard of. And Smith was in love with the whole process.

"I found my thing," he said. "The world of acting unleashed all the artistic impulses within me. It was the first external canvas that felt big enough to hold the landscapes of my imagination. My musical expression always felt narrow and constrained by the limits of my skills and talents. Making music felt like living in a great neighborhood, whereas acting felt like being set free in an infinite universe. As an actor, I would get to be anybody, go anywhere, and do anything: world champion boxer, fighter pilot, tennis coach, galaxy defender, cop, lawyer, businessman, doctor, lover, preacher, genie—I would even get to be a fish. Acting encompasses all the things that I am—storyteller, performer, comedian, musician, teacher."

The Fresh Prince was the highest-rated debut show in the fall of 1990. But even in the craze of producing shows every week, Will was already thinking about movies. After his manager, JL, kept badgering him about where he wanted his career to go, Will finally proclaimed, "I want to be the biggest movie star in the world." JL set about reading every script he could get his hands on. After he had churned through at least 100, he had a conversation with Will about what makes someone a movie star. They came up with three principles: You have to be able to fight, you have to be funny, and you have to be good at sex. If Will was going to make the move into movies, they now knew what they were looking for.

Will and his *Fresh Prince* costar Alfonso Ribeiro used to stand outside of the *Fresh Prince* casting office to check out all the beautiful Black starlets coming through for auditions to be on the show. One day he saw a lovely, slender, petite actress who clearly had a lot of sass. "Who the fuck is *that*?" he whispered to Ribeiro. "She is *not* from LA." He said East Coast recognizes East Coast. It turned out to be Jada Pinkett, who was upset because the casting agent had just told her she was too short to play Will's girlfriend. When he tried to holler at her with an ill-advised "Whatup, shawty?" line, she shut him down immediately.

"Whatever, nigga, move," she said, swatting him away with a hand gesture. He said it was love at first sight—though he quickly got involved after that meeting with another lovely woman, Sheree Zampino. Three months later, he and Sheree were married. The next year they welcomed a son into the world, Willard Carroll Smith III, whom they called Trey.

The Fresh Prince of Bel-Air was a bona fide blockbuster for NBC, running for 148 episodes over six seasons. Though *The Fresh Prince* didn't have the racial edginess found in such shows as *In Living Color* and *The Chappelle Show*, it was enormously popular at a time when rap was still considered dangerous and possibly fleeting. It was a cultural touchstone at a time when hip-hop was still viewed with suspicion.

The idea that a rapper—especially one as young and untested as Smith—could anchor a prime-time hit not only reshaped public perception of rap culture, it cracked open the gates for a new wave of hip-hop stars to cross into mainstream television and film—from Queen Latifah to LL Cool J, from Ice Cube to Ice T. Smith didn't just find his lane—he paved one, proving that charisma, hustle, and the right moment of magic could turn an unlikely opportunity into a generational career.

CHAPTER 18
MARTIN LAWRENCE

Long after Norman Lear introduced white audiences to Black sensibilities with *Sanford and Son* and *The Jeffersons*, and after Bill Cosby crafted *The Cosby Show* with the white gaze in mind, Martin Lawrence exploded onto the scene with a style and swagger that felt revolutionary. His comedy was raw, unfiltered, and unapologetically Black—unlike anything that had ever been seen on television.

But before Martin became a household name, Lawrence was already redefining stand-up for a generation. In 1992, he was tapped as the first host of *Def Comedy Jam*, a late-night HBO series that changed the game for Black comedians. Created by Russell Simmons and Stan Lathan, the show was loud, brash, and deeply rooted in the energy of Black club comedy. *Def Comedy Jam* wasn't just a showcase—it was a launching pad. Bernie Mac, Dave Chappelle, Chris Tucker, Cedric the Entertainer, and Sommore all took the stage on that redbrick set, armed with jokes that weren't softened for mainstream appeal. They spoke in the cadence and language of the barbershop, the cookout, the beauty salon, and the block.

Martin, as host, was the spark. With his gold chains, quick wit, and razor-sharp commentary, he embodied the very ethos of the show—authentic, fearless, and unafraid to tell the truth. He was setting the tone for an entire comedic movement. "Y'all ain't ready!" he'd shout, riling up the crowd like a preacher before a sermon. Every intro was electric. Every set was a moment. Lawrence's presence turned *Def Comedy Jam* into must-see TV for Black America and gave him a weekly platform to hone his voice and connect with audiences nationwide.

In many ways, *Def Comedy Jam* did for Black stand-up what hip-hop had done for Black music—shifting the center of gravity away from white mainstream sensibilities and toward the cultural truths of Black lived experience. And Martin Lawrence, standing in that spotlight, became the face of that shift. It's impossible to overstate how much that show contributed to the depth and breadth of Black comedy. It proved that there was an audience—millions strong—for comedians who didn't want to "cross over," but instead wanted to speak directly to the people who already knew their jokes by heart.

That same energy bled into *Martin*. Alongside *In Living Color*, *Martin* mined Black culture for humor that spoke directly to the community, as if Lawrence and Keenen Ivory Wayans had spent every Thanksgiving in a Black household, playing spades with the cousins and cracking jokes with the aunties.

"I didn't give a damn what white people thought," Martin said. "I was doing comedy from the reality of my people. I was doing comedy from what I knew and what I grew up with, what my eyes have seen."

The recurring characters on *Martin*—like Hustle Man, Bruh Man, and Sheneneh—were groundbreaking, instantly recognizable, and deeply resonant. They weren't just characters; they were lived experiences, comedic reflections of people the Black community knew all too well. Hustle Man—played by the inimitable Tracy Morgan—could have easily been reduced to a stereotype, a scheming hustler looking to get over. But on *Martin*, he was harmless, even lovable.

"Hustle Man was just a guy out there trying to get his," Martin said. "I knew many hustlers like that—guys trying to get over. Bruh Man was that dude who was always around, always at your house eating your damn food. For no reason. Like, 'Why is he always here?' Sheneneh is my sister, my nieces. And no, they weren't bothered, because Sheneneh is a strong Black woman."

When *Martin* premiered in 1992, it made an immediate impact. Viewers were captivated by Lawrence's versatility—he not only played the brash yet vulnerable radio talk show host Martin Payne but also a host of unforgettable characters, from his overbearing mother Mama Payne to his outrageous next-door neighbor Sheneneh, from the snotty-nosed Roscoe to the smooth-talking, jheri-curled old head Jerome. While Eddie Murphy had played multiple roles in *Coming to America*, Lawrence was the first to master this in a weekly television sitcom.

Fox scheduled *Martin* against NBC's Thursday night powerhouse lineup—"Must-See TV"—and while it never beat *Friends* or *Wings* in the ratings, it siphoned off massive Black and young audiences. The show's cultural impact far outweighed its Nielsen rankings. Phrases like "You go, girl!" "Wazzup!" and "Damn, Gina!" became part of the Black lexicon and still echo three decades later.

For Tisha Campbell, who played Gina, the show's lasting impact was unexpected.

"I never thought it was going to be the iconic show that it was because when I was a kid, I watched the reruns of *I Love Lucy* or *The Brady Bunch*—stuff like that that they still play until this day. And you never think that you're going to be on a show that has lasted 30 years. You never think that a five-year-old is going to walk up to you and go, 'Gina!' or somebody is going to yell at you, 'Damn, Gina!' or 'You go, girl!' or any of the things come from the show. I'm blessed and grateful to be a part of something that has lasted so long."

Beneath the laughs, *Martin* reflected the shifting gender dynamics of the 1990s. Women were making strides in the workplace, and Lawrence's character—though often a loudmouthed, over-the-top chauvinist—was ultimately supportive of Gina's career. His comedic battles with Gina's best friend Pam hilariously embodied the complexities of evolving gender roles, making *Martin* more than just a sitcom—it was a time capsule of a changing era.

Before *Martin*, audiences had caught a glimpse of Lawrence's comedic prowess in *Do the Right Thing*, where he played a wisecracking neighborhood kid with a lisp. He had parlayed an early *Star Search* appearance—where he won once but lost his second week—into a role on the third and final season of the sitcom reboot *What's Happening Now!!* In Hollywood, he honed his craft at the Comedy Act Theater, under the mentorship of Robin Harris. It was Harris who introduced him to Spike Lee, who was looking to cast *Do the Right Thing*.

"You wanna boycott somebody?" Harris's character, Sweet Dick Willie, memorably said. "You ought to start with the *goddamn barber* that fucked up your head."

Spike caught Martin's act one night and was impressed. Lawrence, on his own, decided to give his character a lisp—a creative choice that Spike loved so much he insisted it stay.

"What happened to the lisp?" Spike asked when rehearsals began.

"I took it out," Lawrence said with a shrug.

"No, no, no—do the lisp," Spike insisted. "Please do the lisp."

By 1992, Lawrence was on a meteoric rise. He was tapped as the first host of *Def Comedy Jam*, debuting just months before *Martin* premiered, solidifying his status as the next big thing in Black comedy. With *Martin*, he took full control—serving as star, executive producer, and playing multiple characters.

"I was at the helm of leading it, and I had the freedom to do what I wanted to do. And I gave everybody else the freedom to do what they wanted to do," Lawrence said.

Soon, Hollywood came calling. Columbia Pictures approached Lawrence with a buddy-cop script originally written for Jon Lovitz and Dana Carvey. It needed work, but Lawrence saw potential.

"All you need to do is figure out who you want to do it with," the studio told him.

He initially wanted Eddie Murphy, but when that didn't pan out, his sister Rae had a suggestion.

"What about Will Smith?" she asked.

Smith, then a TV star on *The Fresh Prince of Bel-Air*, had recently proven his acting chops in *Six Degrees of Separation*. Lawrence invited him over for dinner, and within ten minutes, he was convinced.

"Let's have two TV stars get together and blow the movies up!" he told Smith.

They did just that. *Bad Boys* grossed $141 million worldwide in April 1995, holding the number one box office spot for two weeks and launching one of the biggest action franchises in Hollywood.

But behind the success, Lawrence was struggling. The relentless grind of filming *Martin*, hosting *Def Comedy Jam*, and directing a new dark comedy, *A Thin Line Between Love and Hate*, took its toll. In 1996, he was arrested after running down Ventura Boulevard waving a gun and screaming, "They are trying to kill me!"

"It was times when I didn't know who I was," he later admitted. "I was, 'Cut! Action! Let's go!' I was all over the place, baby."

Hollywood took notice—and not in a good way. Offers stopped coming. But then Eddie Murphy called.

"He said he was reaching out partly because of my troubles," Lawrence recalled. Murphy was working on a movie called *Life* and, despite studio pressure to cast Cuba Gooding Jr., he wanted Lawrence instead.

On set, Lawrence found himself surrounded by a comedy dream team: Murphy, Bernie Mac, Anthony Anderson, Bokeem Woodbine, and Guy Torry.

"I was in awe," Lawrence said. "Really, there were days he probably just found me looking at him. 'Martin, Martin, you need to be acting right now.'"

In the late '90s, controversy continued to follow him. Costar Tisha Campbell filed a sexual harassment lawsuit, claiming an increasingly hostile work environment on the set of *Martin*. Things became so tense, she walked away from the show before returning to film the final two episodes after a settlement.

Then, in August 1999, Lawrence collapsed from heat exhaustion while jogging in a fat suit in 100-degree heat for *Big Momma's House*. He slipped into a three-day coma, waking up on a ventilator.

"I just happened to go jogging on the hottest day of the summer, with a wool hat on," he said. "Next thing you know, I woke up three days later."

Recovery was slow. He had to relearn how to walk and talk.

"I was slurring all my words," he said. "I had to get a therapist to help me every day to start working on my mechanics again and get back to what should be normal for me."

The wake-up call came with the birth of his daughter, Jasmine, in 1996.

"She played a big role," he said. "She made me look at the reality of things—either keep getting in these little incidents, or do something more important and help raise your child."

Lawrence went on to star in a string of comic films in the early 2000s—*Big Momma's House, Bad Boys II, Black Knight, National Security, Big Momma's House 2, Wild Hogs, College Road Trip, Bad Boys for Life*.

In 2024, nearly thirty years after the first *Bad Boys*, Lawrence reunited with Smith for the fourth film of the franchise, *Bad Boys: Ride or Die*, a global hit grossing $404.2 million. He also returned to stand-up, coming full circle to the craft that had launched his career with a national tour.

Meanwhile, *Martin* remains a cultural staple, its legacy renewed with each new generation discovering its magic. For Lawrence, the journey has been full of highs and lows—but the laughs, always, remain.

CHAPTER 19
LIVING SINGLE

Before *Friends*—that glossy homage to white urban idleness—there was *Living Single*. Debuting in August 1993, a full year before *Friends*, it was the first sitcom to take a serious, yet joyful, look at the lives of young Black urban professionals—known in the '90s as "buppies." *Living Single* tackled race, relationships, and workplace dynamics in ways that few Black-led shows had before, making it a cultural touchstone for African-American viewers who saw themselves reflected in its six main characters. Throughout its five-season run, it consistently ranked among the top five shows for Black audiences, even outperforming *Martin* in the ratings during its first season. Originally airing on Sunday nights before moving to Thursdays in its second season, *Living Single* helped shape the landscape of Black television. When *A Different World* ended, creator Yvette Lee Bowser looked around and saw what was missing: a strong, authentic Black female voice at the center of prime-time. So, she created one.

"I spent five years on *A Different World* voicing very self-possessed, empowered Black women, on a show created by and run by self-possessed, empowered Black women," Bowser said. "And most of my friends were that or aspiring to be. That was really the impetus behind *Living Single*. It was at *A Different World* that I really learned my art could also play a significant role in my activism. And so I just was very intentional about the characters I was creating and the stories I wanted to tell."

Bowser went from *A Different World*, where she felt her voice was heard and respected, to the writers' room for *Hangin' with Mr. Cooper*, the ABC series starring Holly Robinson Peete and comedian Mark Curry as a former NBA player turned basketball coach. When she got there, she was the only Black writer in the room and the only woman in the room.

"There was an oppressive energy there that first season. And I was just like, 'I'm better than this,'" Bowser said. "I was like, 'Guys, I'm coming off the number two show. I know that my voice has value.' I was not really regarded with respect. And I thought, my gosh, if this is what Hollywood is really like, I will not be here long because I am not one to suffer fools. So I became more determined to develop my own show, in large part because I wanted to develop my own work environment where people like me, you know, new voices, people who had been marginalized, people who had different experiences, would actually be heard and seen. And I was very, very determined to get that show on the air."

Both Queen Latifah and Kim Coles had separate development deals with Fox that hadn't borne any fruit, so in 1993 the fledgling network put them together in a sitcom about roommates in New York City called *My Girls*. Latifah's character even had the name Khadijah, which would be her name on *Living Single*.

Bowser was only twenty-eight at the time, too young to know what the glass ceiling looked and felt like.

"I was a woman on a mission," Bowser said. "I understood the assignment. I got the opportunity thanks to Queen Latifah and Kim Coles, who both had unsuccessful pilots developed for them by writers who were not Black. So when they decided to pair up and they had talent-holding deals with Warner Brothers and Fox, the studio and the network, respectively, they insisted that a Black writer get an opportunity. And I just stepped into that gap. I felt very ready to create and run my own show at twenty-eight years old. Crazy."

In addition to Latifah and Coles, they added actresses Kim Fields and Erika Alexander to the group of women, while T.C. Carson and John Henton played their neighbors and friends. Bowser said she created the four women on the show in her own image—the four different sides of herself. "I've been as ditsy as Synclaire [Coles], as superficial as Regine [Fields], as bitter as Max [Alexander], and as focused and driven as Khadijah [Latifah]."

Friends was introduced a year after *Living Single*'s debut and became an enormous hit almost overnight—it finished eighth of all shows in the ratings that first year, its lowest finish in its decade-long run. Warren Littlefield, who was president of NBC Entertainment at the time, was looking for a comedy involving young people living together after he regretted passing on *Living Single*. It was not lost on the public how similar the shows were. But they drew such different audiences, both were able to thrive—even when they went head-to-head after *Living Single*'s first season when it was moved to Thursday.

While Bowser said she fought many battles with the network over controversial topics, her biggest fight was over Erika Alexander's character, Maxine Shaw. "When I turned in my first draft to the network, the note I got back was they wondered if we could lose this character because she was kind of too strong and maybe we didn't need this many women," Bowser said. "I said, 'Well, to take Max out of the show is to take a big part of me out of the show, and I'd rather not do the show at all. So let me come up with something.' So I came up with the idea that she lived across the street and was just as omnipresent. And I actually got more comedy out of it. I heard what their concern was, but I wasn't willing to take the character out and I wasn't willing to dial her down."

Bowser described her decision to stand up to the network as a "quintessential Maxine Shaw move." It was fitting, given that Maxine—brilliant, bold, and unapologetically herself—became an icon for countless viewers. Over the years, Bowser, Erika Alexander, and others connected to the show frequently heard from fans who credited Maxine with inspiring their careers. In 2022, they commissioned a research study to quantify what they already knew: Maxine Shaw's impact was undeniable. The findings, dubbed the Maxine Shaw Effect, were staggering—one in three Black women lawyers said Maxine directly influenced their decision to pursue law school; 79 percent of Black women professionals said she inspired them to take on leadership roles in male-dominated fields; and 90 percent said she gave them the confidence to speak their minds without fear.

Among those who cite Maxine as a personal influence are Congresswoman Ayanna Pressley, politician and activist Stacey Abrams, and even former New York City Mayor Bill de Blasio. Erika Alexander has said that Vice President and Democratic presidential candidate Kamala Harris personally told her on multiple occasions that Maxine was an inspiration.

Throughout *Living Single*'s run, Bowser was keenly aware of the other Black-led comedies shaping television at the time. There was competition, yes, but also a shared sense of camaraderie—each show pushing the others to be bolder, funnier, and more impactful.

"I would say there was healthy competition, and it was good," she said. "They asked me to create a companion piece for *Martin*. *Martin* is so male, so testosterone charged, my feeling was I was going to create kind of a female response to *Martin*. But I also thought, with the show centering women, it was important to have strong men on the show to balance things out and to offer other points of view. And I think that formula worked out pretty well."

Living Single came at a blessed time for Kim Coles, who had been unceremoniously bounced from *In Living Color* after just one season. A lot of the parts that Coles might have played had gone to Kim Wayans, leaving Coles outside looking in.

"Keenen gave a lot of stuff to his sister. That was hard," Coles said, in an interview with *Entertainment Tonight*. "I will say that I get it now. It was really hard then to see the landscape, to feel that I had all this talent inside of me and all these ideas, and they weren't always encouraged."

When she was dumped, she got a call from her agent telling her not to report to work on Monday.

"It was tough, of course, and it was embarrassing. And it was weird because the show was the hottest thing ever. I couldn't understand what I had done or not done right or wrong."

She eventually had a conversation with Keenen after she scored the *Living Single* gig.

"I got a great apology and a great explanation. He actually said to me, 'I had to let you go, but I knew you'd be all right.' And I'm like, Oh, okay, because I am. The good news was that, though I was released after the first year, I went on to a show where I felt that my talents and gifts and experience could really be fostered. It was tough in the moment, but it was a good thing in the end. I left and had an even better experience and made even more money and the show lasted even longer, so how can I be mad?"

Coles said she had a development deal at Warner Brothers, and the execs were telling her they wanted to do a show about women, their careers, their men. Then they asked her what she thought of Queen Latifah.

"I was like, 'I love her.' And they were having the same kinds of meetings with her, so they put the two of us together," Coles said. "They got Yvette Lee Bowser to create the show and, boom, we were off and running and the cast came together beautifully. Like the first day of work, it was like, Oh, this is going to be a hit."

With Latifah hailing from the Newark area in New Jersey, and Coles from Brooklyn, she said they shared a similar energy.

"And Kim Fields was a legend. She was the only little Black girl that was on TV for years [as Tootie on *The Facts of Life*]. John Henton and I both did stand-up and we knew each other from that world. T.C. and Erika Alexander have the same exact birthday. And once we found that, oh, it was on. We would take trips together and hang out together and celebrate births and deaths and marriages and divorces together. It was really good." Though *Living Single* was known as a "Black" show, Coles said when she's out in public she gets frequent evidence that white people were watching too.

"I remember going to the bank one time, and this little old Jewish man—and I knew who he was because I'm from Brooklyn—he squeezed my arm. He said, 'Hello, beautiful. I love that show with all you beautiful girls. Beautiful girls, I love it. It's wonderful.' And he's nothing like the demographic that they said we had. And yet he was watching because it reminded him of home. Through the years, I've seen the colors and shapes and cultures of people who resonated with that show because we were them."

Because Latifah ran her own magazine on the show, that setup gave *Living Single* the opportunity to have on many stars from different fields who visited the magazine's offices or put on performances. The guest stars who appeared during the show's five-season run included Flip Wilson, Ed McMahon, Cheryl Miller, Branford Marsalis, Deion Sanders, Rosie O'Donnell, Gladys Knight, Eartha Kitt, Brian McKnight, Evander Holyfield, and Chaka Khan. Coles said the show had an informal system where one of the regulars would take a guest under their wing for the week and act as their big brother or sister of sorts, showing them where stuff was, making sure they didn't need anything.

"We just sort of attached ourselves to someone so they could feel comfortable," Coles said. "And my favorite thing is Joyce DeWitt [of *Three's Company*], you know, the sitcom legend, announced to the audience, 'I haven't been on TV in a really long time and I am having such a good time. This is the most fun I have ever had shooting a show.' But that's because John was telling her how pretty she was."

Coles said she was fawning all over Isabel Sanford when Coles was her guide.

"I'm like, 'Oh my God, that's Weezy. She's a legend.' I kept kissing her feet," Coles said.

But one of the most entertaining guest stars was Eartha Kitt. Coles said Kitt didn't have much to say to the women; she much preferred talking to the men, greeting them with an effusive "Hello, darling."

"She came to work wearing a turban, a little warm-up suit and two sets of lashes, like bam bam, and some little wrist weights and ankle weights so she could walk and exercise the whole time," Coles said. "She was fabulous. And we threw a party for her and she was pretending to smoke with the carrot sticks. 'Darling, sometimes you just have to smoke a cigarette.' She's fabulous. It was everything."

Moments like that captured the singular energy of *Living Single*—a show brimming with style, personality, and Black cultural specificity.

But while *Living Single* held its own in the network ecosystem, it was also part of a larger sea change.

By the mid-1990s, Black sitcoms were no longer just an experiment—they were a proven hit with audiences. After the blockbuster success of *The Cosby Show*, *A Different World*, *Martin*, *Living Single*, and *The Fresh Prince of Bel-Air*, network executives could no longer ignore what had become a dominant cultural force. But just as Black creatives had finally carved out a significant space on network television, a seismic shift was underway in the TV landscape—one that would both expand and complicate the visibility of Black life on-screen.

In 1995, two new networks launched almost simultaneously: The WB and UPN. Both networks were scrambling to fill hours of primetime programming, and both made strategic decisions to attract Black audiences—particularly younger Black viewers who had been the backbone of earlier sitcom hits. What followed was an unprecedented boom: a new wave of Black sitcoms that made these fledgling networks relevant, popular, and profitable.

UPN (the United Paramount Network) leaned heavily into Black-led programming from the jump. One of its earliest hits was *Moesha*, starring Brandy Norwood as a smart, independent teenager navigating life in South Central Los Angeles. The cast also included Sheryl Lee Ralph—now known for her Emmy-winning role on *Abbott Elementary*—as Moesha's stepmother, bringing warmth, authority, and complexity to a character who could've easily been reduced to a cliché. *Moesha* struck a chord—not only because it centered a young Black girl in a multidimensional role, but because it blended humor with real issues like racial profiling, gentrification, and Black family dynamics. It ran for six seasons and spawned a successful spin-off, *The Parkers*, which featured Mo'Nique as a boisterous, nontraditional college student alongside Countess Vaughn. The show became a standout for its celebration of full-bodied Black womanhood—both literally and figuratively—at a time when few other shows dared to.

Meanwhile, The WB found success with shows like *The Wayans Bros.*, *The Jamie Foxx Show*, and *Sister, Sister*, which had initially aired on ABC before being picked up by The WB. *The Wayans Bros.* brought the anarchic energy of Keenen Ivory Wayans's *In Living Color* into a sitcom format, with Marlon and Shawn Wayans playing exaggerated versions of themselves. *The Jamie Foxx Show* showcased the comic's versatility—Foxx played a struggling entertainer working at a family-run hotel in Los Angeles, a setup that allowed him to blend slapstick, impressions, and tender romantic storylines. Foxx says in his memoir, *Act Like You Got Some Sense*, that he had been getting a lot of nos from the mainstream networks when he was shopping around his show. He felt that the perception in Hollywood was that his time had come and gone with *In Living Color*. His manager approached him with the idea of pitching the show to The WB.

"I like the people that like me," Foxx told his manager. "If Warner Bros. likes me, let's go there."

Another WB show, *Sister, Sister*, starring real-life twins Tia and Tamera Mowry, offered a rare depiction of Black girlhood and sisterhood, fusing hijinks with heart in a show that appealed across age and race lines.

What united these shows was not just their Black casts, but their Black creative teams. Many were spearheaded by Black writers, producers, and directors who brought a lived-in sensibility to the storytelling. These weren't just shows that featured Black people—they were shows rooted in Black cultural rhythms, comedic timing, and generational knowledge. They made space for jokes about the Nation of Islam and HBCUs, about hot combs and double Dutch, about Jehovah's Witnesses knocking at the door on Saturday mornings.

But just as quickly as UPN and The WB embraced Black audiences, the networks decided to go in a different direction. By the early 2000s, both networks began pivoting toward broader (read: *whiter*) demographics, aiming to compete with the Big Four networks. When UPN merged with The WB to form The CW in 2006, many of the Black shows that had built those networks from the ground up were abruptly canceled or phased out. The shift was clear—and for many in the Black creative community, it felt like a betrayal.

In the end, though, *Living Single* was a cultural landmark. Over the course of five seasons, from 1993 to 1998, the show redefined what it meant to see young, Black professionals thriving on television, offering humor, heart, and an undeniable authenticity that resonated with audiences then and now. Though it never received the same mainstream recognition as some of its successors, its influence is undeniable. The friendships, the love, the laughter—all of it helped pave the way for future shows centered on Black joy and success.

And yet, when the show ended, Hollywood didn't come calling. Erika Alexander, who played the sharp and ambitious Maxine Shaw, described the end of *Living Single* not as a springboard, but as a dead stop. There was no industry safety net waiting to catch her, no offers lined up, no producers clamoring for what came next.

"You could be brilliant at something," she once explained, "but that doesn't mean people are waiting for you to do something else." Hollywood, she said, barely knew what to do with the abundance of Black talent already visible—let alone how to nurture the careers of those who had proven themselves.

"So, it wasn't about what we were going to do next. It was like: 'I guess we gotta go back to pilot season.' Like, it starts all over again," she said.

There were no development deals, no immediate auditions, no next chapter written in advance. It was a sobering contrast: being praised as brilliant while feeling invisible. She recalled the surreal experience of showing up to audition alongside college students just breaking in, only to have them recognize her with admiration and confusion—"What are you doing here?" they'd ask, not realizing that in Hollywood, even proven excellence wasn't enough to guarantee a future.

It was a stark reminder: Even when Black creators and performers delivered undeniable hits, there was no guarantee the industry would catch them on the way down—or build anything for them to step into next. Still, *Living Single* endures. Whether through reruns or streaming, it continues to find new audiences, proving that its legacy, like the bonds between Khadijah, Synclaire, Regine, Max, Kyle, and Overton, is built to last.

CHAPTER 20
CHAPPELLE'S SHOW

If the history of Black comedy has been a steady march toward making public what Black people once said in private, then Dave Chappelle's career serves as a cautionary tale. What happens when the boundary between the two dissolves? Can a Black comedian reveal too much? Chappelle's answer was clear: Yes.

He famously walked away from *Chappelle's Show*—his bawdy, irreverent sketch comedy show on Comedy Central—at its peak in 2005, leaving behind a reported $50 million and fleeing to South Africa in search of peace of mind. The decision stunned the industry. How could someone abandon such a cultural juggernaut?

The breaking point came after taping a sketch featuring a Black pixie in blackface. Chappelle initially thought it had gone well—until he noticed a white crew member laughing just a little too long, a little too hard.

"When he laughed, it made me uncomfortable," Chappelle later recalled.

For the first time in his career, he began to wonder: Were white people laughing with him or at him?

"I felt like some kind of prostitute or something," he told Oprah Winfrey in 2006. "If I feel so bad, why keep on showing up to this place? I'm going to Africa. The hardest thing to do is to be true to yourself, especially when everybody is watching."

Chappelle had taken up the mantle forged by Richard Pryor, Keenen Ivory Wayans, and Martin Lawrence, pushing it further than anyone before him. His radically subversive comedy skewered the famous and the powerful with a rawness that was both hilarious and unsettling. His free-flowing sketches—impersonating Prince, Rick James, and Samuel L. Jackson—became instant classics, their quotability unmatched. The first season's DVD became the best-selling TV box set of all time.

His influence is undeniable. Over the years, Chappelle has collected six Emmy Awards, six Grammy Awards, and, in 2019, the Mark Twain Prize for American Humor. The late Dick Gregory put it simply: "When you mention his name among young folks, it's like mentioning Jesus in a Christian church."

Born in Washington, DC, on August 24, 1973, Chappelle grew up in an intellectual household. His father, William David Chappelle, was a professor and dean at Antioch College in Ohio. His mother, Yvonne Seon (née Reed, formerly Chappelle), was also a professor and administrator, and had once worked in the Congo alongside freedom fighter Patrice Lumumba.

His family's legacy was formidable. His great-grandfather, Bishop William D. Chappelle, was born into slavery in 1857 and later became president of Allen University. He led a delegation of African Americans to the White House to meet President Woodrow Wilson. Dave Chapelle's great-great-grandfather, Robert Chappelle, served in the South Carolina Legislature during Reconstruction. His granduncle, W. D. Chappelle Jr., was a pioneering surgeon who, in 1915, founded the People's Infirmary in Columbia, South Carolina, to provide Black patients with access to healthcare.

Though his parents divorced when he was young, Chappelle remained close to both.

"We were like the broke Huxtables," he once said of his childhood in Silver Spring, Maryland. "There were books around the house, everybody was educated to a college level. We used to have a picture of Malcolm X in Ghana. Last Poets records. We were poor, but we were cultured."

Their home was a gathering place for artists and intellectuals. Folk singer Pete Seeger would visit, as did jazz vocalist Johnny Hartman—the only singer to ever record with John Coltrane. It was Hartman who first saw something special in a young Chappelle.

"I was real comfortable with adults," Chappelle said. "I was cutting up in front of Hartman, and he was like, 'Man, you're a funny kid.' And he says to me, 'You're gonna be a comedian.' And I was like, 'What's a comedian?' And he's like, 'It's a guy who tells funny stories for a living, like Richard Pryor or Redd Foxx.' I said, 'I want to be a doctor.' And he was like, 'Eh—'"

But it was Martin Lawrence, another DC native, who provided the blueprint for what was possible.

"I had a personal stake in his success," Chappelle said. "Every time he did something, it made me feel inspired and really good."

By the time he graduated from high school in 1991, Chappelle was ready to chase his dream. His raw talent made an immediate impact in New York's comedy scene. Whoopi Goldberg dubbed him "The Kid." A killer set on *Def Comedy Jam* led to late-night spots on Letterman and Conan. He made his film debut in Mel Brooks's *Robin Hood: Men in Tights* in 1993.

Even then, he had an independent streak. He famously turned down the role of Bubba, Forrest Gump's best friend, believing the part was demeaning and that the movie would flop.

At just nineteen, Chappelle toured as the opening act for Aretha Franklin. After that, he bounced between failed TV pilots before collaborating with another comic, Neal Brennan, to write the stoner comedy *Half Baked*. Though it became a cult classic, Chappelle was frustrated by the experience, feeling it had been dumbed down from their original vision.

"We left *Half Baked* like leaving a crime scene," he later joked.

Meanwhile, Chris Rock was ascending to the comedy throne. Chappelle felt himself fading into the background. After he left *SNL*, Rock had forged a singularly impressive career: three Grammy Awards for Best Comedy Album, four Primetime Emmy Awards, and a Golden Globe nomination. He was ranked number five on Comedy Central's list of the 100 Greatest Stand-Ups of All Time (Chappelle is ranked forty-three) and number five on *Rolling Stone*'s list of the 50 Best Stand-Up Comics of All Time (Chappelle is ranked nine).

"When Chris Rock was real big, the word was, I was irrelevant; they don't need you," Chappelle recalled. "I almost felt like I was in his shadow. People would come up and say, 'Chris, can I have your autograph?' I would say to myself—this is a young man's ego—'I wish just once that people would say that I'm the best. I just want to touch it. I just want this industry to admit it.'"

In time, they would. But the cost of that admission would be greater than he ever imagined.

Chappelle recalled sitting in front of the TV one night when he saw a segment on Hugh Hefner and *Playboy After Dark*, Hefner's offbeat variety show from the late '60s.

"I said I should do a show like that, that's weird. I said, 'Let me call Neal up.' We started talking about variety shows; we wanted to do something that was real personal. I don't know, the word 'personal' kept coming up."

Partnering with Comedy Central—a network riding high from the controversy and success of *South Park*—Chappelle and co-creator Neal Brennan launched *Chappelle's Show*. With instantly iconic skits like "Charlie Murphy's True Hollywood Stories," "The Racial Draft," "When Keeping It Real Goes Wrong," and "Wayne Brady's Show," the series made an immediate cultural impact. But despite its success, Chappelle often questioned whether it was worth it, clashing with network executives over creative control.

"The bottom line was: White people own everything, and where can a Black person go and be himself or say something that's familiar to him and not have to explain or apologize?" Chappelle told writer Kevin Powell in a 2006 *Esquire* profile. "Why don't I just take the show to BET—oh, wait a minute, you [white people] own that, too, don't you?"

One of those battles came over the now-legendary Rick James episode, where Chappelle, playing James, infamously stomps on Eddie Murphy's white couch with muddy boots. The skit was laced with profanity, including gratuitous use of the N-word. The network sent so many notes on language that, if followed, the episode would have needed over forty bleeps to censor the profanity. Chappelle went to the executives to explain why he used the N-word so frequently in the sketch.

"So now I'm sitting in a room, again with some white people, explaining why I say the N-word," he said. "It's a sketch about Rick James, and I don't want to air a sketch with that many bleeps over it; it will render it completely ineffective. Give me another week and I'll just come up with something else. Run a rerun. No, we can't run a rerun, we've got ad buy-ins and blah, blah, blah. Okay, well then, fine, I don't want to do it, then."

A compromise was reached—the episode aired with a disclaimer, the only one in the show's history. But the frustration lingered.

"It's an awful, awful position to put yourself in. . . . It's something that is unique to us. White artists are allowed to be individuals. But we always have this greater struggle that we at least have to keep in mind somewhere."

In *Esquire*, Powell examined the weight Chappelle carried as a Black comedian.

"For sure, it is Chappelle's birthright to talk, provocatively, in his art, about race in America," Powell wrote. "Yet somewhere in that process of journeying from a grossly underestimated comic to the funniest man in America, Dave Chappelle began to feel trapped by the reactions from the suits, from the fans, from the media, from the scholars, from that voice inside his head. These jokes are dangerous in the wrong hands, he would say. That pressure, from all sides, from himself, would lead you, if you were living inside Dave Chappelle's head, to make a mad dash away from the money, real and projected, the fame, the pressures to do season three, of being labeled a brand, an icon, a genius."

Chappelle was especially disturbed when people called him "crazy" for walking away from a multimillion-dollar deal and fleeing to Africa. He pointed to other celebrities who had suffered public breakdowns—Mariah Carey stripping on *TRL*, Martin Lawrence running through Ventura Boulevard waving a gun, screaming, "They are trying to kill me!"

"So let me ask you this—what is happening in Hollywood that

a guy that tough [Lawrence] will be on the street waving a gun, screaming, 'They are trying to kill me'?" Chappelle asked during an episode of *Inside the Actors Studio*. "Yeah, what's going on? Why is Dave Chappelle going to Africa? Why does Mariah Carey make a $100 million deal and take her clothes off on *TRL*? A weak person cannot get to sit here and talk to you, so what is happening in Hollywood? Nobody knows. The worst thing to call somebody is crazy; it's dismissive. I don't understand this person, so they're crazy. That's bullshit. These people are not crazy, they're strong people. Maybe the environment is a little sick."

In the fallout from Chappelle's departure, Neal Brennan, perhaps inadvertently, revealed how little he understood his longtime collaborator.

"Dave would change his sketches so much, and it just got to the point that the show never would have aired if he had his way," Brennan said. "He would come with an idea, or I would come with an idea, pitch it to him, and he'd say that's funny. And from there we'd write it. He'd love it, say, 'I can't wait to do it.' We'd shoot it, and then at some point he'd start saying, 'This sketch is racist, and I don't want this on the air.' And I was like, 'You like this sketch. What do you mean?' There was this confusing contradictory thing: He was calling his own writing racist."

Chappelle later reflected on how success, speed, and constant praise had left him feeling lost.

"If you don't have the right people around you, and you're moving at a million miles an hour, you can lose yourself," he said. "Everyone around me says, 'You're a genius!'; 'You're great!'; 'That's your voice!' But I'm not sure that they're right."

Through it all, Chappelle clung to the example of Richard Pryor, calling him the "highest evolution of comedy."

"You know those evolution charts? He was the dude walking upright," Chappelle said. "There was an article I had read after he died, I think said it best: The mark of greatness is when everything before you is obsolete, and everything after you bears your mark. And what a precedent he set, not just as a comic, but as a dude, the fact that someone was able to open themselves wide open like that, and it's so hard to talk in front of people or to open yourself up to your closest friends, but to open yourself up for everybody? Yeah, I free base, I beat my women, I shot my car—and nobody's mad at Richard for that. Somehow they just understand, and when I was going through this thing this year, that is the example I would think to myself. That gave me the courage to just go back on the stage."

Chappelle mostly lay low after he walked away from his show, popping up unexpectedly at comedy clubs and occasionally doing extended runs at venues such as Radio City Music Hall. He won an Emmy for his *SNL* monologue following Trump's 2016 election. In 2016, he signed a groundbreaking $20 million–per-special deal with Netflix; the first two programs became the most-watched comedy specials in the platform's history.

Chappelle and Chris Rock represent the stunning evolution of the Black comedian. Generations removed from Bert Williams and his efforts to bring dignity to minstrelsy, these two men became the biggest stand-up comics in the business—using wit and sharp social critique rather than playing the fool.

Their success underscores a deeper truth: Black people know America's reality better than anyone—having lived through its worst and surviving to tell the tale.

That's what Chappelle and Rock have been: American truth tellers. The two-headed conscience of the nation. Just as the bully's victims can best speak to his abuses, no one is better equipped to describe America—its contradictions, its absurdities, its cruelties—than those who have endured them firsthand.

For more than a century, Black comedians have been witnesses, keen observers of a country that has often ignored their voices. They haven't always felt free to testify, but they were always watching, waiting.

And when the world was finally ready to hear the real story of America, it knew exactly where to turn—to America's conscience: the Black comedian.

CONCLUSION

Punch Lines and Progress

The history of Black comedy in America is more than just a chronicle of entertainment—it's a story of cultural resilience, innovation, and an ongoing fight for representation in a society that often sought to silence, distort, or overlook the Black experience. From the vaudeville stages to the golden age of '90s sitcoms, Black comedy has not only shaped American entertainment but has also been a force for social change, pushing boundaries, challenging stereotypes, and redefining public perceptions of Black identity and humor.

It began in vaudeville, where Black performers, despite being confined to racist caricatures, carved out spaces for themselves in mainstream entertainment. Even under these constraints, they used humor as both a survival tool and a form of subversion, weaving in satire and wit to challenge the racial limitations of their time. These early pioneers laid the foundation for generations to come, proving that comedy could be both an art form and a weapon of resistance.

As the twentieth century progressed, Black comedians steadily gained greater visibility across radio, film, and television. By the 1970s, shows like *Good Times* and *The Jeffersons* brought Black family life into living rooms across America, offering audiences stories of both struggle and success. But it was the 1990s that marked a true golden age—a cultural renaissance for Black sitcoms fueled by a potent mix of political change, economic growth, and media disruption.

By the time Bill Clinton entered the White House in 1993, the cultural climate had shifted again. A renewed national focus on multiculturalism and middle-class opportunity—alongside crime policies that disproportionately harmed Black communities—influenced the narratives unfolding on TV. At the same time, the economic boom of the '90s fueled the rise of a Black middle class with greater spending power—a demographic advertisers began courting in earnest. Networks like Fox, UPN, and The WB capitalized on the moment, building programming slates that reflected the full spectrum of Black life.

This renaissance wasn't accidental. It was the result of shifting politics, economic realignment, and a media industry suddenly open to new voices. For Black audiences, it was a rare era of representation, resonance, and visibility—a moment when the sitcom became a mirror, finally reflecting back the richness and complexity of Black life in America.

Living Single showcased independent, ambitious Black women in ways that directly influenced later mainstream hits like *Friends*. *The Fresh Prince of Bel-Air* brought class tensions within the Black community into focus, proving that wealth and success didn't require assimilation. Meanwhile, *Martin* delivered raw, high-energy comedy that continues to shape stand-up and sketch comedy today.

These sitcoms captured the full spectrum of Black life: love, ambition, struggle, and joy. Their influence extended far beyond television, shaping music, fashion, and language. Hip-hop was deeply embedded in their DNA, whether through guest appearances from icons like Tupac and the Notorious B.I.G. or the use of R&B and rap-infused theme songs. Fashion moments—from Will Smith's bold streetwear to Maxine Shaw's power suits—became iconic cultural touchstones. Catchphrases like "You go, girl!" "Did I do that?" and "Wazzup, wassup, whassup?!" became part of everyday slang, cementing the era's influence on popular culture.

The explosion of Black sitcoms in the '90s reflected a changing America. But by the early 2000s, many of these shows disappeared as networks, after building their foundations on Black audiences, pivoted toward whiter ones. Yet, the legacy endures. Decades later, reruns, reboots, and cultural references keep these sitcoms alive, proving that Black '90s comedy didn't just make people laugh—it shaped a generation.

And for some, that generation's influence would lead to creation. On September 11, 2000, *Girlfriends*—created by Mara Brock

Akil—premiered on UPN and quickly became a landmark in American television. The series followed the lives of four Black women—Joan, Maya, Lynn, and Toni—as they navigated careers, relationships, and personal growth in Los Angeles. For Akil, the seeds of her career were planted much earlier, through a sitcom that had once inspired her to dream beyond the newsroom.

"There's a point in high school where you have to start thinking about your future," she recalled. "The thing I loved most was writing, but the only career I could imagine at the time was journalism. So, I thought, 'Okay, I'll go to journalism school, become a journalist, and maybe one day I'll write novels.'"

That path shifted dramatically after she started watching *A Different World*—especially during Debbie Allen's transformative tenure as executive producer and director. "Debbie took *A Different World* to a new height. She allowed us to see the world. I couldn't wait to get to college," Akil said. "In fact, *A Different World* was still on when I was in college, and because of that show—and how well it was done—I started to consider being a screenwriter."

That spark became a calling. "I picked up a book and learned some technique. I wrote my first script, and I remember after I wrote the first scene, I thought, 'This is love. I'm in love.' I fell in love with screenwriting. And it's because I could see myself—I could see stories. I could imagine the stories I wanted to tell—all from the inspiration of *A Different World*."

In many ways, Akil's journey completes the circle—a generation raised on Black sitcoms stepping into the writers' room to tell their own stories. *Girlfriends* was both a spiritual heir to the '90s sitcom boom and a fresh, nuanced evolution of it—proof that the tradition of Black comedic storytelling is not only enduring but ever-expanding. That tradition continues today through a new class of creators and showrunners like Issa Rae (*Insecure*), Lena Waithe (*The Chi*), and Quinta Brunson (*Abbott Elementary*), who are redefining what television can look like—sharp, layered, genre-blurring, and specific.

Because ultimately, the history of Black comedy isn't just about making people laugh. It's about making people *see*.

ACKNOWLEDGMENTS

Toni Morrison once said, "If there's a book that you want to read, but it hasn't been written yet, then you must write it."

This is that book for me.

But no one writes alone.

To be a writer is to forever carry a debt to the people, stories, and experiences that shape your words. I'm deeply grateful to those who supported and inspired me throughout this journey.

To my wife, Beth—your support was my anchor, and your encouragement the fuel. You are my first reader, my sounding board, and my grounding force.

To our son, Jacob—your brilliance, sharp sense of humor, and curious mind remind me what all this is for. You inspire me to keep pushing, to keep listening, to keep learning.

To my mother and late father, Lynnca and Gary Sr.—my greatest champions, whose constant belief in me has been a steady, unshakable force.

And to my brother, Gary Jr.—with whom I spent countless hours watching shows like *The Arsenio Hall Show* and *In Living Color*, sharing a connection rooted in something that felt uniquely ours. Thank you for being a source of pride, perspective, and purpose.

This book owes so much to the extraordinary talent and dedication of Nick Chiles. From concept to completion, your insight, ideas, and tireless work helped bring this book to life in ways I couldn't have foreseen. I'm grateful for your sharp eye, your partnership, and your unwavering commitment to getting it right.

My enduring gratitude to Dylan Colligan, Mat Lattimer, and the outstanding team at Javelin—your support and steady guidance have been invaluable. I'm deeply thankful to have had you in my corner every step of the way.

I owe a great deal to my editor, Adenike Olanrewaju, whose clarity of vision and care for this material elevated it at every stage. Your thoughtful edits and deep understanding of the work helped shape its final form, and your early confidence in this project meant more than you can imagine.

To my friends-I-call-brothers who served as my unofficial focus group: Jordan Rouss, Joe Carlos, Bradley Hardy, Travis Brown, Nick Gaffney, Chris Eaglin, and George A. Peters II—your honest feedback and thoughtful direction were crucial and much appreciated.

To the comedians, writers, performers, and producers who contributed to the cultural legacy explored in these pages—thank you for breaking boundaries, expanding our understanding, and giving us the gift of laughter. In particular, I owe a special thanks to those who sat with me during interviews and shared their stories. Your insights illuminated much of this work.

A special note of gratitude to Robert Raben, Donald Gatlin, and Bob Barnett for your invaluable insight and counsel and to Stephen Battaglio for generously sharing archival research that enriched my reporting.

Thanks to Sharon Rockefeller, Sara Just, Amna Nawaz, and my *PBS NewsHour* colleagues for your support and shared commitment to elevating stories that matter.

Lastly, to the readers of this book—thank you for your curiosity and for engaging with this history. I hope this book leaves you with a deeper appreciation for the transformative role comedy plays in our collective journey.

—Geoff Bennett, 05.25.25

BIBLIOGRAPHY

Books

Bogle, Donald. *Brown Sugar: Over One Hundred Years of America's Black Female Superstars.* Bloomsbury Academic, 2007.

Bogle, Donald. *Toms, Coons, Mulattoes, Mammies, & Bucks: An Interpretive History of Blacks in American Films.* Continuum, 1995.

Cook, Kevin. *Flip: The Inside Story of TV's First Black Superstar.* Viking, 2013.

Du Bois, W. E. B. *The Gift of Black Folk: The Negroes in the Making of America.* The Stratford Company, 1924.

Du Bois, W. E. B. *The Souls of Black Folk: Essays and Sketches.* A. C. McClurg & Co., 1903.

Fletcher, Tom. *100 Years of the Negro in Show Business.* Burdge & Company, Ltd., 1954.

Forbes, Camille F. *Introducing Bert Williams: Burnt Cork, Broadway, and the Story of America's First Black Star.* Basic Civitas, 2008.

Foxx, Redd and Norma Miller. *The Redd Foxx Encyclopedia of Black Humor.* Ward Ritchie Press, 1977.

Frierson, Malcolm. *Freedom in Laughter: Dick Gregory, Bill Cosby, and the Civil Rights Movement.* SUNY Press, 2020.

Gregory, Dick and Robert Lipsyte. *nigger: An Autobiography by Dick Gregory.* E. P. Dutton, 1964.

Gregory, Dick and Shelia P. Moses. *Callus on My Soul.* Kensington Publishing Corp., 2000.

Lott, Eric. *Love & Theft: Blackface Minstrelsy and the American Working Class.* Oxford University Press, 2013.

Markham, Dewey "Pigmeat" and William A. Levinson. *Here Come the Judge!* Popular Library, 1969.

McLeod, Elizabeth. *The Original Amos 'n' Andy: Freeman Gosden,*

Charles Correll and the 1928–1943 Radio Serial. McFarland & Company, Inc., 2005.

Peisner, David. *Homey Don't Play That! The Story of "In Living Color" and the Black Comedy Revolution.* 37 Ink/Atria, 2018.

Pryor, Richard. *Pryor Convictions: And Other Life Sentences.* Pantheon Books, 1995.

Randolph, Peter. *From Slave Cabin to Pulpit: The Autobiography of Rev. Peter Randolph.* James H. Earle, 1893.

Sanello, Frank. *Eddie Murphy: The Life and Times of a Comic on the Edge.* Birch Lane Press, 1997.

Saul, Scott. *Becoming Richard Pryor.* HarperCollins, 2014.

Smith, Will and Mark Manson. *Will.* Penguin Press, 2021.

Starr, Michael. *Black and Blue: The Redd Foxx Story.* Applause Theatre & Cinema Books, 2011.

Toll, Robert C. *Blacking Up: The Minstrel Show in Nineteenth-Century America.* Oxford University Press, 1974.

Watkins, Mel. *On the Real Side: Laughing, Lying, and Signifying—The Underground Tradition of African-American Humor that Transformed American Culture, from Slavery to Richard Pryor.* Simon & Schuster, 1994.

Watts, Jill. *Hattie McDaniel: Black Ambition, White Hollywood.* Amistad, 2007.

Wayans, Damon. *Bootleg.* Harper Paperbacks, 2000.

Whitaker, Mark. *Cosby: His Life and Times.* Simon & Schuster, 2014.

White, Jaleel. *Growing Up Urkel.* Simon & Schuster, 2024.

Williams, Elsie A. *The Humor of Jackie Moms Mabley: An African American Comedic Tradition.* Garland Publishing, Inc., 1995.

Articles

Coates, Ta-Nehisi. "Ebonics! Weird Names! $500 Shoes!" *The Village Voice*, May 18, 2004, https://www.villagevoice.com/ebonics-weird-names-500-shoes/.

"Dahomey on Broadway; Williams and Walker Make an Opening

at the New York Theatre and Hold It. All Negro Book and Music Played by an All-Negro Cast—The Negroes in the Audience Were in Heaven." *The New York Times*, February 19, 1903. https://www.nytimes.com/1903/02/19/archives/dahomey-on-broadway-williams-and-walker-make-an-opening-at-the-new.html.

Davies, Madeleine. "Comedian Hannibal Buress Called Out Bill Cosby's Rape History on Stage." Jezebel, October 20, 2014, https://www.jezebel.com/comedian-hannibal-buress-called-out-bill-cosbys-rape-hi-1648597247.

Felton, David. "Richard Pryor: This Can't Be Happening to Me." *Rolling Stone*, October 10, 1974. https://www.rollingstone.com/tv-movies/tv-movie-news/richard-pryor-this-cant-be-happening-to-me-176443/5/.

Gates, Henry Louis, Jr. "TV's Black World Turns—But Stays Unreal." *The New York Times*, November 12, 1989. https://www.nytimes.com/1989/11/12/arts/tv-s-black-world-turns-but-stays-unreal.html.

Grant, Lee. "Acting's No Laughing Matter." *Los Angeles Times*, January 19, 1977.

Marchese, David. "The Interview: Eddie Murphy Is Ready to Look Back." *The New York Times*, June 29, 2024. https://www.nytimes.com/2024/06/29/magazine/eddie-murphy-interview.html.

Powell, Kevin. "The Agonizing Re-introduction of Dave Chappelle." *Esquire*, April 29, 2006. https://www.esquire.com/entertainment/movies/a1122/esq0506chappelle-92/.

Watkins, Mel. "Richard Pryor, Who Turned Humor of the Streets Into Social Satire, Dies at 65." *The New York Times*, December 12, 2005. https://www.nytimes.com/2005/12/12/obituaries/arts/richard-pryor-who-turned-humor-of-the-streets-into-social.html.

Other

"Kim Coles on How Living Single Was the Blueprint for FRIENDS / Leading Ladies of the '90s." Interview by Kevin Frazier. *Entertainment*

Tonight, March 6, 2021. YouTube, 21 min., 19 sec. https://www.youtube.com/watch?v=mC491mPVBcY.

Strong Black Lead (@strongblacklead). "Mara Brock Akil giving Debbie Allen her flowers 🌹 We love to see it! FOREVER is now playing on Netflix." Instagram, May 22, 2025. https://www.instagram.com/reel/DJ-FuYcSw5X/.

INDEX

Abbott Elementary (TV show), 288, 301
ABC, 70, 106, 115, 259
Abdul, Paula, 255
Abrams, Stacey, 285
Abyssinia (musical), 22–24
Academy Awards, 38, 54
Ackroyd, Dan, 211, 219
Adams, Joey, 72
Adderley, Cannonball, 81
Adell, Ilunga, 114–115
The Adventures of Pluto Nash (film), 210–211
African American Film Critics Association, 224
Aiken, James P., 81–82
Aiken, Loretta Mary. *See* Mabley, Moms
Akil, Mara Brock, 300–301
Alexander, Erika, 283–285, 290
Ali, Bardu, 73–74, 108, 110
Ali, Muhammad, 35
Alice Adams (film), 47
Allen, Debbie, 225, 228–230, 301
Allen, Dick, 78
Allen, Tim, 180
All in the Family (TV show), 90, 109, 110, 111, 112, 113, 175
Alma Records, 106
Amazing Grace (film), 84, 114
American Tobacco Company, 22
Amos, John, 112
Amos John, 5
Amos 'n' Andy (radio show)
  Black listeners, 63–64
  characters, 60, 62–63, 64–65, 145
  creation of, 56–57
  debut, 56, 58
  film, 61–62
  name change, 59
  popularity of, 59–61, 65
  Sam 'n' Henry origins, 58–59
  syndication, 59–60
Amsterdam News (periodical), 148
Ancier, Garth, 1, 249
Anderson, Anthony, 280
Anderson, Eddie, 65–67
Angel Heart (film), 225
Another 48 Hrs. (film), 221
Apex Club, 124
Apollo Theater, 42, 72, 73, 196, 199
Armstrong, Louis, 35, 55, 104
The Arsenio Hall Show (TV show), 272
Arthur, Bea, 114
Astaire, Fred, 16
audiences
  Black, 4, 7, 10, 23, 43, 223–224, 234–235
  mixed-race, 7
  segregated, 21, 23
  white, 4, 8, 10, 12, 14, 16, 19–23, 48, 65, 79

Bad Boys (film), 279
Bad Boys: Ride or Die (film), 281
Bailey, Charles P., 42
Bailey, Pearl, 101–102, 116, 119
Barr, Roseanne, 230
Bartlett, Rob, 216
Basie, Count, 55, 132, 135
Beastie Boys, 270
Beatts, Ann, 227–228
Belafonte, Harry, 165, 173, 200
Bell, Darryl, 228–230
Belushi, John, 206, 207, 211
Bend of the River (film), 35
Benny, Jack, 65–67
Benson (TV show), 66
Berkes, Shawn, 173

Berle, Milton, 72
Bernhard, Sandra, 207
Berry, Chuck, 75
Berry, Halle, 221
Besser, Joe, 69
Beulah (radio show), 38
Beverly Hills Cop (film), 212, 220
Beverly Hills Cop III (film), 221
Bicentennial Nigger (album), 205
Big Daddy Kane, 272
Big Momma's House (film), 280
Bill Cosby Is a Very Funny Fellow—Right! (album), 162–163
The Bill Cosby Show (TV show), 171
The Bingo Long Traveling All-Stars & Motor Kings (film), 187
Binkley, Jimmy, 204
Birth of a Nation (film), 31, 51
Birth of the Blues (film), 67
Of Black America (film), 36, 142
Black and Blue (Starr), 102–103, 106
Blackberries (musical), 83
Black Classic Press, 183
Black Comedians on Black Comedy (Littleton), 119
blackface
   Amos and Andy characters, 61–62
   by Black performers, 8
   Kersands's use of, 11
   Mabley's use of, 83
   Markham's use of, 71, 74–75
   by white performers, 16, 31
   Williams' use of, 17, 19–20, 26–28
Black humor
   authentic expression of self in, 218
   for Black audiences, 223–224, 234–235
   private, 43, 70, 78
   public vs. private, 48
   sitcoms, 288–289
   subversive, 2, 80, 234–235, 258, 275, 291–292
   traits of, 14–16
   "twilight zone" of, 75
   white audiences and, 78–79
Blacking Up (Toll), 10

Black Patti Troubadours, 22
Black political consciousness, 4
Black Reconstruction (Du Bois), 51
Black sitcoms, 288–289, 300–301. *See also specific shows*
Blakey, Art, 153
blaxploitation movies, 109, 172, 174, 248
Blazing Saddles (film), 187, 205
Bledsoe, Tempestt, 260
Boarding House Blues (film), 84
Bogle, Donald, 34, 40, 45, 46, 47–48, 52–53, 67–69, 86
Boitano, Brian, 257
Bonet, Allen, 224
Bonet, Lisa, 224–226
Bontemps, Arna, 32
Bootleg (Wayans), 238
The Both Sides of Redd Foxx (album), 106
Bowman's Cotton Blossoms (revue), 83
Bowser, Yvette Lee, 226–228, 282–286
The Brady Bunch (TV show), 90
Brando, Marlon, 107
Bren, Joe, 57
Brennan, Neal, 293, 294, 296
Breslin, Jimmy, 167
Brewster's Millions (film), 209
Bright, Carolyn Elaine, 265–268
Bright, Kevin, 237
On Broadway Tonight (variety show), 198
Brokaw, Norman, 171
Brooks, Mel, 145, 187, 193, 205, 293
Brown, Claude, 203–204
Brown, Garrett, 57
Brown, James, 143
Brown, Jim, 248
Brown v. Board of Education, 181
Bruce, Lenny, 120, 125, 141, 160, 164
Brunson, Quinta, 301
Buck Benny Rides Again (film), 67
Buress, Hannibal, 183
Burkley, Dennis, 116
Burns, George, 107
Bush, George W., 181

Busta Rhymes, 253
The Busy Body (film), 200
Butler, Charles, 45, 46
Butler, Sara, 49
Butterbeans and Susie, 82

Cabin in the Sky (film), 67
Caesar, Sid, 144, 200
cakewalk dance, 21–22, 23
California Eagle (periodical), 48, 50
Callender's Georgia Minstrels, 11
Calloway, Charles, 138
Callus on My Soul (Gregory), 129
Cambridge, Godfrey, 105, 200
Campbell, Bruce, 170
Campbell, Silver, Cosby Corporation, 170
Campbell, Tisha, 278, 280
Cantor, Eddie, 16, 27
Cara, Irene, 244
Carey, Mariah, 295–296
Carlin, George, 141, 142, 241
Carnegie Hall, 81
Carrey, Jim, 3, 235, 250–251, 257, 258
Carroll, Diahann, 109, 140, 170
Carsey, Marcy, 175, 180
Carson, Johnny, 109, 139–140, 145, 162, 165, 245
Carson, T.C., 283
Carter's Army (TV show), 203
Casey, Bernie, 248
Cash, Johnny, 24
CBS, 35–36, 110, 117, 172, 257
Cedric the Entertainer, 187, 223, 276
Central Casting Corporation, 45
Champion of the Freedman (play), 39
Chan Charlie, 68
Chaney, James, 167
Chappelle, Dave, 9, 187, 210, 222, 276, 291–297
Chappelle, Robert, 292
Chappelle, W. D., Jr., 292
Chappelle's Show (TV show), 10, 275, 291, 294–297
Charles, Ray, 178
Charters, Ann, 27

Chase, Chevy, 206, 211
Check and Double Check (film), 61–62
Chess, Leonard, 75
Chess, Phil, 75
Chess Records, 75, 76, 147
The Chi (TV show), 301
Chicago Tribune radio station, 56
The Chinese Cat (film), 68
The Chinese Ring (film), 68
Chisholm, Charlie, 157
Chitlin' Circuit, 35, 71, 100, 102, 139, 145, 147, 195–196
"Chuck Cunningham Syndrome," 261
Chuck D, 233
Church, Thomas Haden, 251
Civil Rights Act (1964), 168
Civil Rights Movement, 65, 109, 120, 128, 142
Civil War, 11
Clarke, A. W., 63
Clerow Productions, 146
Clinton, Bill, 4, 299
Coates, Ta-Nehisi, 177, 182, 183
Coates, W. Paul, 183
Coffield, Kelly, 235, 251
Cohen, Lyor, 270
Cohen, Russell, 270
Cohen, Sidney, 72
Cold War, 4
Cole, Nat King, 93–94, 104, 149
Coles, Kim, 3, 235, 236, 283–287
Collier, Eugenia, 114
colorism, 4
Colpix records, 128
Coltrane, John, 166, 292
Columbia Pictures, 69
comedic tradition, 14–16
Comedy Central, 291, 294
Come On, People (Cosby), 183
The Comic (film), 70
Coming to America (film), 5, 278
Connery, Sean, 167
Constand, Andrea, 184
Conway, Tim, 145
Cook, Alicia, 175
Cook, John Hartwell, 22

INDEX

Cook, Kevin, 132, 141
Cook, Will Marion, 22–23
"coon" character, 20–21, 32–33, 68
Cooper, Ralph, 74
Correll, Charles J., 56–63, 64
Correll and Gosden, the Life of the Party (radio show), 57
Cosby, Anna, 149–150, 162, 170, 174
Cosby, Bill
  activism, 165
  ad campaigns, 174
  affairs, 173
  albums, 141, 162, 165, 168, 169, 171
  assault and rape accusations, 183–184
  The Bill Cosby Show, 171
  birth and early years, 149–151
  Of Black America, 36, 142
  college years, 156–158
  comedy career, 158–167, 169
  Come On, People, 183
  comparisons to Gregory, 147–148, 159–160
  The Cosby Show, 149, 174–180
  death Ennis, 180–181
  A Different World, 224–226, 227
  doctorate, 174
  Fat Albert and the Cosby Kids, 150, 172
  The Flip Wilson Show appearance, 144
  I Spy, 109, 167–170, 176, 197
  jazz obsession, 152–154, 157, 158–159
  military service, 154–156
  Murphy and, 210, 215–216, 220–221
  "Noah" routine, 160, 167
  "pound cake" speech, 181–182
  Presidential Medal of Freedom, 181
  Pryor and, 196–197, 199, 202
  public image, 149
  racial philosophy, 170–171
  Redd Foxx Club partnership, 107–108
  school years, 151–154
  subversive humor of, 2
  The Tonight Show appearances, 147, 162, 165, 167
  TV appearances, 164–165
  Uptown Saturday Night, 173–174
Cosby, Camille Hanks, 161–162, 168, 171, 172–173, 178
Cosby, Ennis, 171, 177, 178, 180–181
Cosby, Erika, 168
Cosby, Erinn, 169–170
Cosby, James, 150, 151
Cosby, Russell, 151
Cosby, Samuel, 153, 160
Cosby, William, 149–150
The Cosby Show (TV show), 1–2, 149, 174–180, 184, 224, 225, 230, 259, 276, 288
Cotton Club, 35
Cotton Comes to Harlem (film), 108–109
Cowboys and Colored People (album), 141–142
'Craps' (After Hours) (album), 203
Crisis (periodical), 25
Crockett, Ronald, 155, 161
Crosby, Bing, 16
Cullen, Countee, 29
Culp, Robert, 169, 176, 177, 197
cultural power, 5
Curb Your Enthusiasm (TV show), 180
Curry, Mark, 283
Curtin, Jane, 211
The CW, 289

Daddy Day Care (film), 214
In Dahomey (musical), 22–23
Dangerfield, Rodney, 217, 241, 242–243
Darin, Bobby, 140, 200
Dark Alibi (film), 68
David, Larry, 180, 242
Davidson, Tommy, 3, 232, 257
Davis, Miles, 152, 153–154
Davis, Ossie, 108, 165
Davis, Sammy, Jr., 71, 77–78, 104, 107, 119, 177, 197, 206
De Blasio, Bill, 285

INDEX 313

Def Comedy Jam (TV show), 276–277, 279, 293
De Havilland, Olivia, 54
Delany, Martin, 16
De La Soul, 272
Delirious (film), 219–220
demographics, shifting, 4
The Devil Made Me Buy This Dress (album), 144
Devine, Loretta, 228
DeWitt, Joyce, 287
Diamond, Selma, 167
Diddley, Bo, 75, 94
A Different World (TV show), 3, 224–231, 250, 282, 288, 301
The Dilemma of the Negro Actor (Muse), 48
Diller, Barry, 1–2
Diller, Phyllis, 84
diversity, 4, 10
Dixon, Vance, 44
DJ Jazzy Jeff and the Fresh Prince, 269–271
Donegan, Dorothy, 94
Don't Be a Menace (film), 258
Dooto Records, 103, 104, 105
Do the Right Thing (film), 233, 251, 252, 278–279
double consciousness, 13–14
Douglas, Buster, 235
Douglas, Mike, 206
Douglass, Frederick, 9, 16
Doumanian, Jean, 211
Dover Opera House, 61
the dozens, 94
Dr. Doolittle (film), 214
Dreamgirls (film), 221–222
Dresner, Zita, 85
Dr. No (film), 167
Du Bois, W. E. B., 17, 25, 51
Dudley, Sherman, 41
Durham, Ernie, 104
Du Sable, Jean Baptiste Pointe, 94
DuSable High School, 94–95, 113
Dyett, Walter, 94
Dyson, Michael Eric, 182–183

Earle, Carla, 253
Earth Girls Are Easy (film), 250
Eastman, Max, 137
Ebenezer Baptist Church, 52
Ebersol, Dick, 206, 211, 217, 219
Ebony (periodical), 106, 113, 170
Eckstine, Billy, 100, 107
Ed Sullivan Show (TV show), 76–77, 199
Edwards, Rob, 250
Edward VII, 23
81 Theatre, 42
The Electric Company (TV show), 172
Ellington, Duke, 55, 135
Elwood, Phil, 203
Emerson Radio, 76
The Emperor Jones (film), 84
Enjoyment of Laughter (Eastman), 137
Ennis William Cosby Foundation, 181
enslaved Blacks, 13–16
"Ethiopian Opera Houses," 12
Evers, Medgar, 128
Everybody Loves Raymond (TV show), 180

Fales, Susan, 227–228
Family Matters (TV show), 178, 259–264
Fargas, Antonio, 248
Farmer, Gene, 114
Fast and Furious (play), 83
Fat Albert and the Cosby Kids (TV show), 150, 172
Fear of a Black Planet (album), 232–233
Fetchit, Stepin, 31–37, 41, 67, 142
Fields, Kim, 283, 286
Fields, W. C., 25, 27
Fillmore, Millard, 12
film
    Black stereotypes in, 31–34, 69–70
    blaxploitation movies, 109, 172, 174, 248
    casting of Black performers, 45
    servant characters, 34, 38, 41, 45–46, 49–54, 68–70
    talking, 31
Firestein, Les, 234

314 INDEX

Fish (film), 18
Fleischann Hour (radio show), 55
Fletcher, Tom, 7, 11
Flip Wilson, You Devil You (album), 109
The Flip Wilson Show (TV show), 109, 142–146, 171
Follies Burlesque Theater, 48
fool persona, 87
Forbes, Camille F., 19, 21
48 Hrs. (film), 212, 218, 220
Foster, Bill, 31
Foster, Pop, 158
The Four Bon Bons, 94
Fox network, 1, 233, 247, 249, 278, 283, 300
Fox News, 207
Fox Pictures, 33
Fox Studio, 35
Foxworth, Jaimee, 262–263
Foxx, Jamie, 3, 4, 191, 223, 256–257, 289
Foxx, Redd, 43, 70, 199, 210, 232, 241
  albums, 76, 100, 103–104, 105–106, 147
  arrests and imprisonment, 97–98, 101
  bankruptcy, 116–118
  birth and early years, 90–92
  "blue" comedy, 103, 105
  Chitlin' Circuit, 102
  club ownership, 106–108, 124
  Cotton Comes to Harlem, 108–109
  death, 117
  drug use, 98, 106, 116
  Filthy Mouth nickname, 101
  on *The Flip Wilson Show*, 144
  in Harlem, 95–99
  Harlem Nights, 117
  Jamie Foxx's name as tribute to, 4
  Malcolm X and, 98–99
  marriages, 100–101, 103–104
  The Redd Foxx Encyclopedia of Black Humor, 16, 99
  Sanford and Son, 90, 110–116
  school years, 92–95
  Sinatra and, 105–106
  subversive humor of, 2
  A Time for Laughter, 200
  The Tonight Show appearance, 109, 139
Frankel, Martha, 233
Franklin, Aretha, 293
Freedman's Bureau, 23
Freedom Spectacular (TV show), 165
Freeman, Morgan, 172
The Fresh Prince of Bel-Air (TV show), 3, 178, 273–275, 288, 300
Friedman, Silver, 216
Friends (TV show), 237, 263, 278, 282, 284, 300
Frierson, Malcolm, 148
Frito-Lay, 257

Gable, Clark, 47
Gaines, Johnny, 149–150
Gantt, Harvey, 148
Gardner, Paul, 159
Gardner, Stuart, 226–227
Garland, Judy, 16
Garrido, Carla, 254
The Garry Moore Show (TV show), 164
Gates, Henry Louis, 178–179
gender dynamics, 278
Getz, Stan, 140
Ghost (film), 196
The Gift of Black Folk (Du Bois), 17
Gillespie, Dizzy, 107, 177
Girlfriends (TV show), 300–301
Gleason, Jackie, 219
Glover, Lillie Mae, 84
Gold, Eric, 255
Goldberg, Whoopi, 144, 196, 293
Gone with the Wind (film), 38, 50–54, 67
Gone with the Wind (Mitchell), 49–50
Gooding, Cuba, Jr., 280
Goodman, Andrew, 167
Goodman, Dana, 269–270, 271
Goodman, Lawrence, 269–270
Good Times (TV show), 5, 112, 113, 299
Gordy, Berry, 204
Gosden, Freeman F., 56–63, 64
Gosden, Freeman F., Jr., 62

Grady (TV show), 115
Grant, Horace, 148
The Great $4,000 Electrical Ball (play), 39
Green, Eddie, 65, 83
The Green Pastures (film), 66
Gregory, Dick, 28, 81, 105, 147, 164, 174, 292
   activism, 122–123, 128–129, 165
   albums, 128
   Apex Club management, 124
   birth and early years, 120–122
   Callus on My Soul, 129
   comedy research, 123–125
   Cosby compared to, 147–148, 159–160
   mainstream success of, 119–120, 126–129
   military service, 123
   nigger: An Autobiography, 128
   at the Playboy Club, 125–126
   school years, 122–123
   subversive humor of, 2
   A Time for Laughter, 200
   The Tonight Show appearance, 162
Gregory, Lucille, 120–122
Gregory, Presley, 120–121
Grey, Brad, 246
Grier, David Alan, 232, 248, 251, 256, 258
Grier, Pam, 190, 206–207
Griffin, Jimmy, 157
Griffin, Merv, 199
Griffith, Andy, 144, 170
Griffith, D. W., 31, 51
griots, 14, 86
Gross, Ben, 169
Growing Up Urkel (White), 262
The Gumps (cartoon strip), 58
Guy, Jasmine, 225, 229–230

Half Baked (film), 293
Hall, Arsenio
   The Arsenio Hall Show, 272
   Coming to America, 5
   The Late Show, 233, 247
   mentorship of Black artists, 4–5
   Wayans and, 243–244, 245
Hall, Jane Aiken, 82
Hallelujah! (film), 31
Hamill, Dorothy, 257
Handy, W. C., 16, 44
Hangin' with Mr. Cooper (TV show), 282–283
Hanks, Catherine, 161–162, 165–166
Hanks, Guy, 161, 166
Hardison, Kadeem, 225, 229–230
Harlem Nights (film), 116–117
Harlem Renaissance, 26, 29, 87, 96
Harlow, Jean, 47
Harris, Betty Jean, 103–104
Harris, Kamala, 285
Harris, Robin, 248, 278
Hart, Kevin, 187, 222
Hartman, Johnny, 292–293
Harvey, Steve, 187, 223
Hayes, Isaac, 248
Hearts in Dixie (film), 31, 34, 41
Hefner, Hugh, 125–126, 294
Heitman, Patricia, 204–205
"Hello Muddah, Hello Fadduh" (song), 163
Helms, Jesse, 148
Hemsley, Sherman, 112–113
Henry, Buck, 196
Hentoff, Nat, 126
Henton, John, 283, 286
Hepburn, Katharine, 47
Here Come the Judge! (Markham), 71
He's the DJ, I'm the Rapper (album), 271
Hickman, Howard, 40
Higgins, Chester, 168
Hi Hat Hattie and Her Boys (radio show), 49
Himes, Chester, 108
Hitchcock, Alfred, 197
Hogan, Ernest, 20
Holiday, Billie, 98
Hollywood Shuffle (film), 244, 248
Holmes, Groove, 153
Holyfield, Evander, 287
Home Improvement (TV show), 180

INDEX

Honeywood, Varnette, 178
Hope, Bob, 16, 55
Horne, Lena, 161, 165, 177
House Party (film), 252
Houston, Whitney, 175
Howard, Moe, 69
Howard, Shemp, 69
Howard, Sidney, 51
Howard University School of Law, 22–23
Hughes, Langston, 29, 32, 87–88
Hughley, D. L., 187
The Humor of Jackie Moms Mabley (Williams), 84
Hunt, Bonnie, 251
Hurst, Viola Anna, 191, 193
Hurston, Zora Neale, 83
Huth, Judy, 184

Ice Cube, 275
Ice T, 275
I'm Gonna Git You Sucka (film), 248–249
Imitation of Life (film), 194
The Impatient Maiden (film), 46
The Improv, 241–242
inclusivity, 4
In Living Black & White (album), 128
In Living Color (TV show), 277, 285, 289
  casting, 2–3, 249–253
  Emmy award, 254
  Fly Girls, 3, 253, 254–255
  Homey the Clown, 256
  musical guests, 253–254
  popularity of, 237
  premiere, 1, 232
  subversive humor of, 221, 234–235, 258, 274–275
  success of, 2, 3
  Super Bowl half-time show, 257–258
Insecure (TV show), 301
Inside the Actors Studio (TV show), 295
Introducing Bert Williams (Forbes), 19
Irene (TV show), 244
Irish Luck (film), 68
Is Bill Cosby Right? (Dyson), 182–183

. . . Is It Something I Said? (album), 187, 205
I Spy (TV show), 109, 167–170, 176, 197
I Started Out as a Child (Cosby), 165, 168

The Jack Benny Show (radio show), 65–67
The Jack Paar Show (TV show), 164
Jackson, La Toya, 221
Jackson, Michael, 221, 257
Jackson, Papa Charlie, 44
Jackson, Samuel L., 5
The Jade Mask (film), 68
Jaglom, Henry, 197
The Jamie Foxx Show (TV show), 288–289
The Jazz Singer (film), 31
The Jeffersons (TV show), 66, 112, 259, 276, 299
Jet (periodical), 113, 168
Jezebel (film), 67
Jim Crow (character), 9
Jimmy's Chicken Shack, 98
J.J. Fad, 271
J. M. Johnson's Mighty Minstrels, 39
The Joey Bishop Show (TV show), 107
Johnson, AJ, 252
Johnson, Anne-Marie, 248
Johnson, Charles S., 29
Johnson, Elwood, 158
Johnson, Jack, 68
Johnson, Joe, Jr., 158
Johnson, John, 113
Johnson, Lyndon B., 81
Jo Jo Dancer, Your Life Is Calling (film), 209
Jolson, Al, 16, 31
Jones, Elvin, 166
Jones, Philly Joe, 153
Jones, Quincey, 90, 115, 171, 272–273
Jordan, Louis, 135, 137
Jordan, Michael, 148
The Joy Boat (play), 83
Judge (periodical), 29–30

Julia (TV show), 109, 170
"Jump Jim Crow" (song), 9
Jump Swinging Six, 96–97

Kael, Pauline, 187
Kay, Monte, 140–141, 142
Kaye, Danny, 177
Keaton, Buster, 24
Kennedy, John F., 81, 165
Kersands, Billy, 7–11
Kersands' Minstrels, 11
Keymáh, T'Keyah Crystal, 3, 251
Keys, Alicia, 175
Khan, Chaka, 287
Killebrew, Evelyn, 100–101
King, Alan, 160
King, B.B., 144, 177
King, Martin Luther, Jr., 52, 201–202
King, Rodney, 4
Kirk, Andy, 98
Kitt, Eartha, 107, 169, 287
Knight, Gladys, 287
Kool Moe Dee, 271
The Kraft Summer Music Hall (TV show), 141, 199–200
Kravitz, Lenny, 225
Kravitz, Zoë, 225
KRS-One, 254
Ku Klux Klan, 31, 149, 167

Lady Sings the Blues (film), 187, 204
Laff of the Party, Volume 1 (album), 103, 104, 105
Lamb, Jean, 155–156
language, use of, 6
Lankkard, Nym, 44
LaRue, Lash, 189–190
Lassiter, James (JL), 269, 274
The Late Show (TV show), 233, 247
Lathan, Stan, 114, 276
Lawrence, Martin, 3, 145, 191, 221, 223, 251, 276–281, 293, 295–296
Leaders of the New School, 254
Lear, Norman, 109–110, 112, 115, 276
Lee, Ed, 33
Lee, Spike, 233, 247, 252, 278–279

Leigh, Vivien, 50
Leno, Jay, 242
Leonard, John, 144
Leonard, Sheldon, 166–167
Leonard Part 6 (film), 227
Lesser, Sol, 32
Let's Do It Again (film), 174
Lewis, Jerry Lee, 75
Life (movie), 280
Lincoln Theater, 74
Lipsyte, Robert, 128
Litman, Arlene, 224
Little, Cleavon, 110, 145
Little David Records, 141–142
Littlefield, Warren, 284
Littleton, Darryl, 119
Living Single (TV show), 3, 282–290, 300
LL Cool J, 232, 253, 270, 271, 275
Locke, Alain, 29
Loma Records, 105
Long, Johnny Lee, 72
Look Who's Here (play), 83
Lopez, Jennifer, 3, 232, 254–255
Lott, Eric, 16
Louis, Joe, 67
Love & Theft (Lott), 16
Lubinsky, Herman, 100
"Lucky Guy" (song), 100
Lyles, Aubrey, 56, 62
Lynch, Vernon, 213–214, 215

Mabley, Jack, 83
Mabley, Moms, 210
  adoption of stage name, 80, 83
  The Bill Cosby Show appearance, 171
  birth and early years, 80, 81–82
  blackface, 83
  Chitlin' Circuit, 35
  film career, 83–84, 114
  on *The Flip Wilson Show*, 144
  Moms, 196
  monologue humor, 80–81
  popularity of, 81, 147
  rapes and pregnancies, 82

Mabley, Moms (*continued*)
  religious beliefs, 85
  stage persona, 80, 81, 84, 85–88
  subversive humor of, 2, 80
  theater career, 83–84
  A Time for Laughter, 200
Mac, Bernie, 117, 187, 223, 280
Mack, Charlie, 62, 271, 272, 276
The Mad Miss Manton (film), 47–48
Maher, Bill, 242
Major Bowes' Original Amateur Hour (radio show), 96–97
Mammy character, 29–30, 40–41, 46, 49–54
Man About Town (film), 67
Man and Boy (film), 171–172
Manchild in the Promised Land (Brown), 203
Manson, Mark, 265
Markham, Pigmeat, 83
  albums, 75–76, 147
  birth and early years, 71
  blackface, 71, 74–75
  Chitlin' Circuit, 71
  Ed Sullivan Show, 76–77
  "Here Comes the Judge" gag, 72, 77–78
  Here Come the Judge! 71
  "Open the Door, Richard," 132
  A Time for Laughter, 200
  touring career, 72–75
Married... with Children (TV show), 1, 2, 233
Marsalis, Branford, 287
Marshall, Thurgood, 230
Martin (TV show), 2, 221, 277–281, 282, 285, 288, 300
Martin, Dean, 201
"Mary's Gone with a Coon" (song), 8
Maude (TV show), 112, 114
Maxine Shaw Effect, 284–285
Mayfield, Curtis, 144
Mayo, Whitman, 115
MCA Records, 171
McCoy, Willie, 135, 137
McDaniel, Etta, 39, 40, 44

McDaniel, Hattie
  birth and early years, 38–39
  blues music, 43–44, 48
  domestic work, 40, 44
  film career, 45–54
  Gone with the Wind, 38, 49–54
  marriages, 40, 44
  minstrelsy, 39–41
  radio shows, 38, 49
  TOBA circuit, 41–43
McDaniel, Otis, 38–39
McDaniel, Sam, 39, 44, 49
McDaniel Sisters Company, 40
McDuffie, Elizabeth, 50
McKnight, Brian, 287
McLeod, Elizabeth, 58, 62–63, 64
McMahon, Ed, 287
McQueen, Butterfly, 53–54
McRae, Carmen, 107
McVea, Sam, 49
The Meanest Man in the World (film), 67
medicine shows, 18, 19
Medina, Benny, 272
Meiklejohn, William, 50
Meredith, James, 88–89
Michaels, Lorne, 206, 211, 246
Mickey Mouse, 16
Miller, Cheryl, 287
Miller, Dorie, 150
Miller, Flournoy, 56
Miller, Paul, 237
Minsky's, 72
Minstrel Show (radio show), 56
minstrelsy
  appeal of to white audiences, 8, 10–12, 13
  Black caricatures, 8, 9, 17
  geographic spread of, 12
  impacts of, 16
  popularity of, 11–12
  on the radio, 56
  segregation in, 8
  show format, 12–13
  "slave bands," 10–11
Miss Bandana (play), 83
Mitchell, Margaret, 49

The Mod Squad (TV show), 170, 203
Moesha (TV show), 288
Molle Minstrels (radio show), 56
Mom persona, 84–85
Moms (show), 196
Monie Love, 254
Mo'Nique, 288
Mooney, Paul, 114, 202, 245, 256
Moore, Tanya, 271–272
Moore, Tim, 68, 70, 83
Morehouse College, 178
Moreland, Mantan, 67–70, 83, 171
Moreno, Rita, 172, 177
Morgan, Tracy, 277
Morris, Earl, 51
Morrison, Toni, 4
Motion Picture Producers Association, 45
Mowry, Tamara, 289
Mowry, Tia, 289
Mulan (film), 214
Mumford, Thad, 227–228
Murphy, Charles, Jr. (Charlie), 212–213
Murphy, Charles Lee, 212, 213
Murphy, Eddie, 187, 196
   The Adventures of Pluto Nash, 210–211
   awards, 212
   Beverly Hills Cop, 212, 220
   bipolar disorder, 219
   birth and early years, 212–214
   children's films, 214
   comedy career, 215–217
   Coming to America, 5, 278
   Cosby and, 220–221
   Delirious, 219–220
   film career, 117, 219–222
   48 Hrs., 212, 218, 220
   Harlem Nights, 116–117
   influences, 210, 214, 215–216
   Lawrence and, 280
   popularity of, 220
   Pryor and, 216, 221
   Raw, 219, 220, 248
   The Royal Family, 117
   Saturday Night Live, 130, 211, 217–219, 246
   school years, 214–215
   subversive humor of, 2
   success of, 210
   Trading Places, 212, 219
   Wayans and, 217, 245–246, 247–248
Murray, Bill, 211, 221
Muse, Clarence, 34, 41, 48
My Brother's Keeper (album), 128
My Son, the Nut (album), 162–163

NAACP, 25, 35, 50, 66, 69–70, 165, 233
A Natural Born Gambler (film), 18
NBC, 56, 59, 109, 110, 113, 115, 142–143, 146, 167, 171, 174–175, 180, 211, 229, 244
Nelson, Bob, 216
The New Negro (Locke), 29
New York Society for Ethical Culture (NYSEC), 148
Next Time I Marry (film), 68
nigger: An Autobiography (Gregory), 128
nightclubs, 30–31
Nixon, Richard, 205
Nobody (Charters), 27
"Nobody" (song), 24
Norbit (film), 222
Norman . . . Is That You? (film), 116
Norwood, Brandy, 288
Not the Cosbys (script), 1–2
NPR, 128
The Nutty Professor (film), 214

Obama, Barack, 4, 5, 183, 207
O'Connor, Carroll, 90, 114
O'Connor, John, 207
O'Donnell, Rosie, 287
Okeh Race Records, 44
In Old Kentucky (film), 33
Old Time Southern Singers, 48–49
100 Years of Laughter (TV show), 106
100 Years of the Negro in Show Business (Fletcher), 7
O'Neill, Eugene, 84

Opportunity (periodical), 29
Optimistic Do-Nuts (radio show), 44, 49
The Original Amos 'n' Andy (McLeod), 58, 62–63
Orlando, Tony, 104
Overton, Ada, 22

Paar, Jack, 119, 162
Page, LaWanda, 93
Parham, Hartzell "Tiny," 43–44
Parker, Alan, 225
Parker, Charlie, 100
Parker, Harold, 195
The Parkers (TV show), 288
The Partridge Family (TV show), 203
Pastor, Tony, 21
Payton, Jo Marie, 260
Peisner, David, 256
Perez, Rosie, 3, 252–253, 254
Perfect Strangers (TV show), 260
Perry, Lincoln. *See* Fetchit, Stepin
Perry, Tyler, 5, 10, 64, 130, 145
Pete, Holly Robinson, 283
Phillips, Esther, 107
Pick, Sam, 44
Pickens, Slimm, 107
A Piece of the Action (film), 174
Pierce, Franklin, 12
Pippen, Scottie, 148
Plantation Party (radio show), 56
Playboy (periodical), 170
Playboy After Dark (variety show), 294
Playboy Club, 87, 125–126
"playing the dozens," 14
Poitier, Sidney, 70, 106, 173–174, 200
Polk, James, 12
Poussaint, Alvin, 178, 183
Powell, Colin, 5
Powell, Kevin, 294, 295
Presley, Elvis, 16, 75, 214, 215
Pressley, Ayanna, 285
Pridgett, Gertrude, 84
Prohibition songs, 25
Pryor, Gertrude, 188–189
Pryor, Leroy "Buck," 188–189, 193
Pryor, Marie, 188–189, 195, 206, 208

Pryor, Richard, 43, 81, 114, 117, 141, 241
  activism, 202
  albums, 186, 203, 205
  birth and early years, 185, 187–190
  at Cafe Wha? 197–198
  Chappelle on, 296–297
  Chitlin' Circuit, 195–196
  Cosby and, 196–197, 199
  death, 209
  drug use, 145, 201, 203–205, 207–209
  film career, 187, 204–205, 209
  fire incident, 208–209
  on *The Flip Wilson Show*, 145
  Harlem Nights, 117
  influences, 201–202, 203
  The Kraft Summer Music Hall, 199–200
  military service, 193–195
  Murphy and, 210, 215–216
  performance films, 187, 208, 209
  at the Redd Foxx Club, 106, 107, 202–203
  The Richard Pryor Show, 207
  Saturday Night Live appearance, 206
  school years, 190–193
  sexuality, 203
  stage personas, 147, 185–186
  subversive humor of, 2
  A Time for Laughter, 200–201
  The Toy, 209, 219
  TV appearances, 198–199
  TV career, 203
  Uptown Saturday Night, 173–174
  use of language, 202–203, 216
  "Wino and Junkie" routine, 204
Pryor, Richard, Jr., 195
Public Enemy, 232–233, 254, 271
Pulliam, Keshia Knight, 175, 178, 260
punning, 14

Queen Latifah, 253, 272, 275, 283–287

race, acknowledgement of, 148
race records, 75–76

INDEX

racial discrimination, 200
racial satire, 120
racial ventriloquy, 56–57
racism, 4, 104, 194, 203, 244
radio
    Black listeners, 63–64
    invention of, 31
    McDaniel on, 44, 49
    stereotypes on, 55–56, 65
    See also specific radio shows
Radio Digest (periodical), 63
Radner, Gilda, 211
Rae, Issa, 301
ragtime, 23
Rainey, Big Memphis Ma, 84
Rainey, Ma, 42–43, 84
Ralph, Sheryl Lee, 288
Randolph, Peter, 15
Rashad, Ahmad, 176
Rashad, Phylicia, 176, 178, 225
Raven-Symoné, 225
Raw (film), 219, 220, 248
Rawitt, Tamara, 233, 248–249, 251
Rawls, Lou, 107
RCA, 115
Reagan, Ronald, 26–27
On the Real Side (Watkins), 13–14, 29, 32, 33, 42, 81, 125
Records, M.F., 106
Red Devils, 39
Redd Foxx Club, 106–108, 202
The Redd Foxx Comedy Hour (TV show), 116
The Redd Foxx Encyclopedia of Black Humor (Foxx), 16, 99
Redman, Don, 73
Red Pastures (play), 83
Reed, Ishmael, 203
Reed, Robi, 252
Reese, Della, 104, 117
Reid, Tim, 207
Reiner, Carl, 167
Reiner, Rob, 167
representation, 3, 224, 262
Reprise Records, 105
Revenge (album), 141

revues, 83
Ribeiro, Alfonso, 274
Rice, Thomas "Daddy," 9
Richard Pryor: Live in Concert (film), 187, 193, 208
Richard Pryor: Live on the Sunset Strip (film), 209
The Richard Pryor Show (TV show), 207
Rickles, Don, 106, 200
Riley, Tony, 236
RKO, 62
The Robe (film), 123
Robertson, Gil, 224
Robeson, Paul, 84
Robin Hood: Men in Tights (film), 293
Robinson, Jackie, 91
Rock, Chris, 3, 187, 222, 251, 297
    awards, 293
    Hall's mentorship, 5
    I'm Gonna Git You Sucka, 248–249
    Smith and, 268
    success of, 293–294
Rock the House (album), 271
Rogers, Timmie, 125, 126, 174
Rogers, Will, 35
Rolle, Esther, 112
Rollins, Sonny, 140
Romano, Ray, 180
Rooney, Mickey, 16
Roosevelt, Eleanor, 50
Ross, Diana, 145, 204
Roth, Manny, 197–198
Rourke, Mickey, 225
Rowan & Martin's Laugh-In (TV show), 77–78, 79
The Royal Family (TV show), 117
Ruben, Aaron, 114
Run-DMC, 270
Rush Management, 270
Russell, Nipsey, 43, 70, 125, 126, 174, 251

Sahl, Mort, 120, 125
Salt-N-Pepa, 271
"Sambo" figure, 9, 125
Sam Hague's Georgia Minstrels, 11

Sam 'n' Henry (radio show), 58–59
Sanders, Deion, 287
Sanford (TV show), 116
Sanford, Fred Glenn, 90–91
Sanford, Fred, Jr., 91, 92–93, 94
Sanford, Isabel, 113, 287
Sanford, Jon. *See* Foxx, Redd
Sanford, Mary Alma Hughes, 90–91, 93–94
Sanford and Son (TV show), 90, 110–116, 276
Saratoga (film), 47
Saturday Night Live (SNL) (TV show), 3, 5, 178, 187, 206, 211, 217–219, 246, 250, 297
Savoy Ballroom, 97
Savoy Records, 100
The Scarlet Clue (film), 68
Scary Movie (film), 258
Schlatter, George, 78
School Daze (film), 252
Schultz, Sheldon "Shelly," 162
Schwerner, Michael, 167
Scott, Hazel, 98, 107
Scott, Jimmy, 100
In Search of Our Mothers' Gardens (Walker), 85
Seeger, Pete, 292
segregation, 2, 7, 8, 21, 23, 89
Seinfeld (TV show), 180, 263
Seinfeld, Jerry, 180, 242
Selznick, David O., 49–52
Seon, Yvonne, 292
servant characters, 34, 38, 41, 45–46, 49–54, 65–67, 68–70
sexism, 4, 203
Shadow over Chinatown (film), 68
Sherman, Allan, 162–164
She's Gotta Have It (film), 247
Shore, Mitzi, 243–244
Show Boat (radio show), 56
Shrek (film), 214
Sidewalks of Harlem (play), 83
Silver, Roy, 160, 162, 170, 171
Silverman, Fred, 115, 116, 172
Silver Streak (film), 187

Simmons, Russell, 270, 276
Simone, Nina, 24
The Simpsons (TV show), 233
Sinatra, Frank, 27, 96, 105–106, 107, 140
Sinclair Weiner Minstrels (radio show), 56
Sister, Sister (TV show), 288–289
Six Degrees of Separation (film), 279
From Slave Cabin to Pulpit (Randolph), 15
slavery, 10–11, 13–15
Smith, Bessie, 42, 75, 86
Smith, Cecil, 111
Smith, Ellen, 265
Smith, Harry, 265, 266
Smith, Jada Pinkett, 268, 274
Smith, Trey, 274
Smith, Will
    Bad Boys movies, 279, 281
    birth and early years, 265–268
    The Fresh Prince of Bel-Air, 273–275
    Hall's mentorship, 5
    rap career, 268–271
    Rock and, 268
    Six Degrees of Separation, 279
    Will, 265, 266, 273
Smith, Willard Carroll, 265–268
A Soldier's Story (film), 246
Sommore, 276
The Souls of Black Folk (Du Bois), 13
Spade, David, 251
speakeasies, 30–31
Spelling, Aaron, 203
Spelman College, 179–180
The Spook Show (Broadway show), 196
Stand Up and Cheer (film), 35
Stanwyck, Barbara, 47–48
Starr, Michael Seth, 98, 102–103, 106
St. Benedict the Moor Mission, 92–93
Stepin Fetchit (Watkins), 36
Steptoe and Son (TV show), 109–110
stereotypes
    "coon," 20, 21, 32–33, 68
    in film, 31–34, 69–70
    Mammy character, 29–30, 40–41, 46, 49–54

in minstrelsy, 8–11
on the radio, 55–56, 58–60, 65
"Sambo" figure, 9, 29, 125
servants, 34, 38, 41, 45–46
simpleminded "fools," 14
thugs and pimps, 244
Still, Charity, 53
Stir Crazy (film), 187
Stoddard, Karen, 85
Stormy Weather (film), 67
"The Streetbeater" (song), 90
Streisand, Barbara, 202
Stringbean, Sweet Mama, 84
Suburban Inn, 44
Sullivan, Ed, 76–77
Super Bowl half-time show, 257–258
Sussman, Morris, 72
Sweet Sweetback's Baadasssss Song (film), 172

Tartikoff, Brandon, 273
Tatum, Art, 98
Taylor, Bayard, 16
Taylor, Leroy, 131–132
Temple, Shirley, 16, 35
Tetragrammaton, 170
TGIF programming, 259
That Nigger's Crazy (album), 186, 205
A Thin Line Between Love and Hate (film), 280
3rd Bass, 254
Thomas, Danny, 167
Three Stooges, 69
Tienken, Richie, 216–217, 247
A Time for Laughter (TV show), 70, 200–201
TOBA (Theatre Owners Booking Association), 41–43, 71, 82
Toll, Robert, 10, 12
Tomei, Marisa, 225
Tomlin, Lily, 144, 193, 207, 241
Toms, Coons, Mulattoes, Mammies, & Bucks (Bogle), 34, 40, 47
The Tonight Show (TV show), 109, 139, 162, 165, 167, 244–245
Toomer, Jean, 29

Torry, Guy, 280
Townes, Allen, 269
Townsend, Robert, 242–243, 244, 245, 246–248
The Toy (film), 209, 219
Trading Places (film), 212, 219
Travis, Dempsey, 94
tricksters, 86–88
Truth, Sojourner, 53
Tubman, Harriet, 53
Tucker, C. Delores, 233
Tucker, Chris, 276
Turan, Kenneth, 220
Turman, Glynn, 229
Tuskegee Institute, 241
Twain, Mark, 16
2 Live Crew, 271
"Two Real Coons," 21
2000 Years with Carl Reiner & Mel Brooks (album), 158
Tyler, John, 12
Tyson, Cicely, 169
Tyson, Mike, 235–236

Uggams, Leslie, 177
United Artists, 248, 249
United Negro College Fund, 241
UPN (United Paramount Network), 288, 289, 300, 301
Uptown Saturday Night (film), 173–174
Urban League, 29
Urkel (TV character), 260–264

Valle, Julia, 92
Valle, Lincoln Charles, 92
Vallée, Rudy, 55, 198
Vampire in Brooklyn (film), 221
Vandross, Luther, 236
Van Peebles, Mario, 172
vaudeville, 7, 16, 21–25, 43, 55, 299
Vaughan, Sarah, 100, 107
VelJohnson, Reginald, 260
Vereen, Ben, 26–28
Victoria, Queen, 9
Virgin Records, 255
Voting Rights Act (1965), 168

324 INDEX

Wachs, Bob, 216–217
Wade, Ernestine, 65
Waithe, Lena, 301
Walker, Aida Overton, 22, 23, 24, 40
Walker, Alice, 85
Walker, George
  birth and early years, 19
  blackface characters, 20–21
  Broadway musicals, 22–24
  death, 24
  vaudeville act, 21–22
  Williams and, 17, 18, 19, 20–24, 39
Walker, Jimmie, 112, 261
Waller, Fats, 55
Walrond, Eric, 26
Walters, Barbara, 116
Warfield, Marsha, 207
Warner, Malcolm-Jamal, 177, 260
Warner Bros. Records, 272
Warner Brothers, 105, 162, 164, 169, 170, 283, 286
Washington, Booker T., 17, 18
Washington, Denzel, 246
Washington, Desiree, 236
Washington, Dinah, 94, 102
Washington, Harold, 92
Watermelon Man (film), 70
Waters, Ethel, 38, 42, 84
Waters, Muddy, 75
Watkins, Mel, 31, 43, 45, 56, 64–65, 67, 75, 126, 209
  On the Real Side, 13–15, 29, 32, 33, 42, 81, 125
  Stepin Fetchit, 36
Watts, Jill, 38, 40, 44, 45, 46–47, 50, 52, 53
Watts, Patricia, 195
Wattstax (film), 205
Wayans, Damon, 2, 223, 232, 234, 238, 239, 240–241, 243, 246, 247, 249–252, 256
Wayans, Devonne, 238
Wayans, Diedra, 238
Wayans, Dwayne, 238, 240
Wayans, Elvira, 238
Wayans, Elvira (mother), 237–239
Wayans, Howell, 237–239
Wayans, Keenen Ivory
  birth and early years, 237–241
  college years, 241–242
  comedy career, 241–245
  Hall and, 243–244, 245, 247
  I'm Gonna Git You Sucka, 248–249
  In Living Color, 1, 2–3, 232, 233–237, 249–258, 277, 285–286
  Murphy and, 217, 245–246, 247–248
  Pryor and, 239–240, 241
  subversive humor of, 234–235
  The Tonight Show appearance, 244–245
  TV appearances, 244
Wayans, Kim, 232, 238, 247, 249–250, 285
Wayans, Marlon, 2, 232, 238–239, 241, 242, 245–246
Wayans, Nadia, 238
Wayans, Shawn, 2, 232, 238, 245–246
The Wayans Bros. (TV show), 258, 288–289
Way Down South (film), 32
The WB, 258, 288–289, 300
"We Are the World" (song), 221
W. E. B. Du Bois, 13
WEBH, 57
Werner, Tom, 175, 180
Wesley, Richard, 173–174
WGN, 56, 58–59
White, Armond, 36
White, Gavin, 157
White, Jaleel, 259–264
White, Melvin "Slappy," 101–102, 125, 126, 174
White, Slappy, 43
White, Walter, 35, 50–51
White Chicks (film), 258
whiteface, 39
white supremacy, 76
Whitman, Walt, 16
Whittaker, Juliette, 192–193, 198
Whodini, 270
Wilder, Gene, 187, 219
The Wild Wild West (TV show), 200

INDEX 325

Wiley, Stella, 22
Will (Smith), 265, 266, 273
William Morris, 171
Williams, Andy, 141
Williams, Bert, 203, 210
   birth and early years, 18–19
   blackface characters, 17, 19–20, 26–28, 62
   Broadway musicals, 18, 22–24
   death, 17, 25–26
   praise for, 17–18, 26
   racism against, 24–25
   subversive humor of, 2
   vaudeville act, 21–22
   Walker and, 17, 18, 19, 20–24, 39
   Ziegfeld Follies, 18, 25
Williams, Billie Dee, 204
Williams, Clarence, III, 170
Williams, Dootsie, 103, 104, 105
Williams, Elisie A., 84, 85, 86
Williams, John, 99
Williams, Mary Lou, 99
Williams, Robin, 207, 242
Williams, Vanessa, 175
Wilmore, Larry, 3, 237
Wilson, Clerow, Sr., 130, 131
Wilson, Cornelia, 130, 131, 132
Wilson, Demond, 110–111, 115
Wilson, Eleanor, 131
Wilson, Ellis, 178
Wilson, Flip, 43, 287
   albums, 141–142
   awards, 144–145
   birth and early years, 130–133
   characters, 138
   Chitlin' Circuit, 139, 145
   comedy research, 137
   cross-dressing characters, 133, 138–139, 142–143, 147
   The Flip Wilson Show, 109, 142–146
   The Kraft Summer Music Hall, 141
   mainstream success of, 130, 137, 144–145
   at the Manor Plaza, 135–137
   military service, 133–135
   at the Redd Foxx Club, 107
   school years, 132–133
   The Tonight Show appearances, 139–140
   Uptown Saturday Night, 173
Wilson, Nancy, 81, 177
Winfrey, Oprah, 291
Winters, Jonathan, 164
Witherspoon, John, 248
WMAQ, 56, 59
womanist, 85
women comedians, 85
Women's Christian Temperance Union, 39
Wonder, Stevie, 177
Woodbine, Bokeem, 280
wordplay, 14
World War II, 69, 74, 97, 150

X, Malcolm, 98–99, 108, 183

Yingst, Margaret, 191
Yorkin, Bud, 110–111
The Young Lawyers (TV show), 203
Youngman, Henny, 72

Zampino, Sheree, 274
Ziegfeld, Florenz, Jr., 18, 25
Ziegfeld Follies of 1911, 18, 25

ABOUT THE AUTHOR

GEOFF BENNETT is the co-anchor of *PBS NewsHour* and an NBC News contributor. A Peabody Award–winning journalist, he has reported on politics at the highest levels, covering the White House and six presidential elections, while also conducting exclusive interviews with cultural icons, global leaders, and groundbreaking artists. His work bridges politics and culture, offering insight into the forces that shape American society. He lives in the Washington, DC, area with his wife and their son.